CRISIS IN LEBANON

Crisis in Lebanon

by

FAHIM I. QUBAIN

THE MIDDLE EAST INSTITUTE
Washington, D. C.
1961

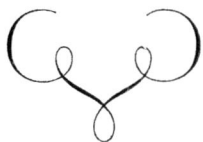

PRINTED IN THE UNITED STATES OF AMERICA
BY THE FRENCH-BRAY PRINTING COMPANY, BALTIMORE, MARYLAND

Contents

CHAPTER

PAGE

I. The Land, Its People and History 1
II. Political History and Government 16
III. The Causes of the Crisis 28
IV. Slide Into Anarchy 48
V. The Civil War 71
VI. The United Nations Debates 89
VII. The American Commitment 111
VIII. Intervention or Internal Revolt? 133
IX. The Political Settlement 154
X. Summary and Conclusion 169
Appendices 181
Index 237

Preface

In this study, I have followed the transliteration system used by the *Middle East Journal*. However, names of individuals and place names in direct quotes have been left as they appeared in the original texts and in the two U.N. maps at the back of the book.

While writing this book, I visited Lebanon three times in 1959 and 1960. Here, I want to express my gratitude and appreciation to the many Lebanese who kindly helped me with information, views and documentary material. They are too numerous to mention by name.

Thanks are also due to the Middle East Institute. For more than three years it has placed its various services and facilities at my disposal, thus enabling me to do research on this as well as other studies. I especially wish to thank Miss Kathleen Brown of the Institute for her patience and many hours of work in proofreading the manuscript and compiling the index.

Many others have helped in a number of ways, but I am alone responsible for all statements and conclusions made in this book.

Washington, D. C.

FAHIM I. QUBAIN

May 10, 1961

CHAPTER I

The Land, Its People and History

THE REPUBLIC of Lebanon, like several other Arab states, was carved out of the defunct Ottoman Empire after the First World War. Prior to 1918, it was an autonomous province restricted to Mount Lebanon, the hill region immediately inland from the coastal strip, and extending some 20-30 miles north and south of Beirut. The French, at the inception of their mandate, expanded the territory of Mount Lebanon into the much larger area of "Greater Lebanon"—the Lebanon of today.

The present political boundaries were delimited on September 1, 1920. From the north and east, the country is bounded by Syria. From the south, by Israel; and from the west, by the Mediterranean.

In area and population, Lebanon is the smallest of the fully independent states in the Middle East. It has an area of 4,062 square miles (about half the size of Israel), and a population estimated in 1956 at a little over one and one half millions.

The country is divided into four natural belts, all running parallel to the Mediterranean coast. First, there is the flat fertile coastal strip—a mere ribbon never wider than four miles, stretching from Ras al-Nāqūrah on the Israeli border in the south, to al-'Arīḍah on the Syrian border in the north. At some points this flat land virtually disappears, and the mountain directly meets the sea.

Immediately east of the coastal strip, and parallel to it, comes the western range—Mount Lebanon, the highest in the Levant. It rises to its highest peak of over 10,000 feet at Qurnat al-Sawda, south-east of Tripoli, and dwindles to mere hills above Sidon. Mount Ṣannīn, north-east of Beirut, is over 9,000 feet.

The Lebanon (the western range) consists of a single up-fold. A geological feature of great importance, and which creates one of the oddities of the Middle East, exists within the up-fold. This is the occurrence of a layer of non-porous rocks which are exposed on the western slopes of the range. Because of this non-porous layer, water is forced to the surface producing large springs—sometimes, as large as small rivers—at the unusually high level of three to five thousand feet above the sea. As a result, the western slopes of the Lebanon Mountains, unlike those of Syria and Palestine, are well-watered and intensely cultivated up to heights of three to five thousand feet above sea level.

The abundance of water and fertile soil at high altitudes and the existence of deep ravines with forbidding cliffs, often several thousand feet in height, have had a deep influence on the history of the Mountain. This made it a refuge and a haven for persecuted minorities. Water and fertile soil made habitation at high altitudes possible, while the deep ravines and forbidding cliffs made enemy penetration from the coastal plain extremely difficult, if not virtually impossible.

The third belt—immediately east of the Lebanon range, is the trough-like plain of al-Biqā' (the Bekaa). It is 70 to 80 miles long and about ten miles wide. Its floor rises gently towards the center, reaching its highest altitude of over 3,000 feet at Ba'lbak, on the watershed between the Orontes and the Liṭānī. To east and west, mountain walls, rising five to seven thousand feet higher still and covered with snow a substantial part of the year, provide a beautiful panorama.

The Biqā' is served by two main rivers: the Orontes (al-'Āṣī) which flows northwards into Syria, and finally reaches the Mediterranean near Antioch in Turkey; and the Liṭānī. The Liṭānī flows southwards until a short distance from the Israeli frontier, then makes a sudden turn westwards and plunges through a deep gorge into the Lebanon range and empties into the Mediterranean. The Liṭānī waters are now being harnessed for irrigation and hydro-electric power.

The fourth belt—immediately east of the Biqā', is the eastern range called the Anti-Lebanon, extending along the Syrian frontier. Some of its peaks rise to a height of over 7,000 feet. Mount Hermon, al-Shaykh which is the southern continuation of the Anti-Lebanon range, rises to 9,200 feet. Unlike the Lebanon, the Anti-Lebanon range has a very scanty water supply (the water seeps to the base), and consequently is sparsely inhabited.

* * *

The climate of Lebanon varies with altitude and proximity to the sea. The existence of mountain ranges close and parallel to the sea restricts maritime influence to a narrow littoral zone.

In the coastal zone, winters are mild, summers moderately hot, and rainfall relatively adequate. The coldest months of the year are January and February with an average temperature of 54° to 57°F. A feature of the spring and even of winter, is the *khamsīn* wind, which has at times raised the temperature in Beirut in January to

79 °F. August everywhere is the hottest month, with an average temperature of 85 °F in Beirut. In the summer nights are oppressive, dew is very heavy and the humidity high (Beirut max. 73° % in June). Because of the heat, the lack of relief at night and the humidity, many town-dwellers (particularly from Beirut) move to the hills during the summer months.

The coast receives over 30 inches of rainfall a year, a comparatively high figure for that part of the world. January is the wettest month, and June through September are rainless.

A remarkable change in climate takes place as one proceeds from the coast to the Mountain zone, even within the short distance of five miles. Here the winters are cold, and snow is of regular occurrence. In the Lebanon range snow may last from two to four months, and the three peaks (Qurnat al-Sawda, Ṣannīn, and Hermon) are snow-clad for at least six months of the year (usually from December to June). The name Lebanon itself, is said to be derived from the Aramaic *Leben* (whiteness) in reference to these snow-capped peaks.

In the summer, there is a wide diurnal variation, so that the nights are cool. Thus Aley, a summer resort only five miles from Beirut, but 2,500 feet above sea level, is cool and pleasant.

The mountains receive between 40 and 50 inches of rain annually. The number of rainy days however is low—an average of 80-85 days a year, so that rainfall can be described as intensive. This has important results: unless the top soil is protected, it would be swept away by the heavy rains. Consequently, a striking feature of the mountain zone in Lebanon, is terracing on a grand scale. In some districts, the hillsides are terraced continuously at intervals of three or four feet.[1]

* * *

The people of Lebanon enjoy one of the highest standards of living in the Middle East and the Lebanese economy is one of the most thriving in the area. For instance, the national income rose from an estimated 919 million Lebanese Liras (£L) in 1948 to 1,090 millions in 1952, and to 1,465 millions in 1956.[2] In other words, assuming the total population to be around 1.5 millions, the average per capita income in 1956 was, roughly speaking, about 300 dollars a year. This, in comparison to the rest of the area, is very high. Furthermore, although there is a great variation in wealth, in Lebanon this fact is not as glaring as in the rest of the Arab world.

The three pillars of the Lebanese economy are agriculture, industry and services.

Agriculture plays a much less important role in the economy of Lebanon than in that of neighboring Arab countries. It accounts for about 19.5 percent of the national income, and only 50 percent of the population depend on it for livelihood. The main limiting factor in agricultural expansion has been the lack of arable land.

Because of the comparative abundance of water, and a variety of soils and altitudes, Lebanon produces a wide range of fruits, vegetables and cereals. In cereals, however, the country is not self-sufficient, and imports the balance of her needs—estimated by the International Wheat Agreement at 75,000 tons a year—from Syria and other countries. The most important fruit products are olives, bananas, grapes, citrus and apples, particularly the last two. In the last decade, there has been fairly heavy investment in apple-growing, so that production rose from 11,000 metric tons in 1944 to 32,000 tons in 1956. It is expected to reach about 100,000 tons in some ten years. Citrus production is about 100,000 tons; grapes, about 80,000 tons; bananas, about 25,000; and olives, about 35,000.[3]

In terms of percentage of the national income, Lebanon is the most highly industrialized Arab state. This sector of the economy (including construction) accounted in 1956 for 15.4 percent of the national income, amounting to £L. 225 millions.[4] Between 1952 and 1956 inclusive, the number of industrial establishments rose from 2,200 to 2,906; and the number of workers, from 19,000 to 24,200. Total industrial investment during these five years came to £L. 970 million, rising from 165 millions in 1952 to 232 millions in 1956.[5]

The largest industries in Lebanon are textiles, manufacture of clothes, cement, electricity, food-processing, sugar, alcohol and alcoholic beverages, soap, wood products and furniture, non-metallic quarrying, and metal industries.

The third and most important element of the Lebanese economy is services, including commerce, tourism, entertainment, entrepôt and transit traffic, international financial transactions, insurance, transport, warehousing, education and various other services. No other country in the world relies as heavily as Lebanon on services for its livelihood. This source provides about 65 percent of the total national income.

Beirut, the capital city, commercial center, and main sea port, is one of the most—and probably the most—important commercial center in the eastern Mediterranean. This is due to several factors, among the most important of which are: first, the port of Beirut has a free market zone, almost completely free of any restrictions on the movement of goods and capital. Second, it has an enviable geographic position as the gateway to the Arab hinterland. This fact has assumed particular importance since the development of the oil industry in the Persian Gulf and the consequent prosperity of that area. Third, over the last three centuries, Beirut developed institutional facilities (warehousing, banking, business connections, etc.) which are not available to the same degree in any other Arab country, except Egypt. Fourth, the Arab economic blockade of Israel, since 1948, has relieved Beirut of any competition from Tel-Aviv, Haifa and their merchants. Finally, around 1950, Western business establishments began to move from Cairo—their traditional center—to Beirut, where they felt they would be more secure. In recent years, Syria has been developing near-by Latakia as a rival port. The volume of business has been so great, however, that so far neither Beirut nor its merchants have been affected to any appreciable degree from this competition.

In addition to trade as such (i.e., purchase, sale and transit of goods), Beirut has become the international financial center of the area. There is hardly any restriction on the movement of capital into and out of the country. In addition to money changers who do a vast amount of business, the number of banks operating in Beirut, increased from seven in 1945 to over 40 in 1957. Most are owned or controlled by foreign interests, mainly European, but also American. Among the latter may be mentioned the Chase Manhattan Bank (1950), the First National City Bank (1955), and the Bank of America (1956).

In addition to trade and finance, Lebanon has benefited directly from the development of the oil industry in the Persian Gulf. The Iraq Petroleum Company has a pipeline which terminates in the port town of Tripoli; and Tapline (Trans-Arabian Pipeline, an associate of the Arabian American Oil Company) has another terminating in Sidon. In addition to transit dues which these companies pay Lebanon,[6] they also employ several thousand workers. Moreover, these pipelines have made possible the construction of refineries to supply the local market.

The geographic location of Lebanon at the hub of international sea, air and land routes, the completion in 1954 of an international airport at Beirut, the development of the entertainment industry, and above all, its pleasant climate, the beauty of its mountains (Lebanon has been called the Switzerland of the Middle East) and its Mediterranean coastline, have made it the tourist center *par excellence* of the Middle East.

Between 1951 and 1955 inclusive, the number of tourists and transit tourists (excluding Syrians), rose respectively from 90,000 and 82,000 to 179,000 (tourists) and 260,000 (transit tourists). Income from this source (again excluding Syrians) during the same period rose from £L. 42 million to 110 million.[7] In 1956, the Beirut airport was estimated to have handled some 450,000 transit passengers, in addition to those entering the country for longer periods of time.[8]

In 1956, it was estimated that Lebanon had over 320 hotels with some 16,000 rooms, employing about 15,000 workers. During the same year, the number of restaurants, cafés and night clubs was estimated to be 1,775, employing some 11,000 workers.[9]

The president of the Hotel Employees and Workers Union estimated that in 1956, nationals of the Arab states, including those from Syria and Egypt, comprised about 50 percent of the tourists and spent, during the summer season alone, an estimated £L. 150 million.[10]

A source of invisible income is the remittances of Lebanese immigrants, principally in the United States. In the past, this source used to play an important role in the economy of the country. In recent decades, particularly since the Second World War, this source has declined both in absolute and relative terms. Today, it accounts for about 14-22 million dollars a year.[11]

As has already been stated, agriculture and industry account for about 35 percent of the national income, while services provide the remaining 65 percent. This heavy reliance on services—which has no parallel anywhere in the world—makes the Lebanese economy extremely vulnerable, since the magnitude of these services depends on international conditions (fluctuations in prices, recessions, political conditions, etc.) over which the Lebanese government has no control.

In recent years, the above situation has caused considerable criticism of government policy, and raised vociferous demands that it take active measures for the development of both agriculture and industry. Moreover, as is usual with almost everything else in the Middle East, the issue, economic in nature, became entangled in internal, regional and international political questions.[12]

In the case of both agriculture and industry, despite the limitations mentioned previously, there is still room for some expansion. However, owing primarily to the opposition of the powerful mercantile interests which are heavily represented in government, so far only limited protection and assistance has been given to these two sectors.[13]

* * *

The most recent census in Lebanon was taken in 1932. However, a rationing census (with rather dubious results), conducted in 1942, came to be recognized as an equivalent. Since then only estimates have existed. The "census" is a political issue in Lebanon. The Christians—primarily the Maronites among them—insist that they are in the majority, although it is commonly believed that this is no longer the case, and that the Muslims are either equal or even superior in numbers. As a result, the Christians have opposed the taking of a census. In this connection, it is of interest to note that the taking of a census was included among the "musts" in the first policy statement issued in 1943 by Riāḍ al-Ṣulḥ, the premier of the first cabinet of independent Lebanon.[14] Nevertheless, no steps were taken in that direction, probably to avoid sectarian discord. In recent years, there has been increasing restiveness among the Muslims (primarily the Sunnis) on this question.

There have been various estimates as to the present population of Lebanon. They are all projections based on the above-mentioned 1942 census. The latest, in 1957, by the United Nations, put the figure at 1,525,000 excluding 102,000 registered Palestinian refugees.[15] Another estimate put the figure in 1956 at 1,450,000 Lebanese citizens, 112,000 Arab refugees, and 13,000 other aliens, thus making a total of 1,575,000[16]. In the absence of any definitive data, this last figure seems as good as any.

Of the total population, over 26 percent live in Beirut, the capital city (450,000); and a further 10-15 percent in Tripoli (140,000), Sidon (Ṣaida) (36,000), Zahlah (20,000) and Tyre (Ṣūr) (12,000).[17]

Lebanon has one of the highest rates of population increase in the world—estimated at three percent a year in 1957,[18] and one of the lowest mortality rates in the Middle East (5.4 per thousand in 1953).[19]

In the past some 15,000 Lebanese used to emigrate each year, principally to the Americas and particularly to the United States. Australia and West Africa have also been main recipients. Emigration was caused in the past by political factors, population pressure on the land, famines and the lure of wealth. Due to immigration restrictions in foreign countries, the above figure has declined in recent decades to 2,000-4,000 a year. The majority of the immigrants have been Christians, but there are many Muslims and Druze as well. Some believe that the Lebanese (or people of Lebanese origin) living abroad number more than those in Lebanon itself.

The most significant aspect of the population in Lebanon is not its geographic distribution, ecological, racial or linguistic structure, but rather its religious distribution. This aspect has been the main theme of political and cultural life for several centuries. Some Lebanese writers would even trace this phenomenon as far back as ancient times.[20]

Lebanon, unlike any other state in the Middle East, is a country of religious minorities, each conscious of its separate identity, jealous of its rights, and a little different from the other in its outlook and orientation. The largest single group are the Maronites who constitute some 30 percent of the total population. It is true, however, that the main divisions lie along Christian-Muslim lines.

The Economic Research Institute of the American University of Beirut, basing its calculations partly on official data, estimated the religious distribution in 1956 as follows:

Muslims and Druze:	*Sub-Total*	*Total*
Sunnis	286,000	
Shi'as	250,000	
Druze	88,000	624,000
Christians:		
Maronites	424,000	
Greek Orthodox	149,000	
Greek Catholics (Melkites)	91,000	
Armenian Orthodox	64,000	
Armenian Catholics	15,000	
Protestants	14,000	
Syrian Catholics	6,000	
Syrian Orthodox	5,000	
Latins (Roman Catholics)	4,000	
Chaldeans	1,000	773,000
Miscellaneous:		
Jews	7,000	
Others	7,000	14,000
Grand Total		1,411,000

The geographic distribution of the main religious communities is of considerable interest. The Maronites comprise the great majority in Mount Lebanon, and predominate in a number of coastal towns. The Greek Orthodox, Greek Catholics, and the Protestants are found in both the towns and villages of central Lebanon. The Sunni

Muslims are almost wholly urban. They are concentrated in Beirut, Tripoli and Sidon. In Beirut, they constitute about one-third of the population, while they virtually dominate Tripoli, as well as the region of ʿAkkār. The Shiʿa predominate in south Lebanon and the Biqāʿ. About three-fourths of the Druze live in the southern half of Mount Lebanon, just east and south of Beirut.

The first people to appear prominently in the historical scene of Lebanon were the Canaanites, who occupied the coastal area adjacent to the mountains around 3,000 B.C.[21] About a thousand years later, they began to be called Phoenicians.

Lebanon was invaded and controlled at one time or the other, by Hittites, Egyptians, Persians, Greeks, Romans and Byzantines. The Roman period which commenced in 64-63 B.C. with Pompey's conquest of the area, was perhaps the most significant.

During the Roman period (including the Byzantine), Greco-Roman culture became wide-spread; Aramaic replaced Phoenician as the language of the country; Christianity displaced all earlier religions and gave the country a "Christian character" which was to remain with it even to this day.

In 634-40 A.D., Lebanon, Syria and Palestine came under the sway of the Muslim Arabs (as distinguished from earlier Arab tribal movements). Gradually, Syria and Palestine were islamized and arabicized, but the penetration of Islam into Lebanon was very slow, and that of the Arabic language even slower. Only in the 13th century was the victory of the Arabic language over Aramaic virtually complete. Nevertheless, Syriac (a branch of Aramaic) continued to be widely spoken in the mountains until the 17th century. To this day, it is still spoken in three Christian villages in the Anti-Lebanon—Maʿlūla, Bakhʿah and Jubbʿadin,[22] and used in the liturgy of some Christian churches.

With the Arab Muslim conquest, Mount Lebanon embarked on its historical role of providing refuge for Christians, and Muslim dissidents and in becoming the home of lost causes.

The Arabs evicted Christians from coastal towns[23] as a military measure and replaced them with Muslims as a counter-balance for the Christians of the mountain.[24] Otherwise, by and large, they left the mountain alone, although Muʿāwiyah (661-680 A.D.) and some of his successors made several atempts to bring the mountain under Arab control, without success.[25]

It was around this time, out of the amalgamation of Mardites (Christians from the Amanus and Taurus mountains) with native and other Christians from Syria, that the Maronites and Mount

Lebanon began to assume a national significance. Some of the Christians who were expelled from coastal towns, together with those who wanted to escape Muslim domination, migrated to the fastness of Mount Lebanon. Later, they were joined by the Mardites.[26]

The Maronites owe their name to the patron saint of their Church, Marūn, an ascetic monk who died about 410 A.D. The founder was the first bishop, Yuhanna Marūn (*d. ca.* 707 A.D.) under whose leadership the Maronite community attained a near independent status.[27] Since the fifteenth century Qannūbīn, cradled in the mountain just below the Cedars, has been the seat of the Maronite Patriarchate. Bikirki, however, is now used in the winter. The head of the church is styled "Patriarch of Antioch and all the East."

Originally, the Maronites held the monothelete doctrine that Christ had two natures (human and divine) but one divine will. They gave up this doctrine, however, in the 12th century, and in 1439 at the Council of Florence united with Rome. Full union was not effected until 1736 at the Synod of al-Luwzayah, when doctrinal and other questions were finally agreed upon.[28] In 1584, Pope Gregory XIII established a Maronite College in Rome which, in addition to training Maronite clergy, produced many distinguished scholars.[29]

The early connection of the Maronites with Rome, their trade with the Italian city states, their support of the Crusaders, and Catholic missionary activity among them, particularly that of the Jesuits, in addition to the disabilities imposed on the Christians by the Muslims, have made them identify themselves with the "Christian" West, and in particular with France.

Louis IV of France, in a letter dated May 21, 1205, is credited with giving the Maronites his protection.[30] Much later, Louis XIV in a circular letter, dated April 28, 1649, instructed his diplomatic representatives to give French protection to the Maronites and to treat them "with all possible charity and gentleness."[31]

Another religious group which came to play an important role in the history of Lebanon were the Druze, who emerged in the 11th century. The Druze owe their name to Muḥammad al-Darazī, a confidant of al-Ḥakīm (996-1031) the Fatimid Caliph of Egypt. Al-Darazī taught that God had manifested Himself nine or ten times in history, and that al-Ḥakīm was the last such incarnation. When al-Ḥakīm was killed, his followers denied his death and maintained that he is only in a state of temporary "absence" from which he will triumphantly return at the opportune time.

The new cult found few adherents in Egypt. But in Syria (to

which al-Darazī fled from the anger of a Cairo mob when he announced his doctrine) the new message struck home in the area at the foot of Mount Hermon. It is here that the movement can be said to have been born. Gradually, the movement worked its way northwards into the mountains. By the time of the Crusades, the Druze had reached and controlled the Shūf district southeast of Beīrut, and had converted such tribes as the Tannūkhs, the Ma'ns, the Arislāns, and Junblāṭs. These families provided, and the last two still provide the leadership.[32]

For sometime the history of Lebanon was dominated by the two religious groups: the Maronites and the Druze. With the migration of Arab tribes, Sunnis and Shia's, primarily to the coastal areas and the plains, and with the presence of various other Christian groups, the confessional structure of Lebanon began to emerge and take definite form.

In 1516-17, the Ottoman Turks under Selim I conquered Syria and Lebanon. A delegation of Amirs from Lebanon went to Damascus to pay him homage. Selim confirmed them in their fiefs, allowed the same autonomy they enjoyed under the Mamlūks, and imposed a comparatively light tribute on them. He was, however, so impressed by Fakhr al-dīn I of the Ma'n family, that he bestowed on him the title of Sultan of the Mountain. The star of the Tannūkhs began to wane and that of the Ma'ns to rise.

The power of the Ma'ns reached its zenith in the person of Fakhr al-dīn II (1586-1635), grandson of Fakhr al-dīn I. He is regarded as the father of modern Lebanon. His brilliant career came to an abrupt end when he was captured by the Turks in 1635, taken to Constantinople, and strangled in the court of one of the mosques there. In 1697, when Aḥmad, the last of the Ma'n line, died childless, the amirs and notables of Lebanon met in a national conclave and elected Amīr Bashīr al-Shihāb as governor. The House of Shihāb ruled the country at the head of a feudal pyramid, for almost a century and a half (1697-1841).

The House of Shihāb reached the pinnacle of its power in Bashīr II, called the Great (1788-1840). Like his famous predecessor, Fakhr al-dīn II, he set for himself the goals of independence, modernization and progress, using for their achievement the same methods of bribery, intrigue, alliances and war. Toward the end of his long and checkered career, during which he went four times into voluntary exile, religious differences and strife assumed a country-wide character the intensity of which had never existed before, thus setting the tone of future political life, and leading to the direct intervention of the Western powers in the internal affairs of Lebanon. This came about with the invasion of Ibrāhīm Pasha and the Egyptian occupation of Lebanon (1831-1840).

The principal contribution of the Egyptian occupation of Lebanon to sectarianism, was the splitting of the Mountain into two hostile, armed and suspicious camps (Christian and Druze), willing and capable to plunge the country into a religious holocaust at the first intentional or unintentional provocation.[33]

The departure of Ibrāhīm Pasha with his Egyptian troops, and the end of Bashīr's rule in 1840, was followed by a brief period (1840-1860) of virtual anarchy in which confessional hate played the primary role. This was further encouraged and fomented by British and French agents, and the Turkish authorities. Lebanon and its people fell prey to international politics, and was left to the mercy of imperial forces which were beyond its control or, for that matter, the comprehension of its people.

After Bashīr II was deposed, the Ottoman Porte directly asserted his authority by appointing the Christian Qāsim al-Shihāb (1840-42, renamed Bashīr III), as Prince of the Mountain. In 1841 shortly after his accession, a small incident (the shooting of a partridge by a Christian on the property of a Druze) touched off the first Druze-Christian conflagration (commonly called in Lebanon, *al-ḥarakah al-ūlā*). The Druze marched on Dayr al-Qamar, a Maronite stronghold, killed off most of its people, and set it on fire (October 14, 1841).

Following the above outrage, Bashīr III was deposed thus bringing to an end the era of amirs, and ushering in the *Mutaṣarrifiyah* Period in which Lebanon, the Mountain, was internationally recognized as autonomous.

In 1842, in an agreement between Turkey on the one hand, and the five Great Powers (Austria, Britain, France, Prussia, Russia) on the other, Mount Lebanon was divided into two districts *(qā'im maqāmiyah),* one Christian in the north, and one Druze in the south. Each was to be governed by a *qā'im maqām* chosen from the local inhabitants by the Ottoman Pasha of Sidon.

The last and most infamous outburst was the massacre of 1860 which continued in unabated and unprecedented fury from April to July and spilled over from Lebanon into Syria.

At last, with the approval of the other Great Powers, 6,000 French troops were landed in Beirut in August 1860. However, they were preceded by Fu'ād Pasha, the Turkish foreign minister, with fresh Turkish troops, who re-established law and order even before the French arrived.

After the arrival of the French, Fu'ād Pasha set up an international commission with himself as chairman and representatives of the five Great Powers as members. After determining the amount of indemnity to pay the Christians (1,250,000 pounds sterling), and meting out various sentences, the commission settled down to the business of setting up a new régime for Lebanon. On June 9, 1861 a new organic statute *(règlement organique)* was signed in Constantinople by France, Britain, Austria, Prussia, Russia and Turkey.[34] Amended in 1864, it remained in force until the outbreak of the First World War.

The statute reconstituted the entire Mountain into an autonomous *mutaṣarrifiyah,* to be administered by a Governor-General *(mutaṣarrif)* appointed by the Porte with the approval of the Great Powers for a term of three years (in 1864 extended to five, and in 1868 to ten years). He had to be a Christian, and (in practice) non-Lebanese.

The statute also created a Central Administrative Council of twelve members (two for each of the Maronites, Greek Orthodox, Greek Catholics, Sunnis, Shi'as and Druze) and charged it with "assessing taxes, administering revenues and expenditures, and rendering its advisory opinion on all questions submitted to it by the governor."

In the 1864 revision of the statute, the Mountain was divided into seven districts as against six previously. Instead of the simple ratio of two representatives for each religious group in the Central Administrative Council, each of the seven districts was allotted a certain number of seats which had to be filled on a confessional basis. Thus the confessional ratio system was introduced for each of the districts, as well as for the Mountain as a whole.

Each of the districts *(qada)* had a sub-governor *(qā'im maqām)* appointed by the Governor from the dominant religious group. Thus there were three Maronites, one Greek Orthodox, one Greek Catholic, one Muslim and one Druze.

The statute abolished feudal privileges, bestowed equal rights on all citizens, and provided for a population census and a land survey. Internal security was to be maintained by local police under the jurisdiction of the Governor, and no Turkish troops were to be allowed in the land. No military service was required of the inhabitants, and no tribute due to the Turkish Porte. Taxes were to be levied to meet local needs only, but if a surplus occurred it went to the

Turkish imperial treasury which, however, had to cover any deficits.

In short, the Mountain, in so far as internal matters were concerned, was virtually separate from the Turkish empire. Just as important is the fact that this autonomy was guaranteed by the Concert of Europe.

Da'ūd Effendi, an Armenian Catholic, was the first and most able governor. He was followed by a series of ineffectual successors. Nevertheless, during the new régime which lasted until the outbreak of the First World War, the Mountain enjoyed cultural flowering, economic prosperity, and public peace which had no parallel anywhere in the Near East. Without question, despite many shortcomings, Mount Lebanon was the best governed of the Ottoman provinces.

An important development took place during this period. Many Druze, motivated by fear and other factors, migrated into neighboring Syria, so that they were greatly reduced in number in Lebanon itself. As a result, the Christian-Druze controversy lost, to all practical purposes, its significance and much of its bitterness.

NOTES

1. Most of the technical data in this section are based on W.B. Fisher, *The Middle East,* London: Methuen, 2nd. ed., 1952, pp. 371-77.
2. United Nations, *Economic Developments in the Middle East 1956-1957,* New York: 1958, pp. 68-69.
3. For statistical data consult the following: *Ibid.,* p. 68; N. A. Ziadeh, *Syria and Lebanon,* London: Ernest Benn, Ltd., 1957, pp. 218-19; R.I.I.A., *The Middle East, A Political and Economic Survey,* London: Oxford University Press, 3rd ed., 1958, pp. 358-60; Y.A. al-Ḥilū, *On the Lebanese Economy,* (in Arabic). Beirut: Dār al-Fārābī, 1957?, pp. 27-39.
4. *Economic Developments in the Middle East, 1956-57,* p. 69.
5. U.N., *Economic Developments in the Middle East, 1955-56,* New York: 1957, p. 37.
6. Both Syria and Lebanon are in conflict with the two companies over transit dues.
7. al-Ḥilū, *op. cit.,* p. 88.
8. *Ibid.,* p. 88.
9. *Ibid.,* p. 87-88
10. *Ibid.,* pp. 88-89.
11. Ziadeh, *op. cit.,* p 242.
12. For criticisms of the opposition on this issue see the following Lebanese writers: al-Ḥilū, *op. cit.,* Fu'ād Ammūn, *The Foreign Policy of Lebanon,* (in Arabic); Beirut: Dār al-Nashr al-'Arabiyyah, 1959, pp. 89-97; Kamāl Junblāṭ, *The True Nature of the Lebanese Revolt,* (in Arabic). Beirut: Dār al-Nashr al-'Arabiyyah, 1959, pp. 163-66.
13. R.I.I.A., *op. cit.,* p. 360.
14. In this connection al-Ṣulḥ stated, "One of the things which must be attended to, in order to insure full and true popular representation, is the conducting of a general census supervised by a group which would combine competence, honesty and impartiality. We shall proceed in this work soon." For full text of the policy statement see, The First Arab Cultural Conference, *Lebanon in the Era of Independence* (in Arabic), Beirut: Dār al-Aḥad, 1947, pp. 5-17.
15. U.N., *1958 Statistical Yearbook,* p. 31.
16. H.R.A.F., *The Republic of Lebanon,* New Haven: 1956, p. 54.
17. The figures for Beirut, Tripoli and Sidon are estimates of the Economic Research

Institute of A.U.B. Those for Zaḥlah and Tyre are from Europa Publications, Ltd., *The Middle East,* London: 5th ed., 1957, p. 252.

18. 1958 Statistical Yearbook, *op. cit.,* p. 31.

19. R.I.I.A., *op. cit.,* p. 357.

20. For instance see Anīs Ṣāyigh, *Confessional Lebanon,* (in Arabic). Beirut: Dār al-Ṣirā' al-Fikrī, 1955.

21. For details on ancient Lebanon, see Philip Hitti, *Lebanon in History,* London: Macmillan & Co., 1957.

22. Philip Hitti, *History of Syria,* New York: Macmillan, 1951, p. 546.

23. Many Christians collaborated with their Byzantine co-religionists against the Muslim Arabs and did constitute a military threat.

24. Ṣāyigh, *op cit.,* p. 57.

25. *Lebanon in History,* p. 245.

26. *Ibid.,* pp. 245-47.

27. *Ibid.,* pp. 247-49.

28. *Ibid.,* p. 406.

29. *Ibid.,* pp. 402-406.

30. For text of the letter see Lebanon League of Progress, *The Lebanese Book,* (in Arabic). New York: al-Hoda Press, n.d. (ca. 1936), p. 219.

31. For the text of the letter see J. C. Hurewitz, *Diplomacy in the Near and Middle East,* Princeton: D. Van Nostrand Co., Ltd., 1956, Vol. I, p. 24.

32. For details see *Lebanon in History,* pp. 257-264.

33. For details see *Ibid.,* pp. 423-425; C. G. Hess, Jr., and H. L. Bodman, Jr., "Confessionalism and Feudality in Lebanese Politics," *The Middle East Journal.* Winter, 1954, pp. 10-26.

34. For full text see Hurewitz, *op. cit.,* pp. 165-68.

CHAPTER II

Political History and Government

IN 1920, Lebanon came under a French mandate which lasted for some twenty years and terminated officially in 1943. During this period several important developments took place:

First, in order to create "Greater Lebanon" *(Grand Liban)*, the French added to the Mountain an area more than twice its own size, comprising the fertile Biqāʿ plain and the coastal zone.[1] In this manner the Sunni population was increased almost eight times, the Shia's four times, while the Maronite population increased only by one third. Thus, no longer could the Maronites claim a "Christian Lebanon."

Second, a new factor appeared—regionalism. While the Maronites favored a French mandate,[2] the population of the annexed areas, predominantly Muslim, were reluctant participants in the enlarged country, and favored inclusion in Syria; and, particularly in the early period, felt the tremendous pull of Fayṣal's Arab government in Damascus.[3]

Third, the French, in addition to reintroducing confessionalism into political life, also introduced for the first time, what is known as "feudality" into politics through the now-famous "list" system. Most of the electoral districts were multi-seat districts. Thus, theoretically, under the "list" system any group in an electoral district could combine to form a list of candidates. Actually, however, owing to the absence of any genuine party organization and to the existence of clan loyalties, the practice resulted in

> the formation of lists centered around a strong clan leader, usually landed. To his list would be attracted members of other—usually minority-confessions in the electoral district on a compromise or payment basis, with a requisite pledge of complete political fealty. Money and clan influence, violence and threats, were the usual electioneering methods, with the result that political power became associated with either clan strength or wealth. As a result, the list system permitted the strong, landed individual to become 'chief of the list.' Thus was the new 'feudality' established.[4]

Fourth, this period saw an extensive spread of the French language and culture, particularly in the cities among Maronites and other Catholics—to the point of their being virtually gallicized.

Many Lebanese in the cities spoke only French at home, could not read or write Arabic, their mother tongue, ate French food, and knew and read only French literature and magazines. Some intermarried with the French, and others considered themselves virtually French.[5] For instance, Emile Eddé (Iddah), a Maronite and three times President under the French mandate—publicly stated during this period that Lebanon was a "Christian island" in a Muslim sea, and that its culture was Western and French.[6]

Finally, during this period "Phoenicianism" and "Mediterraneanism"[7] came into some vogue, mostly among Christians. Both were encouraged and fostered by the French.[8] Both ideas are essentially variations of the same general theme. The first states that the Lebanese are racially and culturally Phoenician in origin and different from the Arabs; the second, that the Lebanese belong to the same racial group that inhabits the Mediterranean basin, and that their culture is "Mediterranean" rather than Arab. In addition, "Syrianism," propagated by the Syrian National Social Party,[9] made considerable headway in Lebanon, Syria, Jordan and Palestine. Fundamentally, this theory states that the inhabitants of the Fertile Crescent, by social interaction, history and geography, are one nation—the Syrian nation, and that they, too, are different from the Arabs.[10]

Concurrently with all these cultural and ideological movements, Arab nationalism in one form or another was competing for position. After the departure of the French it was to gain considerable strength and momentum. Conversely, "Phoenicianism," "Mediterraneanism," and "Syrianism" lost popular appeal and the thin veneer of French culture began to wear off.

* * *

In December 1946, the last French soldier left Lebanon. The broad outlines of the basis of the new independent Republic of Lebanon were laid down in 1943 in an unwritten understanding, or gentlemen's agreement, between the two outstanding Christian and Muslim leaders of the country—Bishārah al-Khūrī, first President, and Riāḍ al-Ṣulḥ, first Prime Minister of independent Lebanon. This was later approved and supported by their respective followers, and came to be known as the National Covenant *(al-Mithāq al-Waṭanī)*.[11]

The Covenant laid down the following principles:

1. Lebanon was to be a completely independent sovereign state. The Christians were to forego seeking foreign protection (i.e., Western and in particular French) or attempting to bring Lebanon under foreign control or influence. In return, the Muslims were to forego

making any attempt to bring Lebanon into any political union with Syria, or into any form of Arab union.

2. Lebanon was a country with an Arab "face" and language and a part of the Arab world—with a special "character." Despite its Arabism, however, Lebanon would not cut off its cultural and spiritual ties with Western civilization which had helped it to reach an enviable degree of progress.

3. Lebanon was to cooperate with all the Arab states and to become a member in the Arab family, provided the Arab states recognized its independence and sovereignty within the present boundaries. In its relation with the Arab states, Lebanon should not side with one group against another.

4. Public offices would be distributed equitably among the recognized confessions, but in technical positions preference would be given to competence without regard to confessional considerations. The three leading positions in the country were to be distributed according to the following convention: President of the Republic, Maronite; the Prime Minister, Sunni Muslim; the President of the Parliament, Shi'a Muslim.

In other words, in relation to the Arab world, Lebanon was to regard itself as an Arab state "with a special character," to cooperate economically, politically, culturally and militarily with the Arab states, act in concert with them on the international level, refuse to align itself in any way with any foreign power against the interests of the Arab states singly or collectively, but in disputes among the Arab states, themselves, was to remain neutral. In return, the Arab states had to recognize its independence and not to make attempts to incorporate it in any unification schemes. The independence of Lebanon was recognized individually by all the Arab states, and collectively in 1944 by the Alexandria Protocol which prepared the way for the Pact of the Arab League.

The constitutional structure reflects the spirit of the National Covenant and the extremely delicate political balance between the various communities in a plural society. This balance is so fragile and sensitive that any degree of internal dissatisfaction or outside pressure can upset it, and cause the machinery of government to break down. Because of this fact it is virtually axiomatic in Lebanon that, for the government to function, it must be acceptable to the important population blocs, at the least.

Conversely, because of this delicate balance; because in order to function the government must not antagonize, the Lebanese government, compared to other governments in the area, is something of a shadow government and the Lebanese people enjoy freedom which, despite many imperfections, has no parallel anywhere in the Middle East. This can be seen in many ways: fear of the police does not exist in Lebanon. Unlicensed parties maintain offices in the main squares of Beirut, publish papers and even put up candidates in parliamentary elections. A thriving press, representing almost every imaginable point of view, publishes attacks on the government—a refreshing phenomenon and one conspicuous by its absence in the rest of the Arab world today. By and large, except during periods of unrest, a relaxed atmosphere predominates in the country, and a spirit of live and let live prevails.

Under the constitution, the President who—by usage—must be a Maronite, is invested with such extensive powers that the system of government may be called presidential. He is elected for a term of six years by the Chamber of Deputies *(Majlis al-Nuwāb)*. He may not, however, be elected twice in succession. This is an important point and one which will be crucial to our entire story. He appoints and dismisses all members of the cabinet including the Prime Minister, and all other public officers not otherwise provided for by law. He is authorized to conclude executive agreements which can be terminated by the signatories after one year, but must bring these to the attention of the Chamber "as soon as the interest and safety of the State permit." He also negotiates all other treaties, but those involving expenditure of public funds or relate to commerce must be ratified by the Chamber before they can come into force.

The President is also endowed with legislative initiative. He may put into effect by decree any bill which the cabinet considers urgent after its consideration by the Chamber without decision for more than forty days. He promulgates laws after adoption by the Chamber, and enjoys the right of suspensory veto which only an absolute majority of the total Chamber can override. He may suspend the Chamber for not more than one month in each of its two sessions; he may call it into an extraordinary session fixing its agenda and duration. And he has the power to dissolve it completely by decree, with the approval of the cabinet.

* * *

The legislature is composed of a unicameral Chamber of Deputies. Members are elected by direct ballot for a four year term.[12] The composition of the Chamber, however, is not determined by individual or party victories at the polls, but on the basis of the size of the various religious communities. In turn, this "size" is not determined by census, but is fixed permanently by legal fiction.

In 1920, it was "established" by the French that the Maronites comprised 29 percent of the total population; the Sunnis, 21; the Shi'as, 18.5; the Greek Orthodox, 9.7 percent and so on down the line to the Chaldeans constituting roughly 0.1 percent of the population.[13] These percentages served then as the basis for the structure and administration of the state, as they still do today.

A glance at Table I will reveal an interesting fact. Between 1943 and 1960, the number of deputies in the Chamber changed from 55 to 77 to 44 to 66 to 99. Yet in each case, the number has been a multiple of eleven. This figure of "11" is derived from the understanding that the composition of the Chamber must be in the ratio of six Christians to five non-Christians.

TABLE I

Composition of the Chamber of Deputies
1943 - 1960

Confession	*Number of Deputies*					
	*1943**	*1947*	*1951*	*1953*	*1957*	*1960*
Maronites	18	18	23	13	20	30
Sunnis	11	11	16	9	14	20
Shi'as	10	10	14	8	12	19
Greek Orthodox	6	6	8	5	7	11
Druze	4	4	5	3	4	6
Greek Catholics	3	3	5	3	4	6
Armenian Orthodox	2	2	3	2	3	4
Protestants	—	—	1	—	—	1
Armenian Catholics	—	—	1	—	1	1
Minorities	1	1	1	1	1	1
Grand Total	55	55	77	44	66	99
Number of electoral Districts	7	7	9	33	33	26

* Refers to the year the Chamber was elected.

Before each election, an electoral law specifies the total number of deputies in the Chamber, divides the country into electoral districts, fixes the numbers of deputies for each district along with their confessional distribution. A candidate must deposit £L 3,000[14] which he forfeits if he receives less than 20 percent of the votes in his district. In 1952, voting became compulsory, under penalty of the law, to all male citizens. In the same year, women over 21 years of age who have at least an elementary education or its equivalent, were granted suffrage.

Members of the Chamber elect the President of the Chamber who, by usage, must be a Shiʿa. Only once so far—in 1947—has this tradition has been broken when the late Ḥabīb Shahla, Greek Orthodox, was elected.

The cabinet is appointed by the President of the Republic. In making his choice, the President must insure equitable confessional representation among its members. Cabinet members may or may not be chosen from among the deputies. They are responsible both to the President and the Chamber. The chief of the cabinet—the Prime Minister, must be a Sunni. Although the Prime Minister acts as a brake on the tremendous power of the President, his authority by comparison is feeble indeed.

As can be readily seen, through the distribution of the three main positions (i.e., President of the Republic, the Prime Minister, and the President of the Chamber) and confessional representation in the Chamber, the Cabinet and most of the important public offices, a system of confessional checks and balances has been devised in the functioning of the government, with supremacy, however, assured to the Christians.

Although this has enshrined confessional division, perpetuated the *millet* mentality, prevented the development of loyalties to a higher ideal and inhibited the evolution of democratic political institutions along Western lines; at the same time, it has been a stabilizing factor, for it has meant government by consent and concession, and made the assumption of dictatorial powers by a single individual a rather remote possibility. Further, this delicate equilibrium has acted as an effective safeguard of personal freedom and individual liberties, for any serious violation of the constitution infringing on communal rights, would inevitably precipitate a severe crisis, and possibly an armed rebellion.

Confessionalism has also inhibited the evolution of a genuine party system, and directed political activity on confessional lines. In a certain sense, parties in Lebanon are pointless, for the voter is restricted by law in his choice of candidates to a Sunni, a Shiʿa, a Maronite, and so on down the line. This is reflected in the existing influential parties in Lebanon. They are all based on confessional and/or clan foundations, and have hardly any programs or real party organization. Parties with ideologies, programs and organization, cutting across confessional and clan loyalties, are still weak and ineffective. Some political combinations are formed for limited objectives, as for instance in 1952 and 1957-58, but usually they disappear once the immediate objectives are achieved.

Since 1943, when Lebanon became officially independent, the

country has had three presidents: Bishārah al-Khūrī (1943-52), Camille Sham'ūn (Chamoun) 1952-58, and the present incumbent, Fu'ād Shihāb.

In 1943, Bishārah al-Khūrī and his Prime Minister, Riāḍ al-Ṣulḥ,[15] became national heroes when the French arrested them, thereby precipitating an international crisis.[16] Al-Khūrī remained popular until 1946. His prestige tailspinned in 1947 when, through fraudulent elections, he brought in a puppet Chamber which, on May 22, 1948, adopted a constitutional amendment enabling him to succeed himself. Another puppet Chamber, fraudulently elected in April 1951, proved to be the beginning of his political demise. The government machinery became riddled with graft, corruption and nepotism. In 1952 he was forced to resign, whereupon he virtually retired from the political scene until 1958. He was succeeded by Sham'ūn.

* * *

Insofar as the Sham'ūn Administration came to power under unusual circumstances, and to the extent that the events immediately preceding its assumption of power provide a framework for evaluation of future policy, it is important to recite those events in some detail.

Sham'ūn's opposition to the al-Khūrī administration dated back to 1948 when he resigned his cabinet post as Minister of Interior. In his letter of resignation (dated May 19, 1948), he cited as among the principal reasons for his resignation: the projected amendment of the constitution to enable al-Khūrī to be re-elected, something which he felt "should never be done, lest a precedent of amending the constitution for personal reasons be established;" the failure of the administration to root out corruption and bribery, to introduce civil and financial laws consonant with the modern world, to plan Lebanese economic and fiscal life on a sound basis, to reform the electoral law which "so far has prevented the people from returning their own choice," and to safeguard public liberties, especially the freedom of the press. In concluding his letter, he said, "I feel I should tender my resignation, and devote myself to collaboration with national circles which share such views with me."

After the April 1951 elections which returned another puppet Chamber, an opposition developed inside the Chamber known as the National Socialist Front (N.S.F.). It was essentially an alliance of Junblāṭ's Progressive Socialist Party, Eddé's National Bloc, and the National Call Party under the leadership of al-Bazzī. From its inception, the N.S.F. was joined by independent but influential deputies such as Sham'ūn, Franjiyah (Frangíe) 'Usayrān, Ḥājj and Ghassān al-Tuwaynī.

Outside the Chamber another opposition alliance made up of three parties—the Phalanges, the National Organization, and the National Congress, was formed and called itself the Popular Front.

On September 9, the country witnessed a spectacle unique in the annals of politics—a Prime Minister, while still in office, officially denouncing his Chief, the President. Sāmī al-Ṣulḥ, the then Prime Minister, in reporting to the Chamber of Deputies, read a statement denouncing al-Khūrī and his family and citing specific examples of irregular dealings, traffic in influence, and scandals in business transactions. "Men of authority who rule without being responsible," he said, "interfere in every affair of the State. They interfere with justice and request judges and other officials to follow their own policies and serve their party aims at the expense of justice and law. Woe to the judge or official who refuses such requests." He further implied that the President had large sums of money hidden in foreign banks. In concluding his speech, he said, "They have impoverished and opposed the people . . . Gentlemen! how can you expect us to continue our work in this suffocating atmosphere . . . and how can there be any reform before the source of evil is rooted out?"[17]

On the same day (September 9), the Cabinet, dissociating itself from the speech of its Prime Minister, resigned. The President dismissed Sāmī al-Ṣulḥ and appointed a caretaker government composed of three officials.

The trial of strength between the President and the Opposition began moving speedily to its climax. The Opposition, which now had the support of al-Ṣulḥ and al-Yāfī, issued a call for a two-day general strike to be held on September 15 and 16. The President, on the other hand, was able to induce Ṣā'ib Salām, a Beirut deputy and a respected businessman, to become Prime Minister. The latter, pressed by the threat of a strike and finding no takers, formed a small cabinet of three members besides himself on September 14. Salām prudently and tactfully allowed the strike to take place, and it went off without incident.

On September 17, fourteen deputies[18] addressed notes to the President requesting his immediate resignation. Although the large majority of the Chamber was still loyal to the President, nevertheless Salām advised him to resign, arguing that although he had the support of a majority in the Chamber, he no longer enjoyed the confidence of the people. Salām himself resigned on the same day.

At this stage the army entered the picture and then decided the issue. General Fu'ād Shihāb, the Chief of Staff, made it clear that the army would try to keep law and order, but would not fight against the people. In other words, the army would remain neutral.

Al-Khūrī, unable to find a reputable person to become Prime Minister or to depend on the support of the army and desiring to avoid a civil war, resigned on the morning of September 19th. On September 23rd, the Chamber unanimously (with one blank) elected Sham'ūn President.

Sham'ūn's candidacy to the Presidency was supported by the National Socialist Front (N.S.F.) which spearheaded the movement for the resignation of al-Khūrī. Sham'ūn was one of its leading members.

In return for this support, which meant virtual assurance of his election, in an unpublicized document dated September 21, 1952, signed and witnessed by Kamāl Junblāṭ, Ghassān al-Tuwaynī, Camille Sham'ūn, Anwar al-Khaṭīb, 'Abdallah al-Ḥājj, and Emile al-Bustānī; Sham'ūn pledged himself "on my honor and convictions" to pursue and put into effect the following policies:[19]

1. The independence and integrity of Lebanon; non-alignment with any foreign government, and maintenance of friendly relations with all the Great Powers (art. 1).

2. To abstain from using the influence and prestige of his office for personal monetary gain and self-aggrandizement, or for the benefit of relatives and friends (arts. 2 & 3). Also, to close down his law office if elected (art. 4).

3. To put into effect the programs of the Front, "particularly that for which the strike took place." (art. 5).

4. To amend the electoral law and to dissolve the existing Chamber of Deputies (art. 6).

5. To abolish "secret funds" in all government departments, with the exception of the ministries of interior, finance and foreign affairs (art. 7).

6. To insure that appointments and promotions in government departments shall be exclusively on the basis of merit and competence, and by examination (art. 8).

7. To refuse absolutely to appoint any person with a tarnished reputation to a ministerial or any other post, or to be guided by confessionalism (art. 10).

8. Not to take any action contrary to the declarations and criticisms formerly made by the Front (art. 11).

The year 1952 coincided with the beginnings of a socio-political revolutionary movement in the Arab world. Syria was in the throws of revolutionary upheavals, while Egypt had just overthrown King Fārūq and all he stood for. All over the Arab world there was a general feeling of revulsion and disgust with the "old guard." In Lebanon, itself, after several years of corruption, graft and nepotism, the public was hungry for reform.

In such an atmosphere, Sham'ūn possessed qualifications which commended him to various segments of the Lebanese public and to the Arab world in general. He was comparatively young (b. 1900) and endowed with considerable personal charm. He was born in Dayr al-Qamar—a Maronite stronghold—to middle class parents, rather than to one of the great feudal families. A lawyer by profession, he was known to hold liberal and reformist ideas. In local politics, he was, at one time or another, one of the leaders of the Constitutional Bloc, minister of finance and of interior. He also had experience in international affairs: he had represented the Lebanese Government in London, the United Nations and the Arab League. He professed to be an Arab nationalist, advocated close Arab cooperation and had extensive personal contacts with Arab leaders, particularly those of Syria, Saudi Arabia and Iraq.

* * *

During the first few years in office the Sham'ūn administration showed promise of measuring up to the expectations of the public from it.

With some help from international factors, the Lebanese economy soared to unprecedented heights of prosperity, making the standard of living in Lebanon the highest in the Arab world. "Real" wages of the common man were higher than in neighboring countries.

Although there was general prosperity which was visible in every walk of life, the greater part of the incoming wealth went into the coffers of a small mercantile class, thus, in actual practice, widening the gulf between the wealthy few and the common man. Second, the dependence of the Lebanese economy on services for the greater part of the national income made it extremely vulnerable. Hence, both situations, by their very nature, foreshadowed future trouble.

Politically, too, the new administration brought a breath of fresh air into government. For a while, there was little corruption, graft or scandal. An attempt was made to reform the civil service and some 300 officials were dismissed. This attempt not only failed but resulted in the addition of a new layer of Sham'ūn appointees to the already overloaded administrative apparatus.

The new administration also made a reformist attempt to destroy the "big list" system and its resultant companion—political feudalism. In November 1952, Sham'ūn, by holding the threat of dissolution over its head, forced a reluctant Chamber — a holdover from the Khūrī administration—to adopt a new electoral law. On May 30, 1953, when Emile Laḥḥūd, a deputy from Mount Lebanon, and his allies tried to make an issue of the new law, Sham'ūn dissolved the Chamber anyway, thus removing the last external vestige of the al-Khūrī administration.

The 1952 electoral law was a violent departure from the past. It made voting compulsory to all men, and granted suffrage to all women meeting primary school requirements. It divided Lebanon into 33 electoral districts, compared to nine previously. Eleven of the districts were to elect two deputies each, while the remaining 22 districts were allotted only one each. Thus the new Chamber would be composed of 44 deputies, distributed among the various confessions (see Table I), as against 77 formerly.

Regionally, in line with Sham'ūn's professed beliefs, Lebanon began to take a much more active part in Arab affairs. In June 1953 visas were abolished for all nationals of the Arab states. Sham'ūn visited Saudi Arabia, Egypt, Iraq, Syria and Jordan; Lebanon was visited by King Sa'ūd (before his accession), King Fayṣal and King Ḥusayn, and by President Shishaklī of Syria.

In the numerous quarrels between the Arab states Lebanon generally took a neutral position and at the same time played the role of peace-maker. This policy was expressed by President Sham'ūn as late as 1955 when the signing of the Baghdad Pact split the Arab world into two hostile camps. He said in February 1955:

> The preservation of the unity of the Arab front and the cooperation among the Arab League states is vital and should be placed above all other considerations . . . Every one of us gives due appreciation to the arguments made in support of the Iraqi-Turkish agreement on the one hand, and the objections to its conclusions on the other. What is important is to find a solution reconciling the opposite points of view, thus safeguarding the Arab League from the danger threatening it.[20]

Internationally, Lebanon maintained for a while friendly relations with all the Big Powers. It accepted economic and technical aid from the United States, signed trade agreements with East Germany (December 1953) and the Soviet Union (April 1954) and stepped up its exports to Czechoslovakia (December 1954).

By and large, until the end of 1954, Lebanon enjoyed peaceful and prosperous existence. Serious attempts were made at administrative and electoral reform but failed. She took a neutral position between the Arab states and played the role of peace-maker among them. At the same time, she maintained friendly relations with all the Big Powers and avoided becoming involved in the East-West conflict, or joining an international alliance.

The year 1955, however, was the turning point. Internal dissatisfaction including personalisms; regional tensions, particularly the upsurge of Arab nationalism under the dynamic leadership of President Nāṣir (Nasser) and the East-West conflict, were the factors which converged on Lebanon, interacted with each other and gradually but inexorably led to the crisis of 1958.

NOTES

1. The area of Lebanon—the Mountain was some 3,200 square kilometers. That of the annexed areas was 6,930 square kms.

2. See Muhammad Darwazeh, *Arab Unity* (in Arabic), Beirut: al-Maktab al-Tijārī, 1957, pp. 349-50. Also see by the same author, *On the Arab Movement* (in Arabic), Sidon: al-Maktabah al-'Aṣriyyah, 1950, Vol. II, pp. 125-30.

3. *Ibid.*, pp. 130-133.

4. Hess and Bodman, *op. cit.*, p. 16, Violence, purchase of seats and of votes, and fraud, have become standard procedures in Lebanese elections. For a graphic description see Eugenie Abu Chadid, *Thirty Years of Syria and Lebanon,* Beirut: 1950, (Post-script, 7-15). Also on the Lebanese elections of 1947, see *The Black Book of the Lebanese Elections,* New York: Phoenicia Press, 1947; and the National Bloc, *The Crime of 25 May,* n.p. (Beirut) 1947 (in Arabic).

5. An observation from the personal experience of the author.

6. *On the Arab Movement,* vol. II, p. 129.

7. This also found some vogue in Egypt and was propagated by such men as Ṭahā Ḥusayn. See his *The Future of Culture in Egypt.*

8. Nabīh A. Fāris and Muḥammad Tawfīq Ḥusayn, *This is the Arab World* (in Arabic), Beirut: Dār al-'Ilm Li al-Malāyīn, 1953, pp. 192-197.

9. The Syrian National Social Party is often referred to in Lebanon as the "Parti Populaire Syrienne." Hence, throughout this book we shall use the "P.P.S." designation for it.

10. See for a full discussion of the philosophy of the Syrian National Social Party, Anton Sa'ādah, *The Ten Lectures,* Beirut: 3rd ed., 1956. (In Arabic.)

11. For a good exposition of the National Covenant and its implications see, Joseph Mughaizal, *Lebanon and the Arab Question,* Beirut: 1959, pp. 88-122. (In Arabic.)

12. The four year term was first instituted in 1952.

13. H.R.A.F., *The Republic of Lebanon,* New Haven: 1955, Vol. II, p. 546.

14. This was reduced from 5,000 liras in 1952.

15. al-Ṣulḥ was assassinated in Amman in 1951 by members of the P.P.S. in retaliation for the execution of Anton Sa'ādah, their leader in 1949.

16. For details of the crisis see Munīr Taqī al-dīn, *The Birth of an Independence,* Beirut: 1953. (In Arabic.)

17. For the full text of the speech, see Sāmī al-Ṣulḥ, *Memoirs of Sāmī Bey al-Ṣulḥ,* (in Arabic) Beirut: Maktabat al-Fikr al-'Arabī, 1960, pp. 224-227.

18. The fourteen deputies were: Sham'ūn, Junblāṭ, Eddé, Franjie, Munlā, Karameh, Tuwaynī, Khaṭīb, Ḥājj, Dhwaq, Bazzī, Tosbat, Ṣulḥ and Yāfī.

19. For full and verbatim text of the document (in Arabic) see, *The True Nature of the Lebanese Revolt,* pp. 57-58.

20. Part of a message from Sham'ūn to Sāmī al-Ṣulḥ. *Radio Beirut,* February 3, 1955; 0500 GMT.

CHAPTER III

The Causes of the Crisis

THE LEBANESE crisis which began in earnest with the murder of al-Matnī, a newspaperman, on May 8, 1958, and lasted through August 8 of that year, was fundamentally caused by a division in the soul of Lebanese society. All other factors are either external manifestations or subsidiary derivatives. This division involves the concept which the Lebanese holds of his identity, the nature and function of his country, its relation to its Arab neighbors and to the world at large, but particularly to the Christian West.[1]

It is these concepts which condition the responses of various segments of Lebanese society to internal and external stimuli; and conversely, determine the depth and extent of the impact of new forces on them and, consequently from this, their cultural, spiritual and political orientation. In turn these concepts are the responses both to the physical environment and to historical processes that have been long in the making.

These diverse concepts too often held by a number of distinct groups, neither of whom command a clear majority, create severe stresses on the conduct of the affairs of the state both internal and external. A combination of two or more groups—dissatisfied with the conduct of domestic or foreign policy, can precipitate a national crisis, and if there is an equally strong opposition, cause what would amount to a civil war. This, fundamentally, is what had caused the crisis of 1958.

* * *

Another fundamental factor, related to but different from the first, is Arab nationalism on the one hand, and the protection mentality of the Christians on the other.

For centuries—from the Arab-Muslim conquests in the 7th century until modern times, the Christians, as *dhimmis* (a protected trust), lived on the fringes of social life, never full members of the community, sharing neither its responsibilities nor its rights.

On the other hand, since the genesis of European colonialism, the Christians were continuously used as one of its instruments; had themselves learned to depend on it for protection and, in some cases, for acquiring social and governmental positions superior to those of their Muslim compatriots—positions to which by the logic of numbers, they were not entitled.

With the disintegration of Western hegemony over the Arab world, the Christians found themselves without protectors. Some of them are subconsciously afraid of the future. Thus, despite the rise of secular Arab states, some Christians, particularly in Lebanon, have not as yet made a full transition from the mentality of protection to that of full citizenship in a national state.

This is also due in part to Arab nationalism which itself is still in a state of flux. A concept borrowed from the West, where even there it is still subject to a variety of interpretations, Arab nationalism, despite its vigor and reality, has not yet conclusively defined either its framework or content, or its relations to the Church.[2] Most responsible Arab writers and political leaders see in Arab nationalism a secular movement embracing all "Arabs" with no regard to racial origin or religious affiliation. Of these may be mentioned Sāti' al-Huṣrī, the most prominent and prolific writer on the history and theory of Arab nationalism, and the Egyptian Khālid Muḥammad Khālid who, though a graduate of al-Azhar, insists on complete separation of Church and State. Certainly, this is the view held by President Nāṣir of the UAR, and such pan-Arab parties as the Ba'th and the Arab Nationalists' Movement.

On the other hand, there are counter-currents as illustrated in the Muslim Brethren movement and other similar groups, and in the writings of such men as Ahmad al-Zayyāt, Muḥammad al-Ghazālī, Sayyid Qutub, and others. Moreover, in all the Arab countries, the question of Church and State has not yet been resolved in daily practice. This is evidenced by the fact that most of the Arab constitutions declare that the country is a Muslim state, and by the existence of religious courts for each of the religious communities—Muslim as well as Christian sects. Further, in one Arab state, Arab Christians are prohibited from entering certain areas and cities, merely because they are Christians; and conversely, in Lebanon, a Muslim by the accident of his birth, cannot, by established tradition, aspire to certain political positions. Finally, to the Arab masses, nationalism is still a vague notion, identifiable and synonymous with religion.

The above is not intended as a criticism of Arab nationalism. On the contrary, this situation is to be expected. It merely points out that Arab nationalism is still intellectually in a process of formation and growth. In the West, the same process took some four centuries to be completed.

Most Christians in the Arab world have not only accepted Arab nationalism and identified themselves with it, but have become some of its most ardent participants and advocates. Lebanon, however, is an exception to this general rule. With regard to Arab nationalism, Lebanon presents what might be described as a split-personality. Lebanon and Lebanese Christians gave Arab nationalism its first impetus in the 19th Century. Today, Beirut, through its publishing houses, is next only to Cairo as a center from which ideas of Arab nationalism radiate to the rest of the Arab world. Prior to the advent of the republican regime in Egypt, it even superseded Cairo in this respect. And yet, Arab nationalism is least accepted among the Christians in Lebanon. They view it with misgiving, and suspect it of being a Muslim movement in which Christians would return to their status of centuries past as second class citizens.

* * *

The direct causes of the crisis can be divided into three: internal, regional and international. This compartmentalization is intended only for purposes of identification. In actual practice, these factors were inter-related and interdependent.

The internal causes can be reduced to five basic elements: (1) Muslim dissatisfaction, (2) corruption, (3) personalisms, (4) the 1957 elections, and (5) the attempt of President Sham'ūn to succeed himself. The latter two elements will be discussed in Chapter IV.

Muslim Dissatisfaction

Muslim dissatisfaction arises from the feeling that they are second class citizens in Lebanon. This feeling has existed since the time of the French mandate but was aggravated and brought to the forefront by the events which transpired during the last two years of the Sham'ūn administration.

Muslim grievances range over the whole spectrum of political, social and economic life. The best and decisive positions are controlled by the Christians. The Muslims, for instance, would like to see the constitution amended to provide for an increase in the powers of the prime minister and a corresponding decrease in the powers of the president. They feel that if the structure of the state is to be governed by numerical ratios, then this entitles the prime minister —who must be a Sunni Muslim—to more power than he has under the present constitution.

Similarly, the best and most influential positions in the civil service, the army, and in private business are in the hands of the Christians. Not only do the Christians outrank the Muslims in government jobs, but they also far outnumber them. Aside from its implications as to the control of the affairs of the state, the Muslims also feel that since about half the annual budget of the government is spent on salaries, this deprives many Muslims of a source of livelihood to which they are entitled by their numbers. They would like to see government jobs equally divided between Christians and Muslims both as to numbers and ranks, in addition to some regulation which would prohibit discrimination against Muslims in private employment.

The Muslims also complain about educational opportunities open to their children. Although Lebanon is the most advanced Arab country in the field of education and educational services and has reduced illiteracy to 20-30 percent, yet both elementary and secondary education are still basically functions of private foreign and native institutions, most of them denominational. For instance, in 1954, of more than one hundred secondary schools in the country, only five belonged to the state. This, in effect, has resulted in limiting educational opportunities for Muslim children for two reasons: first, some of these schools, particularly the secondary, charge tuition fees which some Muslim parents because of their lower economic status cannot afford; and, second, the great majority of these schools are Christian denominational (native or mission) schools, geared primarily to serve children of the Christian faith and by their nature tend to exclude Muslim children.

The Muslims thus want a vast expansion in state school facilities, to equalize opportunities for their children, particularly in Muslim rural areas; or preferably, full assumption by the state of all elementary and secondary school education. They argue, with justice, that parochial schools—whether native Christian, Muslim or mission—perpetuate religious division and prejudice, while a national school system, through a unified syllabus, would not only reduce confessional tension, but also indoctrinate children of different faiths in loyalty to a national ideal.

Finally, the Muslims complain that the economic and social services of the state, particularly under the Sham'ūn administration, have glaringly benefited Christian areas to the detriment of their Muslim counterparts. They contrast the comparatively high standard of living of the Christian peasantry in the Mountain with that of the Muslim peasantry in the Biqā' plain, for example, where a poverty-stricken population lives with no pure water and poor medical and social services. They further point out that the economic development, which has brought great wealth to the country during the Sham'ūn administration, has been largely concentrated in Beirut and the

Mountain and benefited primarily the Christians and a few wealthy Muslims.

As has been pointed out, these inequalities are not of recent origin, but have existed for many years. However, a greater awakening among the Muslim population, coupled with events during the Sham'ūn administration to be discussed later, aggravated them, brought them to the forefront, and made Muslim demands for their amelioration much more vociferous. Alone, they would not have produced the 1958 crisis, but they were among the many cumulative factors which supplemented and complemented each other.

In 1954 these grievances, along with a number of others, were published in a pamphlet entitled *Muslim Lebanon Today.* Also, a general congress representing "Muslim parties, associations and organizations" in Lebanon was held on November 5, 1954 in Beirut. On behalf of this congress, Muḥammad Khālid, then president of the National Organization, sent a letter, signed also by fourteen other Muslim leaders, to Sāmī al-Ṣulḥ, then prime minister. The letter, dated December 10, 1954, demanded the following:[3]

1—Abolition of confessionalism.

2—Equitable distribution of government positions and jobs among the various denominations.

3—Amendment of the constitution to provide a balance between the authority of the three branches of the government.

4—Conducting a general non-confessional census.

5—Immediate implementation of the plan of economic union between Syria and Lebanon.

6—Implementation of the objectives of the 1952 *coup d'état.*

7—Preservation of Lebanon's Arab reality and combating imperialist currents in Lebanon.

8—Implementation of financial and administrative decentralization in all parts of Lebanon.

The letter and the pamphlet elicited a Maronite reply on August 20, 1954, in the form of an open letter to President Sham'ūn, by Pierre Jumayyil, leader of the para-military Maronite organization, the Phalanges. For comparative purposes, important parts of the letter are paraphrased below:[4]

In his letter Jumayyil argued that he also wanted "the realization of social justice, and the distribution of offices on a basis of equality." This meant "that offices must be allocated according to character, training and productivity, regardless of sectarian origin.

. . . Accordingly, Christians would not be compelled to pay 80 percent of the taxes, while non-Christians pay only 20 percent."

He also agreed with the Muslims in demanding a "general census and the application of Lebanese laws to all those who apply for citizenship . . ." However, this census must include Lebanese immigrants, and the government must register "the hundreds of thousands of immigrants in an appropriate period of time."

He disagreed with the Muslims' demand for the "realization of economic union with Syria." This, he argued, means that Lebanon "should surrender unconditionally to a Syrian union that would destroy its freedom and sovereignty, and reduce it to a mere satellite of Syria."

He favored the Muslim demand for abolishing "religious sectarianism." As a first step, he suggested that religious personal courts be abolished, thus "all Lebanese citizens would have to submit to a civil legal code that would apply uniformly to every one in Lebanon." But would the Muslims agree to this, he asked, or "do they have a hidden objective in demanding the abolition of sectarianism? Are they aiming at putting a certain definite group in power?"

As for the Muslims' desire to amend the constitution, he maintained that the aim of this is "either to put a stop to the power of the President of the Republic, or to distribute the power between him and the Prime Minister equally. It is obvious that the only reason for this is that the President is Christian and the Prime Minister is Muslim . . . This demand with its accompanying agitation, has increased the suspicion of all Christians and put them on their guard. They are afraid that this demand for an amendment of the constitution may turn out to be a step imperiling the existence and future of this country . . ."

Corruption

The Sham'ūn administration for some time managed to maintain a reputation for integrity and fair dealing—at least in comparison with the former administration.

Once the new government had established itself, however, rumors and accusations of "corruption" began to spread and increase. In nature and scope they were similar to those leveled against the former administration of President al-Khūrī. They range from personal enrichment by the President, his relatives and friends, to creating unnecessary lucrative government posts for followers and friends, embezzlement of public funds, bribery, business deals, corruption and miscarriage of justice, and even protection of prostitution.

Whether these accusations were founded in fact or not—and

apparently some of them were true—they were believed by a large segment of the public. One such rumor which had wide public acceptance among both friend and enemy in Lebanon, is that President Sham'ūn is a member of the British Intelligence Service. Some even go as far as assigning him a number. This is believed not only by the general public, but also seriously by some political leaders. It was mentioned to me by several of them and it was mentioned in print by Mr. Junblāṭ in his book *The True Nature of the Lebanese Revolt,* already cited.

Personalisms

Politics in Lebanon is a highly personal affair. With the exception of a few ineffective "ideological" parties, political groupings revolve around personal leadership—usually a clan leader, a city notable or a semi-feudal lord.

In his bid for power, President Sham'ūn managed not only to antagonize most of the influential leaders of the country—both Christian and Muslim, but also attempted to liquidate them from the political scene. Hardly a leader of any real influence remained on friendly terms with him. In a country like Lebanon, this amounts to political suicide.

It was, therefore, natural that—in addition to their political convictions—these leaders would exploit and fan public discontent to bring about the fall of an administration, whose chief they regarded as their personal enemy.

Regional Factors

It will be recalled that, according to the National Covenant of 1943, Lebanon should maintain close friendly ties with all the Arab states, and a neutral position in any conflict between them. Also, that Lebanon joined the Arab League on condition that the Arab states collectively recognize its independence and sovereignty, as enunciated in the ministerial declaration of 1943. This was the subject of a special annex in the Alexandria Protocol of 1944.

During al-Khūrī's administration (1943-52), Lebanon followed a meticulously neutral policy, and in general, stayed out of intra-Arab political affairs, though it acted in conjunction with them on the international level. When the Sham'ūn administration assumed power in 1952, it also maintained a neutral position for some time, but in addition, it followed a much more aggressive "Arab policy" than the previous administration in the sense of identifying itself with the Arabs and Arab political life. This was in line with the announced convictions of President Sham'ūn who regarded himself then as an Arab nationalist.

Eventually, however, Lebanon foundered on the shifting sands of Arab politics, which in turn caused internal and regional repercussions. It should be noted that during this period (1952-58), the Arab world was being shaken by socio-political upheavals which had no parallel in the area for many centuries. These upheavals were apt to create severe stresses throughout the region.

Thus, the principal regional factors which contributed to the 1958 crisis were (a) relations with Syria, (b) relations with Egypt, (c) polarization of Arab politics into an Egyptian-Iraqi conflict, and (d) the Arab unification movement. It should be noted that all these factors were inter-related, and in their turn, related to international factors.

Relations with Syria

One of the major irritants between Syria and Lebanon are the divergent economic policies of the two countries. Up to 1950, they enjoyed an economic union which had dated back to the early days of the mandate. Custom revenues were divided between them in the ratio of 44 percent to Lebanon and 56 percent to Syria.[5] Under this arrangement Lebanon followed a *laissez faire* policy and developed into an importing agent.

On March 13, 1950, the Syrian government broke the economic union. It adopted a policy of economic nationalism, including high tariffs, restrictions on imports and movement of capital, encouragement of agriculture and local industries, and discouragement of foreign capital. The policy reached a climax in 1952 with Decree No. 151 providing for the Syrianization of all foreign business. Lebanon, on the other hand, not only continued in its *laissez faire* policy, but expanded it, including free trade, free money movement, and encouragement of foreign investment.

Since 1950, negotiations—with no results—have been going on intermittently for either an economic union or common economic policies. Syria generally insisted on complete economic union covering economic policies, custom legislation and high tariffs, while Lebanon insisted on free trade. In 1953 a "temporary" agreement was reached—and renewed several times since, which permitted the exchange of local agricultural and industrial products, subject, however, to the payment of duty. Following the failure of negotiations for economic union in 1955, the 1953 agreement was renewed again in March 1955, but this time, *sine die.*

The economic issue soon became a political question. First,

whenever one of the two countries was displeased, it instituted economic measures against the other, causing retaliation in kind. Second, the *laissez faire* policy of Lebanon caused considerable dissension among the Lebanese themselves. Some saw in it a policy harmful to Lebanon itself, and advocated a policy similar to that of Syria; and on the other hand, they saw in it—through foreign economic expansion in Lebanon—a threat to the economy of Syria in particular, and of the Arabs in general.

Finally, the question of economic union became the subject of severe political debate in Lebanon. Some supported it strongly, seeing in it benefits to Lebanon and Syria and to the Arabs in general;[6] while others, mostly Maronites, opposed in any form, as they saw in it an infringement on the sovereignty of Lebanon and a step towards political union.[7]

Another cause of irritation between Syria and Lebanon has been the question of political refugees. Since 1949 Syria has gone through a number of *coup d'états,* and in each case, several of the opposition find political asylum in Lebanon. This naturally does not please the group that happens to be in power in Syria at the time.

In 1955, two events contributed further to the deteriorating relations between the two countries: the murder of Colonel Adnān al-Mālikī and the exchange of state visits between Sham'ūn and Celal Bayar, President of Turkey.

On April 22, 1955, Colonel Adnān al-Mālikī, adjutant to the Syrian Chief of Staff, and a member of the Ba'th Party, was shot dead by a member of the P.P.S.—who also shot himself immediately afterwards. The party as such was accused of being an accomplice in the murder.

During the investigation, several army officers and government officials—all members of the P.P.S.—were dismissed from service, while a large number of party members were arrested. Other members escaped to Lebanon.

The party organs in Lebanon (where the party was then officially illegal, but nevertheless operated in the open) attacked the Syrian government, which protested. It was even suspected that the Lebanese government was harboring some of the culprits and that Sham'ūn himself was implicated. When Syria requested that a number of Lebanese nationals—members of the P.P.S.—be handed over for trial, and Lebanon rejected this request, relations between the two countries reached almost to the crisis level.

The exchange of state visits between Sham'ūn and Bayar added fuel to the fire. In April 1955 Sham'ūn paid a state visit to Turkey and was later followed by his prime minister, Sāmī al-Ṣulḥ. At the end of the visit a joint statement was issued pointing out the traditional friendship between Lebanon and Turkey and that Turkey is the front line of defense of the free world; that there is no conflict of interest between Lebanon and the Arab states on the one hand, and Turkey on the other, to stand in the way of strengthening of friendly relations and cooperation. In June 1955, President Bayar and his prime minister returned the visit. Significantly, however, no communique was issued at the termination of the visit.

In Syria and among the opposition in Lebanon, these visits were the subject of considerable criticism and suspicion. At that particular time, relations between Syria and Turkey were strained, and there were rumors of Turkish troop concentrations on the Syrian border. Thus, the exchange of visits was criticized as a further manifestation of hostility by Sham'ūn and his administration towards Syria.

Secondly, it was seriously suspected that the visits were a preliminary to Lebanon's joining the Baghdad Pact. Both Sham'ūn and his prime minister denied that this was the purpose of the visits, and emphasized that Lebanon would maintain a neutral policy between Egypt and Iraq, but the statement was never fully believed. In fact, King Sa'ūd, in a verbal message to Sham'ūn, accused Lebanon of favoring Iraq under a false guise of neutrality.

The year 1955 can be regarded as a dividing line in the relations between the two countries. From there on, by and large, they continued to deteriorate. Although Lebanon insisted that she was neutral, and did on many occasions try to heal the rift between Iraq and Egypt, it was regarded as in the Iraqi camp. By early 1957, the hostility between Syria and Lebanon came into the open.

The bad relations between the two countries, both economic and political, contributed to the 1958 crisis in two ways: first, Syria regarded the Sham'ūn administration as unfriendly to it, and worked towards its downfall; and second, this created a split within Lebanon itself. One group supported the position of the Sham'ūn administration, while another felt that Syria was justified in its grievances and supported it against the administration.

Relations with Egypt

As in the case with Syria, the relations between Lebanon and Egypt began to deteriorate in 1955, although they did not reach serious dimensions until after the Suez Crisis in 1956.

In November 1956, the Lebanese Government issued a call for a summit Arab conference which was held in Beirut on November 13 and 14. Both 'Abdallah al-Yāfī and Ṣā'ib Salām, Prime Minister and Minister respectively, then in the cabinet, have told this writer that the invitation was made at the express promise of Sham'ūn to them personally, and to other Arab governments that Lebanon would take some action against Britain and France. However, Sham'ūn denied this and told this writer that he made no such commitment.

In any case, following the conference, Lebanon took no action, aside from expressing its solidarity with Egypt. It should be noted that Egypt, Syria, and Sa'udi Arabia severed their relations with both France and Britain; and Iraq and Jordan with France. It was hoped that Lebanon would at least withdraw her ambassador from London as a token gesture, but she refused to do so. Immediately after the conference both Yāfī and Salām resigned (thus bringing down the cabinet). They later claimed that their resignation was in protest against Sham'ūn's bad faith, and his refusal to take an "Arab stand."

When the 1957 Lebanese elections took place, the rift between the two countries came into the open. Both the Egyptian and Syrian press and radio commenced a violent personal campaign against Sham'ūn, Sāmī al-Ṣulḥ and Charles Malik, branding them as traitors and imperialist lackeys. In turn, the Lebanese Government banned all Egyptian papers during the whole period of the election campaign.

By the beginning of 1957 Lebanon was regarded as unfriendly to both Syria and Egypt. This appreciation of the political relations between the two countries was accepted by the public in Lebanon itself. One group blamed Egypt and Syria, while another blamed the policy of Sham'ūn.

As in the case of Syria, the bad relations between Egypt and Lebanon contributed to the 1958 crisis in two ways: Egypt consistently worked against the Sham'ūn administration and incited the Lebanese public against it; and, second, the Lebanese people split into two main blocs: one supported Sham'ūn and his policy, and the other opposed him and worked for his downfall and the downfall of his policies.

The Polarization of Arab Politics

In addition to the private quarrels of Egypt and Syria as such, with Lebanon, the polarization of Arab politics into two hostile camps, with Egypt leading one and Iraq the other, was also a main contributing factor.

This polarization involved much more fundamental issues than the question of political leadership of the Arab world. It included also such diametrically divergent concepts as revolutionary republicanism versus monarchial gradualism; aristocratic conservative government versus socialist or semi-socialist state; cooperation with the West versus independence from the West.

The polarization—political, conceptual and attitudinal in nature —split the Arab world as it had never been split before. The split was on two levels; governmental and popular. On the governmental level the traditional alignments and antagonisms went with the wind, and a new line-up emerged—that of the kings against the republicans, of traditional government against revolutionary government. In this rigid division, Lebanon was unable to steer a clear neutral course and, whether by design or misadventure, she found herself essentially in the Iraqi camp.

On the popular level, the cleavage cut across state lines and political boundaries—Lebanon being no exception—with the majority of the Arab public, ideologically at least, favoring the nascent republicanism.

Two new factors—virtually absent before—appeared on the Arab political scene. Formerly, politics was an exclusive occupation of "gentlemen" to be conducted behind closed doors, with little said outside, except general statements on Arab solidarity. This had certain advantages. It allowed for genuine negotiation, compromise and withdrawal from rigid positions without losing face. Recently, however, the masses began to have considerable influence on political decisions, mostly through extra-constitutional means. Hence the appearance of the second factor; the extensive use of blatant propaganda to influence the general public.

Immediate political considerations brought together strange bedfellows. Ideologically, for instance, there is little common between the medieval Kingdom of Yemen and the governments of Egypt and Syria. Similarly, some of the opposition leaders in Lebanon who rode the Nāṣir "bandwagon" are generally the semi-feudal types which Nāṣir had been liquidating from Egyptian political life. In fact, some Lebanese intellectuals—in the opposition themselves—have dubbed the crisis in Lebanon, "The Revolt of the Pashas."

In Lebanon, the cleavage on the popular level took an acute character and, because of the structure of the country, carried with it confessional overtones. While, in most of the Arab countries, the masses were behind the Egyptian block irrespective of the attitude of their governments, in Lebanon, the contrary was true. There was a sharp split, with one faction supporting the Egyptian bloc, and the other opposing it.

"Nasserism" and Arab Unity

In addition to the polarization of Arab politics, what has come to be known as "Nasserism" and the upsurge of Arab nationalism in a drive for unity under Nāṣir's banner, were related contributing factors. It is not the purpose here to evaluate or judge "Nasserism," but rather to point out its impact on the Lebanese crisis. Egypt's adoption of Arab nationalism is comparatively new, and basically dates back to 1955. By the beginning of 1956, Egypt was in full swing in its new course as a full-fledged "Arab" state.[8] Its new constitution of February 16, 1956, officially declared that "Egypt is an independent and sovereign Arab state. . . . and the Egyptian people are part of the Arab nation," thus making Egypt the second country to include such a provision in its constitution, Syria being the first.

Egypt not only espoused the Arab cause, but also gave it aid and comfort both moral and material, whether in Algeria, Tunisia, Morocco, or the protectorates of the Persian Gulf. To the millions of inarticulate Arabs, the *Voice of the Arabs* became the voice from the skies, which in the dreariness and hopelessness of their daily lives, verbalized their thoughts, dreamt their dreams, and above all spoke to them of hope—hope that the day of their deliverance from poverty, disease, corruption and foreign rule, would soon come! Nāṣir himself addressed them as "my brethren."

Between 1955 and 1958, Nāṣir was able to perform one daring feat after another: the British evacuation of the Suez Canal in 1954—a question which has preoccupied Egypt for more than seventy years; the arms deal with Russia—which was hailed in the Arab world as a declaration of independence from the West; the ouster of Glubb Pasha from Jordan—which was regarded as a personal victory for Nāṣir; the nationalization of the Suez Canal Company—which in addition to its economic implications, was viewed as a daring retaliation for insult; the union with Syria—which was cheered as the dawn of Arab unity; and even the ignominious defeat in the Suez War was turned into a spectacular international victory.

To the Arab masses Nāṣir's victories were personal, with which they identified themselves as individuals. This, together with real reforms Nāṣir carried out in Egypt, his simple personal life, his uncanny ability to fathom the feelings and thoughts of the masses and verbalize them, made him the idol of the Arab masses everywhere.

The loyalty of a large majority of the Arab masses and of a large segment of the intelligentsia enabled Nāṣir to take actions which directly or indirectly affected other Arab states without adequate consultation or approval of the respective heads of states. Second, rightly or wrongly, other Arab leaders began to feel that they were being treated by Nāṣir not as members of a bloc or as equals, allies and partners, but as subordinates who had to follow his lead irrespective of their views.

Finally, the Arab heads of states found themselves in the uncomfortable and embarrassing position of no longer being certain of their authority or the security of their positions in their respective countries. In a certain sense, a "shadow government" composed of Nāṣir supporters existed in each of the countries, in addition to the legal government. Whenever a divergence of views occurred between Egypt and the country concerned the "shadow government" followed the Egyptian lead, thus causing a split in the country resulting usually in disturbances ranging from demonstrations to virtual civil war. In Lebanon, an intellectual favoring the opposition, explained to this writer, "Those common people behind the barricades in al-Basṭa (a quarter of Beirut) fought neither for Ṣā'ib Salām nor for 'Abdallah al-Yāfī, not even for reform, but for Nāṣir's image and the vision of the future he opened for them."

The result was that Nāṣir, sooner or later, quarreled with virtually every Arab leader: Nūrī al-Sa'īd of Iraq, Ḥusayn of Jordan, Sa'ūd of Saudi Arabia, Sham'ūn of Lebanon, and Bourguiba of Tunisia. Only the leaders of Syria remained on friendly terms with him. At any rate, the Arab leaders accused Nāṣir of conspiring to overthrow them, and the expulsion of the Egyptian military attaché from Arab capitals became a frequent occurrence; while Nāṣir for his part, accused them of being foreign agents—an accusation usually followed by violent radio and press attacks on their personal lives and conduct, and the corruption of their governments, which, in some cases were only too true. Thus, the character of the quarrels changed from impersonal divergence of views to personal and bitter animosities.

This is essentially what happened between Presidents Nāṣir and Sham'ūn, a factor which was not an insignificant element in precipitating the Lebanese crisis of 1958. The rivalry between the two was visible in such simple things as the display of their pictures in public places. Supporters of Sham'ūn and Nāṣir would display pictures of their respective "leaders" in prominent public places in the towns of Lebanon, and then each would try secretly to tear down the pictures of the other side. This trend became so serious that the government banned all such displays in public places.

The upsurge of the unity movement under Egyptian leadership

and the union of Syria and Egypt into the United Arab Republic produced two opposite reactions in Lebanon:

Among the Christians, particularly the Maronites, there was genuine fear and conviction that the U.A.R. in collaboration with Muslim elements in Lebanon, were planning the annexation of the country. Thus, the old dormant specter of "Christians in a sea of Muslims" was revived. It should be noted that Muslim political and religious leaders in Lebanon repeatedly affirmed their dedication to the independence of Lebanon and to the 1943 National Covenant; and that President Nāṣir on many occasions denied any designs on Lebanon and publicly declared his respect for its continued existence as an independent state.

As for the Muslims and other Arab nationalists, they were cheered by the unity movement and greeted with jubilation the Syrian-Egyptian union.

At any rate, whether out of honest conviction or for political purposes, President Sham'ūn in his speeches and in his actions, began to pose as a "Christian" leader, and apparently imbued followers with the conviction of a "Muslim threat."

The question arises: was there a serious threat to the existence of Lebanon as an independent state? If the question refers to the future, then the answer has to be yes. Arab political literature regards Lebanon as an Arab country, and its future incorporation in a partial or full Arab union is taken for granted. This view is held not only by Arabs outside of Lebanon, but also by some Lebanese—Christians as well as Muslims. Certainly Kamāl Junblāṭ, the Druze leader,[9] and other members of the opposition hold this view and regard the National Covenant as only a temporary measure. But such a position rests on consent rather than force, and as such cannot be included in the category of a "threat."

But was there a threat to Lebanon's independence emanating from the U.A.R. and from the opposition in Lebanon? For a proper answer, it would be desirable to analyze the interests of each of the groups involved: the U.A.R., Muslim members of the opposition, and Christian members of the opposition.

As for the U.A.R., all the external evidence available indicates that the forcible annexation of Lebanon at this time would not be in its interests. To be sure, it would probably have liked to see Lebanon "join" but not "forced" into union. In support of this argument, we have two sets of external evidence.

1. The repeated declaration of President Nāṣir that the U.A.R. respects the existence of Lebanon as an independent state.

2. The annexation of an "unwilling" Lebanon would certainly have created manifold domestic and international problems for the U.A.R., which at this juncture in its development it could do without, and which may even have led to the disruption of the union between Syria and Egypt, and possibly retarded the unity movement under the leadership of Nāṣir. It should be remembered that the move for the creation of the U.A.R. was initiated by Syria, that Egypt joined the union reluctantly, and that even disregarding the 99 percent favorable vote in the plebiscite, there is incontrovertible evidence that the majority of the Syrians were in favor of the union. On the other hand, up till now, the Syrian-Egyptian union is still largely a legal fact rather than an established reality. Economic, social and administrative union is yet to come and numerous other problems remain to be solved. Thus, to force Lebanon with its multiple confessional structure and conflicting tendencies to a U.A.R. union that has not yet been digested, would indeed be folly—and President Nāṣir, no matter what his real motives and intentions are, is not known for the lack of foresight and tactical timing. A Lebanon united with the U.A.R. at this time would be a serious liability; an independent, friendly Lebanon is an invaluable asset.

As for the Muslims in Lebanon, who certainly comprised the majority of the active opposition, they can be divided into two groups: the political leaders, and the common people. There is no question that, conceptually and emotionally, both groups were committed to the possibility of an eventual political union with Syria and Egypt. Yet, disregarding their declarations of loyalty to an independent Lebanon, their political or economic interests were and still are in conflict with their ideal of such a union.

It has already been pointed out that the majority of Christian and Muslim political leaders in Lebanon are "traditional style" politicians. This is a class which Nāṣir has been constantly attacking and actively liquidating from political life in Egypt. To this extent, then, the interests of the Muslim leaders in Lebanon are in conflict with Nāṣir's program. Second, the Muslim leaders in Lebanon have the example of their counterparts in Syria. There, the leaders of the country either retired from the scene or surrendered effective political control. In contrast, the Muslim leaders in an independent Lebanon wield tremendous power. Even if they did not have to surrender their political power, the significance of their role would be changed from leaders in an independent state to provincial leaders in a large state.

Similarly with the Muslim common man. Despite his numerous legitimate grievances against the Lebanese Government, and what he feels to be his lower status, he is still generally better off than his counterpart in the Syrian region of the United Arab Republic. His real wages are higher, his standard of living is better and the social services available to him are superior in both quality and quantity. Moreover, as a result of the 1958 crisis, there is reason to believe that the state will devote more attention to him and to his welfare. Thus, there is little incentive for Muslims to desire a union with the U.A.R. aside from general and genuine sympathy with the idea of such a union.

As for the Christian members of the opposition, their loyalty and dedication to an independent Lebanon is self-evident and requires no proof. Certainly, to suggest that men like Henri Far'ūn and Philippe Taqlā, in addition to the Maronite Patriarch, desired the annexation of Lebanon to the U.A.R. is ludicrous. They did believe, as many Christians do today, that the era of foreign protection is over, that the welfare of Christians in Lebanon and the rest of the Arab world rests on their divesting themselves of their minority mentality, and on their identification with their fellow Arabs, and that Lebanon's existence as an independent state depends primarily on its active cooperation with the Arab people and identifying herself with them and with their welfare. They sincerely felt that Lebanon under the Sham'ūn administration had deviated from this cardinal principle.

At any rate, fear—real or imaginary—of the unity movement under the leadership of President Nāṣir, by a segment of the Lebanese population, and support for it by another segment, were important factors in bringing about the 1958 crisis.

International Factors

The triangular rivalry between the West, the Soviet Union and communism, and Arab nationalism under the leadership of President Nāṣir, for predominance in the Arab world, was also an important factor in precipitating the Lebanese crisis. By 1957, the Soviet Union had become a Great Power with *de facto* influence in the area. Conversely, the influence of the West, particularly after the Suez Crisis, had declined virtually to the vanishing point. Also, between 1957 and 1958 the area was subjected to the tensions of the cold war on a scale and in an intensity it had never experienced before or since.

Arab nationalism under the leadership of President Nāṣir which, for purposes of identification only, we shall call "Nasserism" (and which had the wholehearted support of the majority of the Arab people irrespective of the positions of their governments), sought to achieve the following three main objectives:

1. Liquidation of all foreign spheres of influence—economic as well as political—in Arab areas.

2. The creation of an "Arab polity" independent of both East and West—exclusively in what is believed to be Arab interests, as defined by the Arabs and not by any other source.

3. The achievement of political unification of Arab lands "from the Atlantic to the Arab Gulf."

In pursuit of these objectives, "Nasserism" rejected all Western alliances and defense pacts, maintained a sustained propaganda war on Western influence in the Arab world, collaborated with the Soviet Union—on a temporary basis—in its attacks on the West, evolved "positive neutrality" into a doctrine and accepted Soviet technical, economic and military aid with "no strings attached."

The international rivalry split the Arab governments into two main camps over foreign policy. One camp, under the leadership of Iraq, saw in the application of "Nasserism" a reckless and disastrous policy of paving the way for communist penetration which would ultimately lead the Arab world into subjugation to Soviet-communist domination.

On the other hand, "Nasserism"—supported by the majority of the Arab people, recognized no such immediate threat from the Soviet Union or from communism. Conversely, it saw in the various Western defense plans for the Middle East, including the Baghdad Pact and the Eisenhower Doctrine, an attempt to involve them in an East-West conflict in which they have no interest, and a new form of "collective imperialism" whose primary purpose is to perpetuate the subjugation of the Arabs to the West, under the guise of defending them against Soviet aggression and communist penetration.

In the meantime, the events which transpired during 1957 contributed to the deterioration of the relations between the United States and Egypt and Syria. The Soviet Union with the decided advantage of an outsider, posed as the disinterested friend of the Arabs, and basked in a warm sun of popularity. Conversely, after the Suez crisis, the British and the French withdrew from active political participation in the area, and the mantle of leadership in this respect fell on the United States.

The United States in 1957 had an initial advantage because of the position it took in the Suez crisis, but soon this advantage was dissipated. Its policy in the Middle East then, rejected any neutralist position and seemed to insist on the doctrine of "those who are not for us are against us." It sought to isolate both Egypt and Syria. With regard to Egypt, in addition to the various economic measures, the U. S. government regarded Nāṣir as the villain of the peace in the Middle East, and attributed to his machinations everything that happened in the area. The U. S. press was no less hostile. *The New York Times* was the most bitter and violent. In one editorial after the other, it called Nāṣir "an ambitious dictator" and compared him with Hitler.[10]

As for Syria, its relations with the United States reached the crisis level. By mid-1957, Syria had come as close to the Soviet Union as possible short of becoming a satellite. On August 12, 1957, the Syrian Government announced the discovery of an "American conspiracy" to overthrow it.[11] In September, Syria accused Turkey of concentrating its troops on the Syrian frontier in preparation for an attack on it, put its army in a state of readiness, and on October 16, appealed to the United Nations—three days after Egyptian troops landed in Syria to help it repel any Turkish attack. As soon as the matter reached the U.N. General Assembly, what might be described as the "Syrian affair" petered out gradually.

Thus, as can be readily seen, during 1957, and 1958, the policies of the United States on one side, and Egypt and Syria on the other, were hostile to each other.

When the Eisenhower Doctrine was proposed, Egypt and Syria rejected it, and attacked it mercilessly.[12] Lebanon, however, accepted it in the joint American-Lebanese statement issued at the end of the Richards Mission on March 16, 1957.

The adoption of the Eisenhower Doctrine divided Lebanon into two main groups: one composed of the administration and its immediate supporters. A large part of the Maronite community and such political organizations as the Phalanges and the P.P.S., approved the Doctrine; while the rest of the country, including a majority of the influential leaders—Christian and Muslim—and probably a majority of the population opposed it.

Opposition to the Eisenhower Doctrine in Lebanon rested on two main counts: first, it was argued that Lebanon's adherence to the Doctrine brought it openly into the East-West conflict in favor of the Western camp and second, by adopting the Doctrine, Lebanon was siding with the United States against Egypt and Syria. On both grounds it was argued that the administration had violated Lebanon's traditional policy established in the 1943 National Covenant. This policy states that Lebanon must maintain a neutral position on the international level, and support the Arab states against any foreign state.

The Eisenhower Doctrine did indeed bring Lebanon into an international cold war. It committed it to the side of the United States, and conversely, committed the United States to the support of Lebanon and its government. Secondly, it increased the tension within Lebanon itself and split the population into two hostile camps. Thirdly, the Egyptian and Syrian governments came to regard the Lebanese government as in the enemy camp, and as a threat to their own security, thus they began actively working for its removal or overthrow. And finally, the Lebanese government was subjected to an intense and sustained attack by the Egyptian and Syrian press and radio. This was complemented by Soviet attacks and the attacks of communist parties in the Middle East.

NOTES

1. See for an excellent exposition of these conceptions, Albert Hourani, *Syria and Lebanon,* London: Oxford University Press, 3rd ed., 1954, pp. 133-35. See also Kamāl Junblāṭ, *On The Course of Lebanese Policy,* Beirut: Dār al-Ṭalī'ah, 1960, pp. 37-133. (in Arabic).

2. On the confusion in understanding Arab nationalism, see Isḥāq Mūsā al-Ḥusaynī, *The Crisis of Arab Thought,* Beirut: 1954, pp. 11-12. (in Arabic).

3. For full text see Sāmī al-Ṣulḥ, *op cit.,* pp. 452-456.

4. For an English translation of the full text of the letter, see *Christian Lebanon Today,* already cited.

5. This was revised in 1943 as follows: 40 percent to each of Syria and Lebanon, and 20 percent to be distributed according to actual consumption.

6. On all these points see *On the Lebanese Economy,* and *Lebanon and the Arab Question.* Both have been cited.

7. On this point see Pierre Jumayyil *The Phalanges Said,* n.p. (Beirut) n.d. (1957?). In Arabic.

8. For an excellent study of the development of Arab nationalism in Egypt, see Anīs Ṣāyigh, *The Arab Idea in Egypt,* Beirut, 1959.

9. *The True Nature of the Lebanese Revolt,* pp. 95-125; and *On the Course of Lebanese Policy,* pp. 79-91.

10. See for instance "News of the Week in Review" in the *New York Times* of February 2, 1958, and the editorials in the issues of February 3 and 4, 1958.

11. For details see *Mideast Mirror,* August 18, 1957, pp. 2-5.

12. For attacks on the Eisenhower Doctrine, see the following propaganda pamphlets all published in Cairo with the exception of one in Damascus. 'Abd al-Raḥmān al-Khamīsī, *No . . . Mr. Eisenhower,* Cairo: n.d. (*ca.* 1956/57); 'Adil Amīn, *American Lies About the Eisenhower Doctrine,* Cairo: n.p., n.d. (*ca.* 1956/57); A. B., *Richards Solves the Palestine Problem,* Cairo: n.p., n.d., (*ca.* 1956); Bashīr Ka'dān, *The Eisenhower Doctrine,* Damascus: 1957; Muḥammad 'Abbās Sayyid Aḥmad, *The Eisenhower Doctrine,* Cairo: 1957. All are in Arabic.

CHAPTER IV

Slide Into Anarchy

Formation of the United National Front

OPPOSITION to the Sham'ūn administration began to become somewhat vocal as early as 1955. That year, when the Baghdad Pact was formed, Lebanon was trying to feel its way in the new new regional complex, and there was intense political activity. Lebanese politicians traveled extensively in the area. Junblāṭ and other leaders charged the administration with preparing to join the Pact, and opposed the exchange of state visits between Presidents Sham'ūn and Bayar (of Turkey). Others criticized the government for refusing to hand over to Syria P.P.S. leaders allegedly implicated in the murder of Col. Adnān al-Mālikī. Some even went so far as to accuse Sham'ūn of being connected with the P.P.S.

In November 1956, following the meeting of the Arab heads of states on the 13th and 14th when Lebanon refused to take any positive action against France or Britain to express its sympathy with Egypt, 'Abdallah al-Yāfī—then prime minister, and Ṣā'ib Salām, a cabinet member, resigned in protest (or so they later claimed). A new cabinet, with Sāmī al-Ṣulḥ as prime minister, took office. A few points about the composition of the new cabinet are of interest. Sāmī al-Ṣulḥ was known in political circles as a rather pliant politician willing to take orders from above. Charles Malik—known for his pro-Western and particularly his pro-American sympathies, became foreign minister.

Between November 1956 and March 1957 the opposition and the government were gradually drifting into extreme polarities. Up until then, the opposition was an amorphous company of men and political groups, each working independently of the other, many times at cross-purposes. Moreover, they were thought of, and thought themselves, as the opposition which normally exist under a democratic form of government. Difference of views—yes, but not to the point of revolution.

In March and April (1957) (the first political moves were being made for the forthcoming parliamentary elections to be held in June. On March 16, the government officially accepted the

Eisenhower Doctrine. This evoked a storm of protest from various quarters. The cabinet then agreed to hold a parliamentary debate on foreign policy and to submit itself to a vote of confidence from the Chamber of Deputies. The debate took place during the first days of April and lasted for three days. After one stormy session on April 6th, which lasted until 2:30 the next morning, the government won a vote of confidence by a majority of 30 to 1. However, before the vote was taken seven deputies resigned in protest from the Chamber. They were Ḥamīd Franjiyah, Ṣabrī Hamādah, Rashīd Karāmī, 'Abdallah al-Yāfī, Aḥmad and his son Kāmil al-As'ad, and 'Abdallah al-Ḥājj.

The United National Front first appeared on the political scene in April also. Twenty-three political leaders (among them Ṣā'ib Salām, Kamāl Junblāṭ, Ḥusayn al-'Uwaynī, Nasīm Majdalānī, 'Alī al-Bazzī, Ilyās al-Khūrī, Philippe Taqlā, and the seven deputies who resigned from the Chamber on April 6), had on April 1, submitted a memorandum to President Sham'ūn which called for the following measures:

1. The next Chamber should consist of eight-eight members, not sixty-six as the President was reported to want.

2. The present cabinet should resign in favor of a "neutral" cabinet to supervise the forthcoming parliamentary elections (due in June).

3. The immediate cancelling of the state of emergency and of press censorship, both imposed in November 1956 during the Suez crisis.

4. The present cabinet should not enter into agreements with any foreign power until after the election of a new Chamber.

The memorandum warned that if the President did not comply with these demands, the signatories would feel compelled to take "practical steps" as dictated by the interests of the country.[1]

It is important at this point to discuss the composition of the United National Front. In religious coloration, the Front was predominantly Muslim. Its three important leaders were Ṣā'ib Salām, 'Abdallah al-Yāfī (both Sunni Muslims), and Kamāl Junblāṭ (Druze). Moreover, when actual fighting broke out in 1958, it was primarily the Muslims and the Druze who did the fighting, while the Christians remained, by and large, passive. In addition, it is to be noted that in Beirut, Christian areas remained mostly under government control, while predominantly Muslim areas such as al-Basṭa passed to the hands of the opposition. Further, in his recent book, Kamāl Junblāṭ implied that leaders of the opposition purposely failed to supply their Christian supporters with weapons. He wrote, "The mistake the revolution made in the countryside, was its failure to supply Christian groups in the opposition with arms. If we had been careful to distribute some light weapons among our Christian brethren—supporters of the Arab idea—in the mountains . . . they would have resisted isolationist attempts, fought and won. . . ."[2]

It is not to be inferred from the above that the battle was a Muslim-Christian fight. Many Christian political leaders such as Henri Far'ūn, Philippe Taqlā, Fu'ād 'Ammūn, Nasīm Majdalānī, Ḥamīd Franjiyah, Bishārah al-Khūrī, Charles Hilū, René Mu'awwad, among many others, were either members of the Front or other opposition groups. In addition, the opposition received the blessing of the Maronite Patriarch. In fact, the spark which set off the full scale explosion in 1958, was the murder of Nasīb al-Matnī—a Maronite Christian and a severe critic of the Sham'ūn administration.

Some Muslim followers of the opposition and some Christians did regard the fight in purely religious terms and there were incidents along those lines. There was even a real danger that the crisis might degenerate into such a level. The tribute for checking such a trend goes primarily to the stand of the Maronite Patriarch and to the wisdom and restraint of Muslim leaders of the opposition. By and large, it was the Christians, and primarily the Maronites, who regarded the crisis in that light, rather than the other way around .

Politically, the Front was "Nasserist" in orientation. Other than that, it included every shade of political trend from right to left. However, no communist was a member of the Front. There is no question but that the communists were on the side of the opposition and that they did help, but they did this on their own. There was no official tie-up and their aid was not solicited. The communists, however, claim full participation.[3]

In time the Front came to represent, in addition to political leaders and public figures, the following parties: Najjādah—a Muslim youth movement, the counterpart of the Maronite Katā'ib, the *National Organization* (Muslim, but more moderate than the Najjādah), Junblāṭ's *Progressive Socialist Party,* al-Ba'th (pan-Arab socialist), *The National Call* (Arab nationalists), *The Constitutional Bloc* (Maronite, Bishārah al-Khūrī's followers.) This is, of course, in addition to clan followers of particular leaders. For instance, Junblāṭ is the tribal chieftain of several thousand Druze who will do his bidding regardless of the issues.

In addition to the United National Front, what came to be known as the Third Force appeared on the political scene. It was composed of such men as Henri Far'ūn, Yusuf Ḥitti, Muḥammad Shuqayr, Joseph Sālim, Gabriel al-Murr, George Naqqāsh, Bahīj Taqī al-dīn, and Ghassān al-Tuwaynī, among others. The Force was more moderate in its demands than the Front. It came into being primarily to act as a neutral mediator between the Front and the government. As time went by and the lines became more rigid, very little difference in views and attitude remained between it and the Front.

To complement the Front and the Third Force, a Congress of Parties, Organizations and Personalities in Lebanon was formed. Its president was Ḥusayn al-'Uwaynī and the secretary-general, Ḥabīb Rubaiz. The Congress included parties and individuals belonging to the Front and the Force, and in addition, all other organizations and personalities in the opposition but not members of the above two groups. In a certain sense, it was the least common denominator of the opposition. Its primary function was the issuance of statements from time to time, on issues agreed on by every one in the opposition.

It is important to note that at this pre-crisis stage, the objectives of the opposition—primarily the Front—did not include resort to violence or the removal of President Sham'ūn. At this stage, the Front was preparing for a parliamentary election campaign. The elections would be a popular referendum on its policies as opposed to those of the government.

The Egyptian Press Campaign

In Lebanon, as in all other Arab countries, emergency regulations including press censorship were imposed in November 1956, during the Suez crisis. On May 7, 1957, the Lebanese government lifted both the emergency regulations and press censorship to allow for a free election campaign. On the following day, however, it banned all Egyptian newspapers and magazines for the duration of the elections.

Since the early part of 1957 the Egyptian press had not been too friendly towards the Lebanese government and relations between Egypt and Lebanon had been somewhat strained. On March 31, and again during the second week of April, the Lebanese government arrested six persons for distributing leaflets and putting up posters attacking President Nāṣir as a Soviet stooge.[4] On the other hand, there was a feeling that the Egyptian government was encouraging the opposition. On April 11, Kasruwān Labakī, the political commentator of the Beirut daily, *Le Soir,* wrote that he was among those Lebanese who felt closer to Egypt than to Syria and Iraq. But he complained, "We have not renounced this policy, and no one here has betrayed it. But when His Excellency the Egyptian Ambassador behaves like Nāṣir's High Commissioner in Lebanon, when he behaves as if Lebanon were under an Egyptian mandate, when he makes his embassy a refuge for the opposition and chooses his friends entirely from among the enemies of the regime, he does more harm than good to his country."[5]

In April 1957, the Egyptian press and radio commenced a campaign against the Lebanese government which increased in violence with the development of events, and which continued with short interruptions until the end of the crisis in August 1958.

Below are a few samples of Egyptian broadcasts. In this respect, two methods were used: first, direct commentary by the state-controlled Egyptian radio, and secondly, quotations from the Egyptian press by the radio commentator. Usually the press quotations were much more violent. By "quoting" in a review of the press, the Egyptian government achieved two purposes. First, it made sure that the views of the Egyptian press were heard in Lebanon and other parts of the Arab world and, secondly, it absolved itself from being directly accused of being hostile to the Lebanese government.

On April 5, when the Lebanese Chamber of Deputies was debating foreign policy, Aḥmad Sa'īd, commentator of the *Voice of the Arabs* told his listeners, in part:[6]

> The government of al-Ṣulḥ accepted the Eisenhower plan; that is, agreed to cooperate with the United States, the ally of Britain and France, who are in turn the two allies of Israel. In other words, it accepted alliance with the aggressors against Egypt and the Arabs. This cooperation and alliance is undertaken by the Lebanese Government with the West, with the United States, Britain and France at the very moment when France and Britain declare that they would stand by the side of Israel if she decided to commit an aggression against the Arabs and at the very moment when the United States supports Israel's ambition against Aqaba and the Canal and when Israel threatens to occupy the Sinai desert at any time.

About the 12th of June, photostats of forged documents purported to be correspondence between Charles Malik (then foreign minister) and Abba Eban, then Israeli ambassador to the United States, began circulating in Beirut. The Lebanese Foreign Ministry immediately issued a denial which was also broadcast, stating that the documents were forgeries, and warning that "should some newspapers decide to publish these forged documents, despite this communiqué, the Foreign Minister will find himself compelled to bring lawsuits against them before the competent courts."[7]

Despite official protests of Lebanon to Egypt, the Egyptian press appeared with such headlines as "Three Secret Messages Exchanged between Charles Malik and Abba Eban." *Radio Cairo* in its review of the press broadcast extensive quotations of which the following (quoted here in part) from *al-Sha'b* is typical:[8]

> This secret correspondence confirms what we said before and what we say about the reactionary governments and the stooges of imperialism, who are now handling affairs in Jordan and Lebanon and trying to stab the Arab people in the back in the heat of their gallant struggle against imperialism, its alliances and its projects.
>
> Charles Malik and such like are merely tools in the hands of imperialism carrying out its will and obeying its orders. They can only live and rule their people under imperialist protection.

The Election Campaign

While the Egyptian press was maintaining a sustained campaign against the Lebanese government, events in Lebanon were not standing still.

During April there was intense political activity by both government and opposition forces. On April 26, the prime minister issued a warning to Muslim religious leaders in the employ of the state such as Shaykh Shafīq Yamūt, president of the Sharī'a Court of Appeals, and others in similar positions, not to engage in political activity. This warning, however, went unheeded.

It will be recalled that, in 1952, the Sham'ūn administration had passed a reform electoral law, and that in 1953 a new Chamber composed of 44 deputies was elected. In April 1957, a new electoral law was passed. It increased the number of deputies from 44 to 66, and re-districted some of the constituencies. The term of the sitting Chamber was due to expire in June, 1957.

On May 12, 1957, the election campaign opened in carnival style with a pro-government procession during which 200 sheep and one camel were slaughtered in the streets and the meat distributed among the poor. On the same day, the United National Front held a rally—with no meat—during which several speakers, including Ṣā'ib Salām and 'Abdallah al-Yāfī, addressed a crowd—of 75,000 according to opposition sources and of 5,000 according to pro-government sources. The platform of the United National Front included the following main points:[9]

1. The constitution should not be amended to enable President Sham'ūn to stand for re-election.

2. Lebanon should be neutral in any dispute between foreign powers.

3. Lebanon should refuse to house foreign military bases or to join foreign military pacts, such as the Baghdad Pact.

4. Any aid tending to restrict Lebanon's sovereignty or to influence her foreign policy should be rejected.

5. Lebanon should pursue a policy of close, impartial and effective cooperation with other Arab states.

6. The existing government should make way for a caretaker government to supervise the elections.

On May 27, 1957, the United National Front warned President Sham'ūn that unless he dismissed the al-Ṣulḥ government within 24 hours in favor of a neutral caretaker cabinet to supervise the elections, there would be a general strike and "peaceful demonstration," beginning May 30. In response, the Prime Minister, Sāmī al-Ṣulḥ, prohibited all demonstrations likely to lead to a breach of the peace, and requested the Ministry of Interior (in charge of the police) to enforce the ban, and the army to be ready to intervene if it became necessary.[10]

Early in the morning of May 30, opposition leaders met their supporters in various parts of the city and prepared to march to a prearranged meeting place—Avenue Fuad I. Police and gendarmes supported by armored cars prevented them, using at first rifle butts and truncheons. As usual in such cases, there is always the question of the first shot. In an official communiqué, the government claimed that the demonstrators "resorted to violence against the security forces by throwing stones and beating with sticks at the beginning, and later by firing on them from the windows of neighboring houses. The security forces were forced to apply the law which calls for the use of arms when attacked violently."[11] Also, on June 1, Radio Beirut broadcast a statement by the Prime Minister in which he accused the opposition of having planned a *coup d'état.*[12] On the other hand, the opposition not only accused the police of firing first, but also of deliberately so doing, and maintained that the demonstrators did not fire at all, since they were unarmed. In any case, in the scuffle that followed firearms and tear gas were used by the police. The army then moved in and took charge. By mid-afternoon, the streets were completely cleared.

When the fight was over, the government claimed that only four men and one woman were killed. The opposition, however, maintained that more than 15 persons were killed and about a hundred wounded. Ṣā'ib Salām received a head wound and was taken under custody to a hospital. Nasīm al-Majdalānī received a shot in his arm. Some 350 demonstrators were arrested and detained in a stable.

From a reconstruction of the events through personal interviews and documentary material, it seems that the opposition's claim that the demonstrators were unarmed was largely true. Furthermore, if the demonstrators were armed—as the government claimed—and shooting at such close range, as they must have been—it then becomes rather difficult to explain how not a single member of the police or the gendarmes was killed or seriously injured. All those killed and seriously wounded were civilians.

The claim of the Prime Minister that the demonstration was not intended to be peaceful and that the opposition was staging a *coup d'état* does not seem to bear close examination. The ability of the police to arrest some 300 to 400 persons, and to inflict such heavy casualties in killed and wounded, is at variance with such a contention.

The fact is that, as subsequent events have shown, the action of the government was a serious blunder. Ṣā'ib Salām, in addition to his former prestige, became a national hero overnight on account of his head wound. The civilian dead became martyrs and stories of police brutality and torture—whether true or not—became prevalent. In a certain sense, from that day on, the Sham'ūn administration ceased to be a government in the proper sense of the word. Instead of the re-establishment of order, terrorism and lawlessness spread. The opposition, instead of being reduced to impotence, grew in strength until it virtually became another government, existing side by side with the legally constituted authorities.

One last point in this connection should perhaps be dwelt upon. The Prime Minister claimed that "those agitators either lost their minds or have been driven to this by foreign persons or bodies . . ." Although not mentioned by name, this was a veiled reference to the Egyptian government. In addition, pro-government papers commented extensively on Egyptian, Syrian and communist influence on the demonstrations.

The nature of the allegations preclude any definite proof. However, it is a known fact that the leaders of the opposition were very friendly and had close ties with the Egyptian Ambassador in Beirut, Brigadier 'Abd al-Ḥamīd Ghālib. It is also a known fact that the Egyptian and Syrian governments were hostile to the Sham'ūn administration and in sympathy with the opposition. Thus, from *prima facie* evidence it is reasonable to conclude that, at least, the Egyptian Ambassador was kept posted on the plans of the opposition and that, in turn, the Egyptian and Syrian governments helped the opposition with both advice and funds.

As to the charge of the communist influence, it can be dismissed as an attempt on the part of the government and its supporters to discredit the demonstration and the opposition for home and international consumption. In all probability, the communists did play a role in the demonstration, for this is their practice. But it must have been an independent one, not connected with the United National Front. The communists, all through the Lebanese crisis, were an unwanted and embarrassing ally of the opposition.

Following the riots Ṣā'ib Salām, who was in the hospital, went on a hunger strike "until the government of Sāmī al-Ṣulḥ resigns," and the United National Front continued the general strike in the main cities, which, however, was not effective. At this juncture, General Shihāb, Commander of the Army, entered the scene as a mediator. After several meetings with the opposition, a compromise was arrived at:

1. All measures adopted by the commanders of the gendarmerie, the police and the *Sûreté Générale* regarding the "granting of permits, the imposition of penalties, and the deployment of forces, shall be subject to the approval of the Commander of the Army." In other words, General Shihāb was placed in control of all the security forces of the state.

2. Two new "neutral" ministers, Dr. Yusuf Ḥitti and Muḥammad 'Ali Bayhum, were added to the government as state ministers to ensure that the elections would be fair and free.

3. The above two, together with two other ministers—Majīd Arislān and Muḥammad Sabara, were formed into a committee to "examine complaints concerning election affairs, conduct the necessary investigations, and express views thereon."

The United National Front claimed that several other concessions were made by the government, but the above three were the only ones officially announced. In any case, on the midnight of June 2, the general strike was called off, and Ṣā'ib Salām stopped his hunger strike. It should be noted that, on May 31, the government confiscated issues of five opposition papers and deported several Syrians and Egyptians. The Syrians, however, returned a few days later.

The elections were held on four successive Sundays, beginning with June 9. This was intended to reduce violence and to enable the security forces to deal with it. On June 9 Beirut and South Lebanon, with 11 seats each, went to the polls. On the 16th Mount Lebanon with 20 seats. On the 23rd, al-Biqā' with 10 seats. And on the 30th, North Lebanon with 14 seats.

The election results were a sweeping victory for the government. Its candidates won over two-thirds of the seats of the new Chamber, while the opposition came out with only eight seats.

Cumulative circumstantial evidence indicates that the elections—by and large—were fraudulent. Even without knowledge of the particular circumstances, the figures themselves seem open to question. For instance, in the Beirut district, government candidates won 10 seats out of 11, while only one member of the opposition—Nasīm al-Majdalānī—managed to squeeze through. At the same time, it is hard to explain, except by assuming some irregularities, how the two opposition leaders Sa'ib Salām and ʿAbdallah al-Yāfī—traditional deputies for Beirut, highly respected and with a large popular following—were defeated. In Mount Lebanon, all 20 seats were won by government supporters.

Kamāl Junblāṭ, an honest and popular politician, an idealist who distributed his land holdings among his people, a traditional Druze leader with a faithful following, and founder of the Progressive Socialist Party, was also defeated. His defeat was effectively insured by gerrymandering his traditional district to include pro-government Christians who would not vote for him.

Conversely, strong pressure was brought to bear to insure the election of some candidates, as in the case of Dr. Charles Malik. The opposing candidate, a formidable opponent, Fu'ād al-Ghusn, was brought to the President's palace, and after two meetings with Shamʿūn—lasting, it is said, a total of nine hours—was induced to withdraw. The opposition claims that al-Ghusn's life and the life of his family were threatened,[13] while other sources state that "it was pointed out to him that if Dr. Charles Malik were defeated this would be interpreted by Egypt and Syria in particular, as a defeat of the Eisenhower Doctrine, which Lebanon was the first to accept.[14]

In any case, the withdrawal of Ghusn (who was compensated with an ambassadorial post) left the field wide open for Malik, with a communist who did not have the slightest chance of success, as an opposing candidate. In fact, the presence of the communist candidate heightened the election drama, the results of which had already been determined.

On June 17th, two "neutral" ministers — Yusuf Ḥitti and Muḥammad Bayhum—who were brought into the cabinet for the express purpose of supervising the elections and insuring that they would be honest, resigned because they could no longer "tolerate the general atmosphere." Although they could not find any fault with the technical details, they however hinted that "pressure of various kinds has been brought to bear on the voters."[15]

By and large, the press was cynical about the elections. *L'Orient,* a Beirut daily, and a government supporter, argued that "candidates of all colors had been buying votes wholesale, so nobody could complain," while according to some papers, a vote at the town of Zaḥlah, was worth as much as £L500 (approximately $155) just before the polling closed.[16] One pro-government publication ambiguously stated, "the vote was as free as ever possible in the Arab world."[17] Pierre Jamayyil, a government supporter, leader of the Phalanges, who himself was elected, was more open. In a reply (which appeared in the Lebanese daily *Le Soir* of July 15, 1957) to the question "Does your party believe in the legality of the parliament of 66 and its representative character?", he said, ". . . the parliament which has just been given to us, represents in my opinion, only ten percent of the population of the country—at the moment the real parliament is in the street."

In any case, there is little doubt that the elections were neither honest nor free, and that the new Chamber was packed—in many respects similar to its counterpart elected ten years earlier in 1947. The election campaign was conducted in an atmosphere of tension and bitterness, and was indeed the signal for mass violence which continued to increase in intensity until the end of the Sham'ūn administration. This will be discussed later.

The United National Front refused to recognize the election results. It charged that President Sham'ūn interfered openly and effectively in the elections, that "pressure and intimidation were exercised and most of the state machinery was used in various ways to falsify the will of the voters," and that new elections should be held. It further stated that the Front was considering the legal aspects of this "violation of those parts of the constitution which define the powers and responsibility of the President of the Republic."[18]

In fairness to the Sham'ūn administration, the fact should perhaps be pointed out that it had no monopoly on this practice. Its interference in the elections was not as glaring and as naked as the usual practice of its neighbors. In the Arab world, generally, elections are a procedural fiction rather than a constitutional reality. In most cases—in countries which bother to go through the motions of an election at all—only those candidates approved and hand-picked in advance by the administration usually win. Other Arab governments have never had a parliamentary system at all, while others have recently dispensed with such, as contrary to the public good. Lebanon today is the only Arab country where elections are held with a degree of genuine freedom.

The Spread of Terrorism and Arms Smuggling

Immediately following the elections, there was a lull and some relaxation of tension. On July 10 the ban on Egyptian papers was lifted, and two days later Charles Malik was able to announce that relations with Egypt had improved and that "we love Egypt as we love ourselves." The Ba'lbak International Festival was due to open on the 25th with famous theater companies and troupes performing.

The relaxed atmosphere, however, proved to be of very short duration. No sooner had life settled back to a measure of normalcy, when bombings, clan feuds, sabotage, gun-running and clashes between armed bands and the gendarmes in mountain areas began to occur, and then increase in their frequency and in their damage to life and property. This state of affairs continued until the crisis began in earnest in May 1958.

It should be kept in mind that during these months when terrorism and arms smuggling were increasing in Lebanon, tension in neighboring countries was reaching the boiling point. Syria was going through a series of "plots" culminating in the so-called "American plot" and the crisis of Turkish troop concentration. Both Syria and Egypt were at odds with Jordan, and the feud was being waged in a radio war and in a series of plots and counterplots.

Nor were the relations between Syria and Lebanon cordial. Syria regarded the Lebanese government as having "sold out" to the West, and believed that Beirut was the main base for all sorts of conspiracies against its security and independence. Conversely, the Lebanese authorities, particularly Sham'ūn, Sāmī al-Ṣulḥ and Charles Malik, believed that Syria was going communist and will soon become a Russian satellite—although they never expressed this belief openly—and that the spread of terrorism in Lebanon was basically due to the activities of the Syrian *Deuxième Bureau.*

During this period, relations between Syria and Lebanon deteriorated very rapidly. Syrian papers had been under ban in Lebanon for several months, and the ban on several Egyptian papers was reinstituted. Both Radios Cairo and Damascus were being jammed. As terrorism increased, accusations against the Syrian intelligence service also increased, and deportation of Syrians become more frequent. Armed bands were allegedly crossing and re-crossing the frontier between Syria and Lebanon—usually escaping into Syria after clashes with Lebanese security patrols. Arms smuggling from Syria increased.

On November 22—Independence Day in Lebanon—an incident heightened the tension between the two countries. The official celebrations which were held under the patronage of President Sham'ūn were boycotted by the opposition, who instead paid their respects to the Maronite Patriarch. Nor did the Syrian government send a representative. Instead, a delegation of 17 Syrian deputies proceeded from Damascus to congratulate the Maronite Patriarch—Monsignor Paul Ma'ūshī, as a tribute to his "patriotic acts in defense of Lebanon's Arab nationalism." Allegedly, however, they were prevented from entering Lebanon by the border guard on the instructions of the authorities in Beirut.

Akram al-Ḥaurānī, Speaker of the Syrian Chamber of Deputies, telegraphed his counterpart in Lebanon, "it was most astonishing action, but the bonds of neighborliness and the unity of our struggle cannot be weakened by such actions." He further telegraphed the Patriarch, "Syrian Arabs regard you as embodying the essence of nationalist dignity and honor." The patriarch considered this "arbitrary action" as having been "directed against me personally." 'Abdallah al-Yāfī wrote in *al-Siyāsah,* "What are the leaders trying to do? . . . Did they think that by preventing the Syrian deputies from entering Lebanon they would be paralyzing any popular movement that might have been intended for Independence Day?" In a Chamber Debate on November 27th, Kāmil al-As'ad, an opposition deputy said, "The people (i.e. the Lebanese) share the view of the Syrian parliamentary delegation that there is no official authority that deserves to be congratulated for Independence Day other than the Maronite Patriarch." Commenting on the affair, the Syrian Minister of Propaganda said this showed "the depths to which the rulers of Lebanon have sunk."

On November 25th, the Lebanese government issued a denial stating in part that "there were about 50 cars in front of theirs at the border, so that they were asked to wait while formalities were being completed . . . but after five minutes the deputies drove back for no apparent reason . . . There had not been any order to ban the deputies and, in fact, they were not prevented from entering Lebanon." The Prime Minister, Sāmī al Ṣulh, charged on December 3 that the whole incident was intended to fabricate a crisis. He further denied and deplored a reported allegation by Akram al-Ḥaurānī that the deputies were turned back at foreign instigation.

In the meantime, the state of tension and division in Lebanon itself, is illustrated by a near fist fight during a Chamber debate on January 29, 1958. Mr. George 'Aql, one of Sham'ūn's most ardent supporters, attacked the Egyptian and Syrian governments. Ṣabrī Ḥamādah, a member of the United National Front, counter-attacked the Lebanese government. Accusations and insults were exchanged, but colleagues prevented them from fighting. The sitting was then suspended at 11 p.m. to prevent a general fight.

The Union and Nāṣir's Damascus Visit

On February 1, 1958, President Nāṣir and President al-Quwwatlī of Syria signed documents declaring the merger of Syria and Egypt into the United Arab Republic.

The announcement caused immediate repercussions in various parts of the Arab world. In Lebanon, the government on the same day banned demonstrations to avoid any possible trouble. On February 2, Lebanese schools run by the Islamic *al-Maqāṣid* charitable organization, and attended by some 15,000 children, closed down in celebration of the union. On February 5, many schools closed down throughout Lebanon, and despite the government ban demonstrations were held in Beirut, Tripoli, Sidon and Tyre, and Egyptian and Syrian flags were flown over large buildings, in addition to street decorations. In Tripoli, there were minor clashes between the demonstrators and the police who tried to disperse them. In Beirut, the police used fire hoses for the same purpose.

On February 9, a delegation representing the United National Front visited Damascus to congratulate President al-Quwwatlī on the birth of the UAR. He told the delegation, "The new republic is the best guarantee of Lebanon's existence. Lebanon is invited to join it whenever she may so desire by merger, or by federation, with the right to maintain her own integrity and special position." ʿAbdallah al-Yāfī, a leading member of the United National Front, told Syrian reporters in Damascus that the new republic was a better guarantee of Lebanon's independence than "all the foreign guarantees in which some Lebanese believe." Ṣabrī Ḥamādah, former Speaker of the Lebanese Chamber of Deputies, said, "The great majority of the Lebanese people and members of the United National Front want union with the United Arab republic, but we do not like to take any step before all the people are convinced of the advantages of the union, for this might pave the way for subversive elements and imperialist hangers-on in Lebanon to threaten the independence of the country." Rashīd Karāmī, who led a delegation of 30 men from Tripoli, said, "The present hesitation and reluctance of Lebanon is temporary. In the long run Lebanon will devote herself to Arab nationalism in a way which will satisfy Arabism." Fu'ād ʿAmmūn, a member of the opposition, also visited al-Quwwatlī. ʿAmmūn is reported to have said that if Lebanon joined the union she would receive many benefits and dispel any threats against her.[19]

President Shamʿūn, however, speaking in a Maronite church in Beirut on February 8, maintained that because of the diverse religions and sects, Lebanon's independence was and had to be perpetual. He further stated that "Lebanon is a sister of other Arab countries and wishes them prosperity without interfering in their affairs. We want others to do likewise and not interfere in Lebanon's affairs." Dr. Charles Malik told the Chamber of Deputies on February 11, "Lebanon is and always will be a country with her own flag, sovereignty, independence and mission in life. She will play her part internationally: she will take part in every good action which might affect her friends."[20] On February 18, President al-Quwwatlī, at a party given in his honor at Damascus, and attended by Lebanese business men, again invited Lebanon to join the union. Lebanon, and particularly Beirut, he said, would be the principal trade center for a population of about 28 million people. Lebanon would be their summer resort.[21]

Apparently in expectation of intensified pressure from the Egyptian-Syrian union, the Lebanese Council of Ministers decided on February 19 to seek powers from the Chamber of Deputies to suppress political propaganda financed by foreign funds if its aim was considered harmful to the country, or likely to cause disturbances. The proposed bill, it was believed, was aimed primarily at curbing Egyptian influence.[22]

On February 24, President Nāṣir, without forewarning to anyone, landed in Damascus. For several days he spent most of his time addressing thousands of cheering crowds who welcomed him with enthusiasm verging on the hysteria.

The welcome was not restricted to Syrians. According to press dispatches, Nāṣir's visits to Damascus "stirred enthusiasm in Lebanon beyond anything that was expected."[23] Thousands of Lebanese from Beirut, Tripoli, Sidon, Tyre and other towns, traveled to Damascus to join the cheering crowds and pay their respects. Taxi fares from Beirut to Damascus rose to £L25 (5 times the normal) and taxi drivers in Beirut, to drum up trade, chanted "To Damascus to Jamal."[24]

On February 25, a delegation representing the United National Front came to pay its respects. It was composed, among others of 'Abdallah al-Yāfī, Ṣā'ib Salām, Kamāl Junblāṭ Aḥmad and Kāmil al-As'ad, Fu'ād 'Ammūn, 'Abdallah al-Mashnūq, Ilyās al-Khūrī, Ma'rūf Sā'd, Dr. Laḥḥūd and Shafīq Murtada. Ṣā'ib Salām, in addressing Nāṣir, said in part:

> The hearts of the free Lebanese have come to you to express their feelings for you. You have been elected President by the people here. However, we come to assure you that, wherever you are and wherever you go, you occupy the place of leadership in the Arab nation . . . I assure you that all the people of Lebanon also lay upon your shoulders a heavy burden. This, O Your Excellency the President, is because you are not responsible for this Arab republic alone, but you are responsible for all

> Arab people everywhere . . . Allow me to emphasize that you are responsible in particular for Lebanon and the Lebanese people feel reassured at this responsibility as they have confidence in you, personally. The Lebanese see in you and in this new homeland which you have founded, the best proof for the preservation of their entity and independence.[25]

President Nāṣir received several other Lebanese delegations and Lebanese personalities, including a delegation of the Maronite Patriarch, Paul Ma'ūshī. He also addressed Lebanese crowds several times.

The stream of Lebanese visitors continued to flow. On March 9, about 5,000 Lebanese lead by Nasīm al-Majdalānī, Shafīq Murtada, Anwar al-Khaṭīb—all deputies—and Kamāl Junblāṭ, cheered and were addressed by Nāṣir.[26] Lebanese visitors to Damascus to pay homage to Nāṣir were estimated at between three hundred and three hundred and fifty thousand.

There is little question that the birth of the UAR and Nāṣir's visit to Damascus, indirectly and without prior intention, helped bring the Lebanese crisis to a head. The enthusiastic welcome with which both the union and Nāṣir were greeted, created a strong fear among certain segments of the Lebanese public, particularly the Maronites, that Lebanon's independence was in danger. For instance, Father Antoine Qurtbāwī, a Maronite priest, took time out to write an article in a Maronite publication, reputed to have close connections with President Sham'ūn, reminding the world that "Lebanon is not Arab, but is the Lebanon—a Mediterranean country whose language is Arabic." He further maintained that the Egyptians are not Arabs either.[27] In addition, illuminated pictures of President Sham'ūn and placards extolling his virtues, blossomed suddenly in the various streets of Beirut. It was officially stated that this was the reply of his supporters to similar tributes to President Nāṣir.[28] Nāṣir's visit also hardened the lines of division between the opposition and its followers, and the government and its supporters, and made them extremely suspicious of each other, and willing to give any move the worse interpretation. This is illustrated in the unrest and riots that took place in late March and early April.

On March 16, five persons were arrested in Tripoli for leading demonstrators shouting slogans in favor of the United Arab Republic. On the 19th, school children played truant, because the authorities ordered pictures of Nāṣir taken down from walls and other public places (portraits of Sham'ūn were also forbidden). On the 21st, there were more demonstrators in Tripoli shouting anti-Sham'ūn slogans and extolling Nāṣir and the Maronite Patriarch Ma'ūshī.

In Tyre, disturbances became serious. In late March, a court sentenced three men to prison terms (one for three years) for allegedly being guilty of contempt to the Lebanese flag during demonstrations in favor of the UAR. In an impassioned article in the Beirut daily *Le Soir,* Kasruwān Labakī charged that the crowds tore the Lebanese flag, trampled on it, and even wiped their shoes with it.[29]

On March 28th, angered at the court treatment of the three men and alleging that they were framed by *agents provocateurs,* the shop keepers closed down and school children stayed home. There was a demonstration. The gendarmes opened fire and wounded six persons. Later that day about 200 women demonstrated in protest and were joined by some youths. Police fired in the air, but no one was injured except that a stray bullet hit a demonstrator and marked him slightly. On April 1, taxi and bus drivers refused to operate the services, shops remained closed and school children stayed at home. On April 2, demonstrators again clashed with the gendarmes, who opened fire. This time, however, with more serious results: four persons were killed and 11 injured. A few of the gendarmes were hurt, but not seriously. Between March 28 and April 2, some 150 persons were arrested in Tyre. After the clash, the government called in the army which took control of the city. It also withdrew the gendarmerie commandant and the district officer of Tyre because of the animosity against them.

The situation was debated in the Chamber of Deputies. Two opposition deputies, Ma'rūf Sā'd and Kāmil al-As'ad, claimed that the flag was never insulted to begin with, and charged that the police had beaten up and tortured some of the persons detained in Tyre. Niqūlā Sālim, a Christian deputy for Jizzin (South Lebanon), said that most of those arrested on March 28th were youths. Communists and Palestinians had not taken part in the first demonstrations, he maintained. Rashīd Karāmī issued a statement from Tripoli that the people of Tripoli support their brethren in Tyre. "The incidents" the statement said, "are not the first and will not be the last of their kind. We believe that they are a series of conspiracies against the people." The United National Front accused the government of arranging the Tyre disturbances so that it could create a situation in which the constitution could be amended and President Sham'ūn stand for re-election in September.[30]

On the other hand, the Minister of Justice, Bashīr al-'Awar, said in the Chamber that the prison sentences had not been confirmed and were still open to appeal, and that they would investigate reports that members of the outlawed P.P.S. had fired on the demonstrators on March 28. Other officials said that most of those detained on March

28 had been released. Kāẓim al-Khalīl, Minister of Economy, in announcing to the Chamber the casualties of the April 2 clashes, said that some of the demonstrators had thrown sticks of dynamite before the gendarmes fired.

The Minister of Justice reported on his investigations on April 3. He made no mention of dynamite, but said that the gendarmes fired as a last resort. "If the government once hesitated to enforce the rule of law, could it ever take action again," he asked. He further claimed that bullets recovered from the bodies of some of the wounded were fired from a type of gun not usually carried by the gendarmerie.

Presidential Succession

The Lebanese constitution specifically prohibits an incumbent president from succeeding himself. It will be recalled that one of the chief factors which brought about the downfall of former President al-Khūrī in 1952, was his violation of this provision through a puppet legislature. At that time, President Sham'ūn, one of the chief leaders of the opposition, felt that the projected amendment of the constitution to enable al-Khūrī to be re-elected "should never be done, lest a precedent of amending the constitution for personal reasons may be established."[31] President Sham'ūn made the same mistake six years later in 1958.

Fear that the President was planning to run for office again had existed before the 1957 parliamentary elections. Although this question did not come out into the open, it was nevertheless one of the main background issues in the campaign.

President Sham'ūn never explicitly stated in public that he would run. This writer, however, was told by a Western diplomat of unimpeachable authority that President Sham'ūn had informed the American, British and French Ambassadors in Beirut of his determined intention to amend the constitution to make possible his re-election.[32]

In any case, by the opening months of 1958, the rumor had become widespread and became one of the chief topics of political discussion in the country. Sham'ūn's supporters in and outside the Chamber of Deputies were preparing the climate by openly advocating his re-election, while President Sham'ūn himself was dropping broad hints to that effect in political speeches usually made during Christian religious occasions.

In January 1958 the Third Force decided to clarify the issue. A delegation representing the group called on the President to ascertain his position. After the interview, they held a press conference (on January 27, 1958) where they announced that they were now fully convinced that the President was determined to run for another term in contravention of the constitution. The statement concluded, "The fact is that the idea of renewal has become so overpowering that we are in a perpetual state of an election campaign, in which the government is using its machinery and resources to win those elements which may participate in the final victory, at the cost of the dignity of the state and justice."

After the Third Force statement, the "battle of renewal" came out into the open. According to Lebanese sources favoring the opposition, Ṣā'ib Salām, 'Abdallah al-Yāfī and Kamāl Junblāṭ were made generous offers if they would support President Sham'ūn's re-election.[33] They charged as well that 'Ādil 'Usayrān was dispatched to Cairo to win President Nāṣir's support in return for various concessions amounting to Lebanon's falling in line with the policy of the United Arab Republic,[34] and that the Maronite Patriarch and former President al-Khūrī were also approached.[35] All these efforts and offers, however, according to these sources, met with failure and rejection.

On March 27, 1958, some 85 leading political personalities and public figures met at the home of Henri Far'ūn in Beirut, organized themselves into a Congress, and elected Henri Far'ūn President; 'Abdallah Yāfī, vice-president; and Kamāl Junblāṭ, secretary. They made several resolutions and issued a manifesto in which they affirmed their dedication to the continued existence of Lebanon as an independent state and to the National Covenant; blamed the administration for the deterioration of law and order; accused Sham'ūn of spreading anxiety concerning the independence of Lebanon in order to serve his own purpose and warned him that if he made any attempt to amend the Constitution to enable him to renew his term of office, this "will justify the people in imposing their will by all means at their disposal."

On the night of the same day, explosives were thrown in an area which includes the houses of Henri Far'ūn, Fu'ād 'Ammūn, and the weekly *al-Ḥawādith,* a supporter of the UAR.

On April 10, the suspicions of the opposition were confimed. On that day, George 'Aql—a deputy and an ardent supporter of Sham'ūn—announced that he would soon propose an amendment to the constitution in the Chamber to enable Sham'ūn to stand for re-election.

On the same day, April 10, some 300 Muslim leaders, including former Prime Ministers, speakers of the Chamber, opposition deputies, and religious leaders, attended a Ramadan dinner party given by the Mufti of Lebanon—Shaykh Muḥammad 'Alāyā. No Muslim member of the government was invited, as used to be the practice. After the party, a statement was issued in which they declared their opposition to any attempt to amend the constitution. The statement declared the "denunciation by the whole country of the present political situation and utmost dissatisfaction with the behavior of the rulers, which has resulted in bloody incidents." The rulers "had spread dissension among the Lebanese people and stimulated hateful feuds to carry out their plan to amend the constitution so as to allow the re-election of the President." These tactics had destroyed national unity, the statement continued. The leaders further declared that, as a sign of mourning, there should be no congratulations on *Bayram* (the end of Ramadan) as Lebanon was suffering from the policy of the present rulers. This was followed on April 17 by a declaration from the Mufti of Lebanon and some 200 leading Muslims that anyone who accepted or offered *Bayram* congratulations would be regarded as having violated the unanimity of the Muslim community.

On April 15, during a debate in the Chamber which nearly degenerated into a fist fight, Ma'rūf Sā'd charged that the government was arming its supporters. The government, he said, had split the population into factions. French imperialism of the past was not alone to blame for sectarianism in Lebanon. This was also due to the policies of certain individuals (i.e. Sham'ūn). He suggested that the government should resign, and the Chamber be dissolved, for they were responsible for the present chaos which might develop into sectarian violence similar to that of 1860.

On April 20, explosives were thrown near the house of the Prime Minister—Sāmī al-Ṣulḥ—while he was receiving visitors who called to congratulate him on *Bayram.*

On April 24, George 'Aql announced again that he would introduce the motion for amending the constitution the following week.

By the end of April, the country was like a powder keg. Only an incident of symbolic significance was needed to explode it. Acts of violence and sabotage had become a daily occurence. On April 10, the first clashes between the followers of Kamāl Junblāṭ, the Druze leader, took place in the Shūf area. The political significance of these first clashes is indicated by the fact that Rashīd Karāmī, Ḥusayn al-'Uwaynī, Fu'ād 'Ammūn, and Henri Far'ūn told General Shihāb, the Army Commander, that the clash was a political event resulting from the government's intention to change the constitution to enable Sham'ūn to run again. They emphasized that the army should be kept out of the controversy. This indicates that the decision for armed action had been taken by the opposition.

On April 13, the army issued an order prohibiting the publication of any information on its activities and movements, and warned that offenders would be imprisoned up to two years.

The Murder of Nasīb al-Matnī

The spark which touched off the armed conflict occurred in the early hours of the day of May 8 when bullets from unknown assassins killed Nasīb al-Matnī. Al-Matnī, a Maronite Christian, was publisher and owner of the Beirut Arabic daily *The Telegraph,* a severe critic of Sham'ūn and his administration, who was also in favor of strengthening relations with the UAR.

Al-Matnī had been at odds with the administration for some time. On July 22, 1957, he was arrested and tried for publishing a report to the effect that the UNF was still considering whether to ask parliament to try President Sham'ūn for violating the constitution by alleged interference with the elections. The prosecution claimed that the report contravened laws forbidding journalists to defame the President. The defense argued that al-Matnī was merely commenting on the general principle that the President may be tried if he violates the constitution. On July 23, UNF announced that it assumed responsibility for the report and that "the action which the front is studying is legal and the constitution clearly provides for it." The Prime Minister, Sāmī al-Ṣulh, then warned all owners that they would be held responsible for the contents of any UNF statements published in their papers, since such statements were usually unsigned. The owners replied that they considered his warning an attack on the freedom of the press. On August 1, the court sentenced al-Matnī to six months imprisonment, commuted to 15 days, of which he had already served 11 while awaiting trial. He decided to appeal.

Almost immediately — while still in prison — the authorities served another warrant on him for publishing an article by Nasīm al-Majdalānī (an opposition deputy), which allegedly defamed the President by reproducing opposition accusations that the government bought votes at the elections.

On November 9, al-Matnī was stabbed twice in the face, while leaving his office in the early morning. He was taken to the hospital. His assailant, who escaped in a car that was waiting for him, was never apprehended.

When he was murdered on May 8, four unsigned letters were found in al-Matnī's pockets, threatening to kill him if he did not abandon his opposition to the government. The last letter was dated April 19. In his last article which appeared in *The Telegraph* the morning of his murder, al-Matnī called on Sham'ūn to resign. "Lebanon's interests, Lebanon's eternal independence, and the interests of the people make it essential for the individual to sacrifice himself for the benefit of the whole," he had written.

The murder shook the country as nothing had done before. The government and Sham'ūn personally were accused of being behind it. The United National Front joined with other political groups to declare a general strike throughout the country, and to issue the following declaration on May 8:[36]

> In view of the overwhelming wave of provocation, terrorism and violence, and the government's persistence in fanning feuds to submerge the country in a sea of blood in pursuance of selfish personal ambitions and an irrational lust which has now become known to everyone, and which has not been effected by advice, or restrained by conscience, religion, or considerations for the nation and the unity of its children;
>
> And in view of this poisoned atmosphere of plots, injustices, feuds and assassinations—the last of which is the assassination of the noble nationalist, Nasīb al-Matnī;
>
> And in view of this ill-omened policy whose every aspect is plastered with blood, and which has spread anxiety and fear, and which has become a constant threat to the security of citizens in their lives, and to women and children in the threat to the lives of their husbands and fathers; as well as being a threat to the commerce and economy of the country;
>
> And to preserve the national being of Lebanon, the unity of its ranks, and the brotherhood of its sects; and to spare the shedding of the blood of its children—the signatories below, who represent various parties, organizations and tendencies in Lebanon, declare the following:
>
> 1. The rulers are responsible for what has happened and what is still happening in the way of provocative actions, and for the consequent feuds, plots, assassinations, and our national duty requires us to spare our fatherland from their calamitous results.
> 2. Denunciation of the methods they (i.e. the rulers) have resorted to, and which would be repudiated by any person of dignity and honor —methods of perfidy and assassinations—the last of its victims being the martyr Nasīb al-Matnī.
> 3. Declaration of a general strike in all parts of Lebanon, while laying the responsibility for it on the rulers who have destroyed the sanctity of law, and struck down the most sacred and dearest spiritual and national values in Lebanon.

The Third Force issued a statement following the same general lines and calling for a strike. In addition, the following organizations, most of which were members of the UNF, issued independent declarations also calling for a strike: The National Organization, the Progressive Socialist Party, the Constitutional Bloc, *al-Najjādah,* the

Popular Front, the Free Press, The Arab Liberation Party, and the Grand Mufti of Lebanon—Shaykh Muḥammad 'Alāyā.

Bishārah al-Khūrī, former President of Lebanon, issued a statement in which he called on all Lebanese to close ranks before this "severe test" and to repel "the wickedness of the intriguers." He referred to "a series of crimes of provocation, contempt of spiritual values, tampering with God's most valuable gifts to men—freedom, dignity and life. Those disfigurers of Lebanon's pure face desire to disseminate dissension and feuds—that spirit which threatens the being of Lebanon, its independence and its national covenant."

Thus the armed conflict, the story of which will be detailed in the following chapter, began.

NOTES

1. *Mideast Mirror,* April 7, 1957, pp. 4-5.
2. *On The Course of Lebanese Policy,* p. 24.
3. Niqūlā al-Shāwī, one of the founders of the communist party in Lebanon and a member of the central committee, claimed that the party "participated in the revolt from the beginning in all parts of Lebanon. Our comrades were behind the barricades. In some areas they were in full command, while in others, they participated in the command with others. A good number of our comrades were killed or wounded." Toufic Mokdessi and Lucian George, *Political Parties in Lebanon in 1959,* Beirut: L'Orient, 1960, p. 96 (in Arabic and French).
4. *Mideast Mirror,* April 7, 1957, p. 23, and *Ibid.,* April 14, 1957, p. 26.
5. *Ibid.,* April 14, 1957, p. 26.
6. *Radio Voice of the Arabs,* April 5, 1957, 1825 GMT.
7. *Radio Beirut,* June 12, 1957, 1100 GMT.
8. *Radio Cairo,* June 15, 1957, 0500 GMT.
9. *Mideast Mirror,* May 19, 1957, p. 15.
10. *Ibid.,* June 2, 1957, p. 8.
11. *Radio Beirut,* May 30, 1957, 1200 GMT
12. *Radio Beirut,* June 1, 1957, 1100 GMT.
13. See the statement of the United National Front on the election of Charles Malik, dated 20 June 1957.
14. *Mideast Mirror,* July 7, 1957, p. 12.
15. *Ibid.,* June 23, 1957, p. 11.
16. *Ibid.,* June 30, 1957, p. 6.
17. *Ibid.,* June 16, 1957, p. 14.
18. *Ibid.,* July 7, 1957, p. 12.
19. All the above quotations are from the *Mideast Mirror,* February 16, 1958, p. 5.
20. *Ibid.,* p. 5.
21. *Ibid.,* February 23, 1958, p. 14.
22. *Ibid.*
23. *New York Times,* February 27, 1958.
24. *Ibid.*
25. *Radio Damascus,* February 25, 1958, 1915 GMT.
26. *Mideast Mirror,* March 16, 1958, p. 7.
27. *New York Times,* March 10, 1958.
28. *Mideast Mirror,* March 16, 1958, p. 10.
29. *Ibid.,* April 6, 1958, p. 2.
30. *Ibid.,* p. 3.
31. See Chapter II, p. 22.
32. The person concerned asked me not to reveal his name.
33. Nawwāf and Nadiā Karāmī, *The Truth about the Lebanese Revolt.* Beirut: 1959, p. 36.
34. *Ibid.,* pp. 37-38.
35. *Ibid.,* pp. 36-37.
36. *Ibid.,* pp. 44-45.

CHAPTER V

The Civil War

HAD THE LEBANESE crisis not had such tragic aspects, it could have been easily described as a comic opera. There was something unreal about the whole affair—a succession of scenes taken virtually *in toto* from Ruritania: an army that would not fight; opposition leaders officially declared "rebels," with warrants out for their arrest, blandly walking the streets of Beirut in broad daylight with no one laying so much as a finger on them; pitched battles between the army and "rebel" forces stopped, so that army trucks could bring water to the rebels and move their wounded to hospitals; a president virtually a prisoner in his own palace for over two months; a parliament that could not meet; opposition leaders, each with a private army of his own, establishing virtually independent government in his locality—levying taxes and administering justice; and a crisis that was long on bitter words, but short on actual casualties.

Unfortunately, the crisis had a grimmer aspect. A comparatively small minority on both the government and opposition sides seemed bent on leading the country into anarchy. While many innocent victims, including women and children, were being killed by stray bullets and maimed by bombs; while the country sank crazily into financial ruin; while the summer resorts—usually bustling with thousands of tourists—remained empty, the stores closed, business activity at a complete standstill; while badly-needed bridges, roads, waterworks, and power plants were being dynamited; while sectarian wounds which had almost healed began to open up again; while a tempest in a tea-pot was bringing the world to the brink of an atomic holocaust, the politicians on both sides, bargained, held conferences and issued statements.

The Revolt Begins

After the murder of al-Matnī on May 9, 1958, the United National Front declared a general strike throughout the country. For the first time however, the Front demanded the immediate resignation of President Sham'ūn and the formation of a "salvation" caretaker cabinet until a new president was elected. They declared that the strike would continue until their demands were met.

Apparently, the strike was declared with the hope that it would bring about the downfall of the administration. This, however, did not materialize. The strike itself proved partly successful. In Beirut, with its cosmopolitan population, for instance, it was far from effective.

In Tripoli, however, the strike took a serious turn, leading immediately to armed rebellion. On May 9, about 1,000 worshippers at the Manṣūrī Mosque tried to demonstrate after prayers, and clashed with security forces. The clash resulted in some 40 persons being injured. On the following day, May 10, the clashes continued, with more serious results: about 10 persons were killed and 60 wounded, some seriously. Demonstrators set fire to the US Information Library, and to the property of the PPS. On the 11th, fighting was resumed. "People's guards" were formed to enforce the strike and to erect barricades. Shops which ignored the strike were burned down or sacked. By nighttime, when a dusk-to-dawn curfew was imposed, the official toll for the three days of violence had risen to 13 dead and 110 injured.

On May 12, the wave of violence reached Beirut. "From early morning anti-government forces began to barricade many of the roads in or leading into the city. The barricades were reinforced with burning oil drums and by setting fire to oil and petrol which were poured across the streets. Cars which tried to break through the barricades were burned or smashed. Police motorcycles were wrecked. Six persons were killed in clashes with patrolling soldiers, well-armed and supported by armored cars mounting machine guns. The strike was now more general in most parts of the city. Explosions were heard. Occasionally there was gunfire. Curfew from 8 p.m. until 5 a.m. daily was introduced. Beirut, usually a lively place after dark, was dead—except for the rumble of explosions now and then. The streets seemed utterly empty, but the few civilians who ventured out soon found there were soldiers and policemen waiting in the shadows to examine their special passes and, if they had none, take them away for questioning. The road to and from Damascus was barred. Beirut was also cut off from the south. A military warning to newspapers and news agencies said there were penalties of up to five years' imprisonment for publishing anything considered as inciting the population, criticizing the army, or even reporting its activities."[1]

On the 9th, after the news of the clashes in Tripoli reached Beirut, during a policy meeting of the United National Front, attended by Ḥusayn al-ʿUwaynī, ʿAbdallah al-Yāfī, Kamāl Junblāṭ, Fuʾād ʿAmmūn, and Ṣāʾib Salām, among others, the decision for armed revolt was taken, and Kamāl Junblāṭ was chosen to start it in the mountains.[2] On May 12, Junblāṭ reached al-Mukhtārah in the Shūf area, his country home and the center of his Druze followers. On the 13th, Junblāṭ's forces attacked the presidential palace at Bayt al-Dīn. The revolt had begun.[3]

The Balance of Forces

Within a few days after the civil strife commenced in earnest, the country became divided into a number of sectors virtually independent of each other, each under the control of a local leader (see map).

Beirut

In Beirut, the Western district, comprising principally Muslim sections such as al-Basṭa quarter, came under the control of the opposition, while Christian sections remained under government control. Opposition-held areas of Beirut were declared by the army as out of bounds to all security forces of the state.

The opposition-held sections were to all practical purposes independent. At the beginning, there were three separate commands under Ṣā'ib Salām, 'Adnān al-Ḥakīm (leader of al-Najjādah party), and Mu'in Ḥamūd respectively. These were later unified into one central command with Mu'in Ḥamūd as Chairman, and Miṣbaḥ Salām, 'Abd al-Karīm al-Zayn, Rashīd Shihāb al-dīn, Yusuf Ḥakīm, and 'Abd al-Raḥmān Darwīsh as members, in addition to a few others. This command soon broke up, however, when Mu'in Ḥamūd arrested two members ('Abd al-Raḥmān Darwīsh and Yusuf Ḥakīm) and imprisoned them in the house of Ṣā'ib Salām. Thereafter, Ṣā'ib Salām assumed full command, choosing as his assistants 'Abd al-Karīm al-Zayn and Rashīd Shihāb al-dīn. Various administrative committees were also organized. The finance committee was headed by Ḥusayn al-'Uwaynī.

Initially, the opposition in Beirut lacked both arms and ammunition. This was soon corrected. Workshops were established to produce explosives, and Junblāṭ headquarters in the Shūf area supplied them with adequate quantities of ammunition, and various types of machine guns, mortars and bazookas. Later a workshop producing machine guns was established.

Two important opposition papers, *al-Siyāsah* and *Beirut al-Masā,* whose plants happened to be in opposition-held areas, continued to publish, though banned by the government, and copies of their editions were smuggled to government-held parts of the city.

Government forces did not venture into opposition-held sections of the city, although government aircraft occasionally strafed the area, and in some cases they were reported to have used napalm bombs. On the other hand, opposition forces infiltrated government-held parts of the city using bombs and dynamite presumably for their psychological effect, to enforce the strike. An average of about fifty explosives were used each day. A survey by this writer of dynamiting and bombing incidents shows that comparatively few people were actually killed or injured by them. They apparently were placed at times when it was reasonably certain that the premises would be vacant. The two worst incidents took place on May 15 and 26, respectively. On May 15, a time-bomb hidden in a bucket in Martyrs' Square, the main center of Beirut, exploded around noon, killing six persons and injuring 20. On the 26th, a time bomb exploded in a crowded tram-car killing at least one person and inflicting various mutilations on some twenty, including the loss of limbs and so forth.

The initial plan of the opposition called for attacking the presidential palace, capturing Sham'ūn and occupying the Beirut internanational airport. Although the presidential palace was attacked several times, for various reasons the plan never succeeded. It is said that one of the principal reasons was dissension in opposition ranks, and more particularly, the arrest and imprisonment of 'Abd al-Raḥmān Darwīsh and Yusuf Ḥakīm.

Although firing and shooting was a daily—and indeed sometimes hourly—occurrence, the only actually heavy fighting in Beirut took place on Saturday and Sunday, June 14 and 15 respectively, in a determined effort for a show-down on the part of both the government and the opposition. Army tanks were brought up against the opposition in intense city-wide street fighting which continued for two days. The house of Sa'ib Salām was shelled and the top floor was destroyed. Conversely, the house of Prime Minister Sāmī al-Ṣulḥ was looted and burned down by the opposition, the presidential palace was subject to intense gunfire, and parts of al-Raml prison were destroyed—making possible the escape of 15 prisoners.

Tripoli

In Tripoli, the second city of the country, and where the revolt first began, the situation was considerably different. Whereas in Beirut little actual fighting took place, by contrast, Tripoli turned into a virtual battlefield. While in Beirut the role of the army was comparatively minor, in Tripoli, it assumed principal responsibility, employing tanks, armored cars and heavy guns. According to opposition sources, 168 persons from among the opposition were killed in Tripoli and its harbor (al-Mīnā).[4] This figure excludes the hundreds of wounded and the fairly heavy casualties killed and wounded among the government security forces. A large number of buildings were demolished in both Tripoli and the harbor, mostly through shelling by the army and less frequently by bombs of the opposition forces.

Tripoli, like Beirut, was divided into two main sections. The Old City with its ancient narrow lanes, with al-Manṣūrī Mosque at its heart, comprising a population of some 40,000 persons, came under the control of the opposition. The overall direction of "popular resistance" was assumed by Rashīd Karāmī, a former Prime Minister. Under Karāmī, an eight-man central command for policy decisions and direction was organized,[5] and execution was assigned to a seven-man Executive Office, with Ṭal'āt Karīm as general commander.[6] A revolutionary court and other appendages of government were established.

The Old City and the harbor were besieged by government forces throughout the crisis, and food as well as other essentials were prevented, for the greater part, from reaching them, although supplies did get through by devious routes from neighboring villages and from Syria. Tripoli suffered the most extensive damage of any part of the country.

Sidon

In Sidon, opposition forces under the leadership of Ma'rūf Sā'd assumed control of the town. The central command was formed under him, with Ṣalāḥ Sā'd assisting him as general commander. Various revolutionary committees—such as finance, ordnance, training, internal security, court and publicity—were also organized. Apparently, opposition forces comprised some one thousand fighters, in addition to those dispatched to the neighboring countryside.

The Shūf Sector

The best organized sector was this Shūf area in south central Lebanon. There, Junblāṭ established the rudiments of a government including armed forces, supply, police, justice, and various administrative units, with al-Mukhtārah, Junblāṭ's home, as the capital. It was also in the Shūf area that the heaviest and most continuous fighting took place. This was due to several reasons: the bitter enmity between Sham'ūn and Junblāṭ; the existence in the Shūf mountains of many Christian villages—mostly Maronite, who were Sham'ūn loyalists; and finally because Junblāṭ was the strongest opponent and apparently was planning to march on Beirut and either occupy it and/or force Sham'ūn to resign.

Some of the battles which received wide publicity in the world press, also took place in the Shūf mountains.

It was stated previously that on May 13, Junblāṭ's forces attacked Bayt al-Dīn, where the famous Presidential Palace is located. Government and opposition accounts of the battle which raged for several days in the mountains vary considerably in detail. Government statements claimed that the attackers on Bayt al-Dīn and the surrounding villages numbered about 300 men,[7] while opposition sources place the number at a maximum of 65 men. In addition, these sources claim that Junblāṭ personally, on May 12, gave an ultimatum to the 40-man palace garrison to surrender, and that the commanding officer pretended acceptance, but that immediately after Junblāṭ's departure, he brought in PPS reinforcements from Bā'aqlīn and stationed them in the houses in the village.[8]

On the 13th, Junblāṭ's forces launched their attack, occupied the greater part of the village, and came short of reaching the Palace by about 50 meters. However, the gendarmerie garrison and the PPS continued to resist. By sunset fresh reinforcements composed of PPS, supporters of Na'īm Mughabghab, and an amoured column, with artillery and air support, came to the rescue, forcing Junblāṭ's men to withdraw to the surrounding mountains. On the 14th, Junblāṭ's forces attacked again, but again were successfully repulsed. It should be mentioned that Mughabghab was one of the most loyal and effective of Sham'ūn's supporters and actually lived in the Presidential Palace during the revolt.

On the 15th, government forces took the initiative and launched a counter-attack, apparently with the object of occupying al-Mukhtārah and capturing Kamāl Junblāṭ. This, too, failed. According to opposition sources, government forces totaled some 600 men, including gendarmes, about 300 followers of the Druze leader, Majīd Arislān (Minister of Agriculture then), and followers of Na'īm Mughabghab and Qahtān Hamādah respectively. These forces were equipped with rifles, automatic weapons, and assisted by armored cars, heavy guns, and air support.

On the 16th, however, Majīd Arislān and his 300 followers withdrew from the battle. Since the 13th Druze religious leaders had been trying to effect peace between him and Kamāl Junblāṭ. They succeeded in doing so, on the 16th. Thereafter, Arislān disbanded his followers, and retired from the conflict, taking a semi-neutral position.

On the 18th, Junblāṭ's forces after a pitched battle were able to occupy the village of Batlūn, destroying one gendarme truck, capturing two, in addition to three jeeps, and three haun guns.

After the fall of Batlūn, Qahtān Hamādah and his followers retired from the scene, thus leaving in the field against Junblāṭ's forces, the gendarmes, the PPS, Na'īm Mughabghab and other Sham'ūn loyalists. Junblāṭ's forces continued to expand as new volunteers from the Shūf villages and from among the Druze in Syria joined him. Skirmishing between his forces and government forces continued.

A short time after the midnight of June 9 and 10, Junblāṭ launched an attack on the village of Fraydīs and occupied it after intense fighting which lasted 36 hours, ten of which were fought in the village itself.

At one point during the fighting, government planes bombed loyalist forces (mistaking them for the enemy) occupying a strategic hill-top, killing six and wounding several others, and forcing them to withdraw from their position, which was immediately taken over by Junblāṭ's forces.

On the 10th, Junblāṭ's forces occupied al-Barūḥ. On the 11th, loyalist forces withdrew from both Fraydīs and 'Ayn Zaḥaltā, after having suffered 40 killed and 120 wounded (against six killed and 20 wounded for Junblāṭ),[9] and the two villages were occupied by Junblāṭ—the latter having declared itself an "open town." A communiqué (No. 17) issued by Junblāṭ claimed that the following were captured at Fraydīs and 'Ayn Zaḥaltā:[10]

138 military rifles
27 machine guns—Hotchkiss and Bren (the Hotchkiss Turkish make)
18 boxes each containing 1,400 rounds (Turkish—1950).
5 hunting rifles
28 PPS fighters
7 gendarmes

On June 13 the army intervened for the first time in the Shūf area. An army force drove off Junblāṭ's forces from 'Ayn Zaḥaltā, but after about two days of fighting, a meeting between the army commander, General Shihāb, and Kamāl Junblāṭ resulted in a 12-point agreement on June 15, which primarily insured the passage of food and unarmed civilians along the route between Bayt al-Dīn and al-Madayrij, but at the same time froze the number of security forces (other than the army) in the positions they occupied then.[11]

Perhaps the most celebrated battle in the Shūf area was that of

Shimlān which began on June 30 and lasted for some six days. The villages of Shimlān, 'Aināb and Qabr Shmūl and the mountain ridges on which they are located and which surround them, are of considerable strategic importance, since they overlook and command the Beirut International Airport. If an enemy force occupied them, it could easily stop all air traffic, including that of military aircraft, by shelling the airport.

Since the government gave no details of the battle except vague and short statements to the effect that the "rebels" were being dispersed, the account given below is based mainly on opposition sources. So are all the statistical data. Therefore, both the account and the figures should be read with that reservation in mind.

On June 30 Junblāṭ mounted an offensive to occupy Beirut. A small group of his forces marched towards "the Radar"—a hill-top which overlooks a number of villages as well as the airport. They were unable to locate the positions of government forces, with the exception of a vacant house in which government loyalists were stationed. They occupied the house the following day (July 1) but had to abandon it after a four-hour battle, when their ammunition ran out.

On July 2, a Junblāṭ force comprising 250 men occupied the village of Qabr Shmūl, as well as the hills commanding the airport, the hills of 'Aināb and the hills around some 15 neighboring villages. They then surrounded Shimlān itself.

The army then intervened at the appeal of President Sham'ūn. Some 1200 soldiers supported by 20 artillery guns, four field guns, armored cars and tanks moved in with an air cover of six jets. In addition, loyalist forces consisting of "gendarmes, PPS, Jordanians and Iraqis" totaled some 900 men, bringing the grand total of government forces to 2,100 men. The battle raged for four days in the hills and villages. 'Aināb itself was occupied and evacuated three times, while Qabr Shmūl was subjected to a concentrated attack by government forces. In the end, Junblāṭ was forced to withdraw. Opposition sources estimate that government forces fired during the battle some 300,000 rounds of ammunition and 3,000 artillery shells, and lost about 300 men in killed or wounded.[12] In one instance during the battle, it was claimed that bodies (killed) of 17 Iraqis, 32 Jordanians, and 55 Bahraynis including a British officer in Arab clothes, were found.[13] In another instance, the bodies of 40 Jordanians.[14] Junblāṭ's losses, according to his communiqué, (which was not denied by the government), came to 22 killed and 20 wounded.[15] In his most recent book, Junblāṭ implied that the failure of his offensive to occupy Beirut was due to the intentional failure of the opposition leaders in Beirut to support him, by suddenly silencing the operations of their forces against the government. He wrote, ". . . Our forces . . . had reached ten kilometers from the capital, Beirut. . . . Suddenly, by strange magic direction, the operations and skirmishes of the popular resistance forces (in Beirut) ceased, and left us alone in the field of battle . . ."[16]

The Ba'lbak and Hirmil Sector

Within a few days from the commencement of the "revolt," the entire countryside bordering Syria came under the control of the opposition forces—with the exception of some eighteen kilometers. There are some reservations to this statement. In this large area comprising approximately half the country, there were government loyalist villages, while in some cases, government forces penetrated this area at one time or another, but they usually retreated after accomplishing—or failing to accomplish—their immediate objective. Also in some cases, posts were maintained. In other words, by and large, government writ was no longer applicable.

Also, this area was not under one command. It was under the control of independent local leaders who maintained separate commands. For instance, the area north of Tripoli, stretching from the coast to the north and north-east border with Syria, was under the control of Karāmī and Ḥamzah. Then moving southwards along the border, each of the following leaders was in control of his respective sectors: Ḥamādah, Ḥaydar, al-'Aryān, and Aḥmad al-As'ad.

In the Ba'albak and Hirmil area, opposition forces primarily under the leadership of Sabrī Ḥamādah, were particularly well-armed, since a readily available source of supply was close by in Syria. Government regular forces withdrew from the sector peacefully. However, some villages were PPS strongholds. This was particularly the case in the village of Nabī 'Uthmān, located only a few miles from the Syrian border. The village was strongly fortified by the PPS. In addition, they had there a fairly large number of fighting men, a camp for military training, and a radio transmitter which, under the name of *The Voice of Reform,* broadcast to Syria inciting the public against the government.

In May, opposition forces attacked the village in force, and after several hours of bitter fighting were able to occupy it. The radio transmitter was destroyed and substantial quantities of arms were captured. Later, PPS members were hunted down in the entire area.

Many of them were killed, while others escaped to government-controlled sections of the country.

The only government force that remained in the area was an army unit stationed in the well-fortified camp of al-Shaykh 'Abdallah. This camp, including a fort, was located south of Ba'lbak on a hilltop which commanded the whole area. In May, opposition forces attacked the camp and the fort with all the men and fire power at their command but the army, with field guns and assisted by the air force, was able to repulse the attack successfully. The army retained control of the hilltop and the fort throughout the crisis. On the other hand, government forces attempted several times to penetrate the area under opposition control but failed.

The Radio War

The civil war in Lebanon was conducted not only on the field, but also on the air. The Lebanese government banned Egyptian and Syrian papers and jammed *Radio Cairo, Voice of the Arabs,* and *Radio Damascus,* so that UAR news whether in print or over the air, could seldom be heard in Lebanon. On the other hand, the state-controlled *Radio Beirut* had a limited range.

During the crisis, six radio stations appeared on the scene in Lebanon. The first to make its debut was *Voice of Reform* which appeared in 1957. Although it claimed to broadcast from Syria, it was believed to be located in Turkey. Later, when the opposition forces attacked the village of Nabī 'Uthmān, they found it to be located there and destroyed it. The station was run by the PPS for the sole purpose of inciting the Syrian people against their government.

On May 16, 1958, a station calling itself *Voice of Free Lebanon* began operating. It gave news bulletins and statements of the opposition, appealed to the public to revolt, and exposed the "criminal gangs of Camille Sham'ūn." It was located in North Lebanon and run by the opposition.

In May, two new stations appeared in Beirut itself. The first, *Voice of Lebanon,* was run by the pro-government Phalanges party from their sections in East Beirut. The second, *The Torch,* was run by the opposition in al-Basṭa quarter.

In June, the opposition Najjādah party established what was perhaps the strongest station of all, *Voice of Arabism.* The station was located at the party headquarters in the opposition-held section of Beirut. It commenced broadcasting on June, 1958, in Arabic, English, French and Armenian for a total of nine hours a day. It was directed by Suhayl Hamawī of the Lebanese News Agency. Just when the civil war was about over, Salām's supporters raided the Najjādah headquarters and confiscated the transmitter — apparently, due to some divergence of views.

In late August, even after the new president was elected, a new station, *Voice of the Revolution,* appeared. Very little information is available on it. It was presumably located in Beirut, and directed by an opposition faction.

By the end of October, all these stations had ceased their operations, leaving the state-controlled *Radio Beirut* alone in the field.

The Role of the Army

The role of the army during the entire conflict was indeed a curious one. On the whole, it maintained a detached attitude, never committed its entire strength to the government and restricted itself to maintaining basic elements of law and order and to upholding the dignity of the state rather than the government. In a certain sense, it held the balance between the government and the opposition. Whenever opposition forces became too aggressive or too successful, it struck, as for instance, the occasion when the Beirut airport was threatened by Junblāṭ's forces. In some instances, it even acted against government loyalists, particularly the PPS. Essentially, the government could not depend on the army to maintain itself in power, or to suppress the opposition. It has been suggested that, had the army taken resolute action—at least in the earlier part of the conflict—the opposition would not have been so successful, and the crisis shortened.

There were several reasons for the comparative inactivity of the army. First, and perhaps the most important, was the attitude of General Shihāb, the army commander. Basically, General Shihāb took the same position he had taken in 1952, when President al-Khūrī was forced to resign. His conception of the function of the army was that it should defend the country against foreign aggression, rather than suppress internal political factions. He regarded the conflict as basically an internal squabble between politicians—and since this was so, it would be in the best interests of the army and of the country not to be involved in domestic politics. If the army did become involved, a precedent would be set and Lebanon would follow the path of other Arab countries.

Second, the calibre of the opposition may have influenced the attitude of General Shihāb. All of the opposition leaders were his personal friends. The government might call them rebels, it might call them communist-influenced, it might issue warrants for their arrest. Such gambits may impress a journalist harassed by his overseas editors for sensational news, but could hardly change the fact that most of the opposition leaders were patricians, descended from ancient families that wielded vast influence on the lives of thousands of people; that they were important religious leaders, former presidents, prime ministers, ministers, and other important government functionaries; that in the past, they had shaped the destiny of the country, and that they would probably shape it for many years to come. In fact, compared with most of them, Sham'ūn, once he were shorn of the presidency, would pale into a middle class nonentity, except for such prestige and glamour as go with having been a president.

General Shihāb—an aristocrat himself—a descendant of the Shihāb amirs who ruled Lebanon for a century and a half, must have taken this factor into consideration in deciding on the policy of the army. Even if he had been able to suppress the opposition, given the political realities in Lebanon, he would then have been reasonably certain that, sooner or later, these leaders would retaliate in one form or another. Since neither he nor the army were affected, political realism dictated that both he and his army should stay essentially on the sidelines.

A third factor which probably influenced General Shihāb is that he himself was a moderating influence. By staying above politics, by not identifying himself and the army too closely with either the government or the opposition sides, he became acceptable to both and in such a role, was able to exert a moderating influence on the bitterness of the conflict, which otherwise he would not have been able to do. It is to be noted that, when the senseless killing and the stream of bitter statements finally died down, he was the only presidential candidate acceptable to both sides. In a sense, this is a tribute to his political vision and wisdom.

Finally, and perhaps most important of all, there was genuine fear expressed in many quarters that, if the army were to take decisive action, it would lose its morale, that many of its members would refuse to fight their brethren, that it would break up into Muslim and Christian factions, and instead of being able to suppress the opposition, one side would support the government and the other the opposition. The army would not only have lost the respect it enjoyed among the Lebanese people but, in addition, the work of many years spent in creating a good fighting organization would have gone to waste. It should also be noted that opposition forces, whenever possible, avoided any clashes with the army because they regarded it as belonging to the nation and because they respected it and respected its commander. This was in direct contrast with their attitude towards the police and the gendarmerie which they called "Sham'ūn gangs."

It is believed that during the conflict, a group of officers, disgruntled with the inaction of the army, had planned to overthrow General Shihāb, take control of the army and suppress the opposition. For one reason or another, this plan did not materialize.

The Role of the Phalanges and PPS

It is clear that Sham'ūn, even before the beginning of the conflict, was never certain that he would receive the full support of the army. He had before him the experience of a former president, when he himself came to power. In 1952, General Shihāb declared that the army would not interfere in any internal conflict. Thus, former President al-Khūrī was forced to resign before the end of his second term.

Unable to depend on the loyalty of the army, the Sham'ūn administration sought other avenues of support. To begin with, it had the police and the gendarmerie whose functions are to maintain internal security. But neither in numbers nor in equipment could these two forces cope with a full-fledged conflagration. The gendarmerie in particular were very poorly equipped.

Hence, in addition to the security forces at its command, the government fell back on civilian loyalists: part of the Maronites and other Christians; the Phalanges, and the PPS.

With respect to the Maronites and other Christians, Sham'ūn was in a difficult position, since he had to compete for their loyalty with other strong Christian leaders in the opposition: the Maronite Patriarch, former President al-Khūrī (who found this an appropriate time to recoup his political fortunes and to pay back the score), the Franjiyahs, and the 'Ammūns, among others. One way of winning Maronite support was to give the conflict a religious coloring, to whip up religious prejudice, and to convince the Maronites in particular, that the independence of "Christian Lebanon" was in grave jeopardy from the "Muslim" opposition. Thus the Arab nationalist of 1952 became the "Christian" leader of 1958. Sham'ūn was partly successful. Most of the lower clergy and several of the bishops deserted the Patriarch and refused to obey his commands. In some instances—it is reported—priests exhorted their flock to support Sham'ūn during Mass. In any case, the Maronite community was split wide open. Some, convinced that this was a religious conflict, supported Sham'ūn; others remained passive; while yet others remained loyal to the Patriarch and other Maronite leaders. The government drew on the support of the loyalists among them. There is little doubt that it armed some of them, at least. They operated mostly in the Shūf mountains under Mughabghab.

The Phalanges are a para-military organization. They started as a youth movement but later developed into a political party. Their leader, Pierre al-Jumayyil conceived the idea in 1936 after a visit to Germany. Today, they claim a membership of 40,000 persons.

The Phalanges were natural allies of the government. Mostly Maronites, fanatically in favor of an "independent" Lebanon, looking towards the West in their cultural and spiritual orientation, suspicious of Arab nationalism, ever fearful that the Christian might be engulfed in a "Muslim sea," they regarded supporting the government as virtually a sacred duty. In addition, their leader made no secret of his fears of Syria and Egypt. Since 1955, time after time, he had kept making statements charging Egypt with using Arab nationalism as a vehicle to achieve its own ends.

Although the Phalanges helped the gendarmerie in some battles in the countryside, their main activity seems to have been concentrated in the cities, particularly Beirut. They helped the police, patrolled streets and fought some battles with the opposition on their own. It is interesting to note that opposition literature on the crisis lacks the acid bitterness with respect to the Phalanges that it manifests towards Messrs. Sham'ūn, Malik, al-Ṣulḥ and the PPS. This attitude may perhaps be explained by the desire of the opposition not to place the argument on a Maronite-non-Maronite basis, and perhaps because they respected them, although they disagreed with both their position and beliefs.

As for the PPS, much of their support in funds and arms came from the Iraqi government. The alliance must have begun sometime around 1954.[17] It was a natural one: first, Iraq had designs on Syria. This was in conformity with the PPS Fertile Crescent concept. Second, Iraq wanted the overthrow of the regime in Syria and so did the PPS. Third, Iraq was against a union between Syria and Egypt and so was the PPS, which did not include Egypt within Fertile Crescent doctrine. Finally, the party needed badly the arms and funds which Iraq could and did provide it with.

The alliance between the Lebanese government, or rather Sham'ūn personally, and the PPS was also to the mutual advantage of both parties. As early as 1955 there were rumors of contact between Sham'ūn and the PPS leadership. Sham'ūn was preparing for his election to a second term, and must have realized that he might need both the moral and physical strength of the party, which numbers in Lebanon some 25,000. Moreover, his ideas with respect to Syria and Egypt were apparently identical with those of the PPS. As for the PPS, Lebanon had become its last refuge in the Arab countries.[18] It was therefore vitally interested in the preservation and perpetuation of an administration that would be lenient towards it and that would close its eyes to its activities. In 1957, the PPS, although still officially illegal, became aggressively active in Lebanon. In the same year, its leader, As'ad al-Ashqar, was elected to parliament; and in 1958, PPS members who had been in prison were suddenly pardoned *en masse* and released. One of the last acts of the Sham'ūn administration was to legalize the party. On September 18, 1958, three days before Sham'ūn was due to retire from office, the PPS was granted a license to operate.[19]

In 1958, a temporary alliance was arranged between the PPS and the Phalanges—presumably through Sham'ūn's intervention. In doctrine the two parties are poles apart. Whereas the Phalanges were fanatically for an independent and sovereign Lebanon, at least in theory, the PPS does not accept or recognize the independence of Lebanon, and works towards a Fertile Crescent Union—including Lebanon. Clashes between members of the two parties took place even up to May 1958—just before the conflagration. The two parties found a temporary meeting ground in the preservation of the Sham'ūn administration and in their pro-Western orientation.[20]

The PPS played a very active role in the conflict—much more so than the Phalanges. In fact, aside from the police and the gendarmerie, they seem to have been the main support of the government. A figure of some 3,000 is probably a conservative estimate of the number of PPS armed men that were actively in the field. They fought alongside government forces in the countryside, waged their own independent battles, and were also very active in the cities such as Beirut, Tripoli, Sidon, Zaḥlah, and so forth.

No group or individual on the government side—not even Sham'ūn himself, had been the target of opposition bitterness as much as the PPS. This may be due to the fact that the PPS is openly opposed to Arab nationalism; had used Lebanon as a base from which to operate against Syria; and is widely suspected of "hiring" itself out to foreign governments.

Failure of Mediation Efforts

Immediately after the commencement of the conflict in May, 1958, mediation by various individuals and groups, including the Maronite Patriarch, Raymond Eddé (leader of the National Bloc),

'Ādil 'Usayrān, the Third Force, and commercial interests, began to try to solve the crisis in a manner satisfactory to all concerned. These efforts, which were conducted behind the scenes at various times, lasted from May to the middle of June, then suddenly ceased when it became apparent that no solution was possible. Negotiations were not resumed in earnest until after the landing of American troops.

All the mediation efforts centered basically on the following solution:

President Sham'ūn to remain in office until the end of his term.

Sham'ūn to make a public statement clearly setting forth his intention not to seek or accept re-election for a second term.

The government of Sāmī al-Ṣulḥ is to resign in favor of a coalition cabinet under the premiership of General Shihāb. This cabinet to remain in office until a new president is elected and the crisis is finished. (It should be pointed out that the appointment of General Shihāb—a Maronite Christian—to the premiership, would have been a violent departure from the traditional division of offices, by which the prime minister must always be a Sunni Muslim. Mediators, however, believed that only General Shihāb, who was also respected by the opposition, could save the country. In all probability, had mediation efforts succeeded, the appointment of Shihāb to the premiership would have been acceptable to the Muslims, and to the opposition. In fact, six Muslim deputies signed a petition requesting Sham'ūn to appoint him Prime Minister.)[21]

The above solution failed, because the parties concerned refused to compromise. On the one hand, the opposition insisted that Sham'ūn must resign "now"; and on the other, Sham'ūn not only refused to resign, but in addition refused to make a public statement that he would not stand for re-election. At a press conference on May 21, the first he had held since assuming office, he stated that he had never encouraged the idea, suggested by some of his friends, of changing the constitution. However, he declined to answer questions as to whether he would or would not stand for re-election.[22] On May 27, the prime minister declared that the government would not try to amend the constitution. He said in a broadcast: "The President has not requested amendment and the government's statements of policy have never mentioned the possibility . . . The government has not been seeking to make an amendment, nor will it do so in the future, and there is no sign that the Chamber of Deputies intends to do so."[23] This statement however, did not satisfy the opposition, and Sham'ūn persisted in refusing to make a public announcement on the subject himself. In reply to a question, "Do you plan to stand for a second term?", made at a press conference on June 25, Sham'ūn replied, "I have nothing to add to the statement made by the Prime Minister speaking in the name of the government."[24]

Finally, the most important element in the whole mediation plan, General Shihāb, declined the office of Prime Minister. At a press conference on May 30, the Maronite Patriarch stated that it was suggested to him by many politicians that General Shihāb should form a government, and that he tried to mediate. "I tried to convince him, but he declined. Later he accepted, but then he telephoned when my private telephone was out of order and I sent my vicar-general to see him. He told the vicar general that he could not accept after all." Urged to explain why General Shihāb decided to decline, the Patriarch replied,

> This is very delicate. I personally see no other man who can form a government, for there is a danger not only of civil war but of religious warfare. I know the situation—I was born here. The trouble with this little country is that we are only 14 years old as an independent country and the work of 14 years has gone astray. I am not a pessimist, but there is a residue of fanaticism and ignorance in some hearts which will take time to cure.[25]

NOTES

1. *Mideast Mirror,* May 18, 1958, p. 3.
2. Karāmī, *op. cit.,* p. 134.
3. The following passages in Junblāṭ's book leave little doubt that preparations for the revolt had been going on at least since the elections in June 1957, and that arms had been sought and received from outside sources. Commenting on his failure in the elections, Mr. Junblāṭ wrote:

"Our failure in the Shūf . . . after Sham'ūn used his armed gangs—gendarmes and civilians—to terrorize the Christian villages to force them to vote against us, was the third incitement in the crisis . . . When I became certain of my personal failure (Mr. Junblāṭ was then at his home—al-Mukhtarah, in the Shūf area) . . . I left the house secretly through a back door, to Beirut, for fear that my brethren would revolt if I remained among them . . . and in fact, a few hours later, news of the Shūfites reached us. They immediately cut telephone lines, congregated on public roads, and carried out provocative acts against the authorities, who accepted them and avoided facing them, for fear that they would develop into something more serious. We tried the impossible to stop such acts . . . For tens of armed men stationed themselves in our house in the Shūf refusing to leave it . . . Our remaining in Beirut near the security forces, who could detain me anytime they wished, was the only guarantee that the revolt in the Shūf would not break out before we have prepared for it . . . From that hour (i.e. after the election defeat), we began to think that the revolt had become inevitable . . . and we began to make preparations for training and arms, since our brethren and supporters then, had only a small number of rifles, perhaps not exceeding eighty. We successfully contacted those who should be contacted (to secure arms) . . . The authorities began to negotiate and bargain with us, as usual, while secretly preparing a blow with which they attempted to strike Rashīd Aghā al-'Aryān, leader of the Rashaya area, and Salmān Abū Ḥamzah, the man responsible for procuring defense weapons and for training." *The True Nature of the Lebanese Revolt,* pp. 83-89.

4. For a list of the names of the 168 persons killed, see Karāmī, *op. cit.,* pp. 256-256(1).
5. The Central Command was composed of the following persons: Ṭal'at Karīm,

Suhayl al-Baghdādī, Dr. 'Abd al-Majīd al-Rāfi'ī, Fārūq Ma'sarānī, Aḥmad al-Mār, Rashīd Karāmī, Zayd Ḥamzah, and Salīm Qasqas.

6. The Executive Office was composed of the following persons: Ṭal'at Karīm, general commander of opposition forces; Suhayl Baghdādī, alternate commander in absence of commander; 'Abd al-Qādir 'Aḍra, secretary-general Muḥammad 'Akkārī and 'Abd al-Laṭīf Karāmī, treasurers; Ilyās 'Āqūrī, and Khālid 'Aḍrah, ordinance.

7. *Mideast Mirror*, May 18, 1959, pp. 4-5.

8. Karāmī, *op cit.*, p. 137.

9. *Ibid.*, p. 163.

10. *Ibid.*, p. 168.

11. For full text of the agreement, see *Ibid.*, p. 172.

12. *Ibid.*, p. 189.

13. *Ibid.*, p. 187.

14. *Ibid.*, p. 189.

15. *Ibid.*, p. 190.

16. *On the Course of Lebanese Policy*, pp. 9-10.

17. A telegram from Faḍil al-Jamālī to the Iraqi prime minister (Nūrī al-Sa'īd) dated April 28, 1954 reads as follows: "Met with Syrian Nationalists (i.e. PPS). Syria facing important developments. The Syrian Nationalists (i.e. PPS) are willing to receive direction from Iraq."

18. The PPS is illegal in all Arab countries, and is actively suppressed in all of them with the exception of Lebanon. Iraq which supported them in Lebanon and Syria, suppressed them on the homefront.

19. It should be noted that in 1957, the party split into two factions: one under George 'Abd al-Masīḥ, which did not cooperate with the Sham'ūn administration; and the other, the larger of the two, under As'ad al-Ashqar. It was the al-Ashqar faction which cooperated with the Sham'ūn administration and which was granted a license to operate. Before the license was granted, however, this group had to take the term "Syrian" out of its name. Thus its official name now is "The Nationalist Social Party." The 'Abd al-Masīḥ faction still maintains the original name, "The Syrian Nationalist Social Party," and although not recognized by the government, it still continues to operate.

20. Both parties are strongly anti-communist.

21. *Mideast Mirror,* June 1, 1958, p. 8.

22. *Ibid.*, May 25, 1958, p. 3.

23. *Ibid.*, June 1, 1958, p. 6.

24. *Ibid.*, June 29, 1958, p. 4.

25. *Ibid.*, June 1, 1958, p. 13.

CHAPTER VI

The United Nations Debates

UNTIL THE LEBANESE crisis began in earnest, the Lebanese Government made no official accusation against the United Arab Republic of general responsibility for the crisis. There were unofficial hints and rumors; there were official protests against particular incidents—but no broad official statements.

On May 13, 1958, Dr. Charles Malik, then Minister of Foreign Affairs, told a press conference in Beirut that interference by the UAR was the principle cause of Lebanon's plight. After citing various incidents, he stated, "All of these incidents are only the latest manifestations of a concealed movement that has been going on for months and indeed, for years, designed to undermine and destroy Lebanon as a free, independent and sovereign state and bring about a radical modification in her fundamental orientation."[1]

On May 18, the government issued a statement which said in part:

> We only asked that our border with sister Syria should be wide open and our relations with sister Egypt be cordial, both before and after the merger, so that knowledge and good fruits of cooperation in a common high standard of living could be exchanged. We never thought the day would come when arms, subversive instruments, and agents of killing and terrorism would flow across the border. That is a reality today, and has been for two years.[2]

On May 21 and 22, the Lebanese Government complained to the Council of the Arab League and to the UN Security Council, respectively. It claimed that the rebellion in Lebanon was in essence inspired, directed, subsidized and armed by the UAR. It pleaded for urgent action, arguing that the security of Lebanon as an independent state was in immediate jeopardy.

In response, the Security Council held its first meeting on the question during the afternoon of May 27. However, in the hope that the Arabs would be able to solve their problems by themselves, it was agreed to postpone discussion of the subject, pending the results of the deliberations of the Council of the Arab League which was then about to meet.[3]

The League Council met in Banghazi. Originally, it was planned to meet in Tripoli, but the Libyan Government, after making all the requisite arrangements, discovered that demonstrations in support of the UAR were being prepared there. Consequently, it shifted the site to Banghazi to avoid embarrassment and possible incidents.[4]

The Council held four sessions, the first during the evening of June 1. Extended negotiations took place, with the delegates of Libya, the Sudan, and the Secretary-General of the Arab League acting as mediators. One of the principal mediators was Muḥammad Maḥjūb, Foreign Minister of the Sudan.[5] During these negotiations some delegations threatened that their governments would leave the League if the Council failed to produce a resolution,[6] while in addition, both the Sudanese and Iraqi delegations declared openly that if the Secretariat, which was heavily staffed with Egyptians, showed any favoritism, this would be another cause for withdrawal from the League.[7]

At the beginning, most of the delegations showed marked sympathy towards Lebanon as a small Arab country appealing for help against the biggest Arab country.[8] The UAR delegation served notice that it would not be bound by any resolution the Council might make, in accordance with its rights under the League Covenant.[9]

A draft resolution, sponsored by the delegations of Libya, the Sudan, Saudi Arabia, Iraq, Jordan, and later by Yemen was proposed.[10] The operative part of the resolution reads as follows:[11]

The Council decides:

1. To put an end to everything that might disturb the atmosphere of serenity among all the member states, by every means;

2. To request the Government of Lebanon to withdraw the complaint submitted to the Security Council;

3. To address an appeal to the various Lebanese groups in order to put an end to the disturbances and to take every necessary measure to settle their domestic disputes by peaceful and constitutional means;

4. To send a committee chosen from among the members of the Council in order to calm the situation and to implement the decision of the Council of the League of Arab States.

As is evident, the above was a compromise resolution. It accused no one, but at the same time attempted to solve the crisis. Apparently, it was acceptable to the Lebanese delegation; the UAR delegation, having failed to modify it, planned not to oppose it. Indications point to the possibility that, had the resolution been implemented, it would probably have solved the problem.

On June 5, 1958, the Lebanese government received the text of the resolution and rejected it.[12] This caused considerable dismay, and even anger, among all the delegations meeting in Banghazi. "The

Lebanese delegation was really shocked by its government's rejection of the draft resolution, formulated after efforts made by day and night, and the leader, Bashīr al-'Awar, who is Minister of Justice, several times threatened to resign."[13] "Backers of the resolution expressed astonishment and disappointment. They complained that 'we have angered the UAR and failed to satisfy Lebanon. We expected the UAR to be arbitrary, but not Lebanon.' "[14] The Sudan Foreign Minister, Muḥammad Maḥjūb, said "he was greatly offended." He added, "I have exerted much effort to satisfy Lebanon, but her delegations lost a big opportunity in its effort to satisfy Dr. Malik and the government."[15]

The draft resolution of the Council of the Arab League was in fact a sensible one. The question then arises, why did the Lebanese government reject it?

From all indications, it appears that the Lebanese government was not seriously interested in solving the issue at the Arab League level. There was little reason to believe that the Arab League would be able to solve the issue, since its past record in this respect was not conducive to confidence, and since its members were so widely split. Thus, Lebanon went to Banghazi expecting failure. Second, Dr. Malik did not even bother to attend the Banghazi meetings but went directly to New York for the Security Council meetings. Third, it should be remembered that the Lebanese government, insofar as direction of policy was concerned, consisted at that time, essentially of Sham'ūn — the President, Malik — the Foreign Minister, and al-Ṣulḥ—the Prime Minister, listed here in descending order of importance. By 1958, these three men were bitter personal enemies of Nāṣir. To them, nothing less than exposing him at the highest international forum would be satisfactory. Finally, there is reason to believe that, by internationalizing the issue at the UN level, Sham'ūn and Malik hoped for foreign intervention with the resulting possibility of Sham'ūn retaining his position as President of the Republic. In addition to the personal satisfaction of Sham'ūn, such a prospect had two further attractions; first, it would be a disastrous setback to the position of the UAR and President Nāṣir in the Arab world; and second, it would have been a severe blow to members of the local opposition—all personal enemies of Sham'ūn, Malik and al-Ṣulḥ.

* * *

When the Arab League failed to reach a solution, the Security Council took up the question in earnest on June 6, 1958.[16] It had become clear by then that the Lebanese issue had been taken out of its local context and now constituted an international crisis involving an East-West confrontation.

The Security Council sessions were stormy and the speeches of the main contenders lengthy polemics. When the representatives of Lebanon and the UAR made their statements, the usual East-West line-up took place. The USA, the UK, France, China and Iraq flatly supported the allegations of Lebanon and urged immediate action.[17] Canada, Columbia, Japan, Panama and Sweden, on the other hand, avoided prejudging the issue, though at the same time they felt that some action should be taken. The USSR flatly rejected the allegations of Lebanon and maintained that the whole purpose of the complaint was to prepare the grounds for Western intervention in the internal affairs of Lebanon.[18]

In the midst of recriminations and counter-recriminations, Sweden proposed a line of action which, on the one hand, made no judgment and, on the other, provided some constructive measures to help Lebanon. The Swedish representative, Mr. Jarring, submitted a draft resolution on June 10 which proved acceptable to everyone, including Lebanon and the UAR—with the exception of the Soviet Union. The following day, June 11, the resolution was adopted by 10 votes in favor and one abstension—that of the Soviet Union.[19]

In accordance with the Security Council resolution, Mr. Hammarskjöld, the Secretary-General, organized the United Nations Observation Group in Lebanon (UNOGIL) which, by July 3, submitted its first report which generally was unfavorable to the Lebanese claim. The formation, activities and reports of UNOGIL will be discussed in a separate chapter. Here it is sufficient to state that, owing to its lack of powers and the particular conditions existing in Lebanon at that time, it was, to all practical purposes, unable to carry out its mandate.

In the meantime, momentous events were taking place. On July 14, a revolution took place in Iraq which overthrew the monarchy and established a republican régime. Jordan was in a state of turmoil verging on anarchy, and a plot to overthrow King Ḥusayn was discovered. United States Marines, at the request of the Lebanese Government, landed in Lebanon on July 15; and British troops—also at the request of King Ḥusayn, were airlifted into Jordan on July 17.

On July 15, at the urgent request of the US Government, the Security Council reconvened to take up the Lebanese case again. The first speaker was Henry Cabot Lodge, the US representative. He officially informed the Council of the landing of American troops in

Lebanon,[20] that they were being sent there at the request of the Lebanese government, and that

> our forces are not there to engage in hostilities of any kind, much less to fight a war. Their presence is designed for the sole purpose of helping the government of Lebanon at its request in its efforts to stabilize the situation brought on by the threats from outside until such time as the United Nations can take steps to protect the independence and political integrity of Lebanon. They will afford security to the several thousand Americans who reside in that country. That is the total scope and objective of the United States assistance.[21]

At the same time, Lodge tabled a draft resolution which called for the dispatch of United Nations contingents to Lebanon.[22] Canada, China, Colombia, Iraq,* France, Panama, and the United Kingdom supported both the landing of American troops and the US resolution. Japan supported the US resolution with reluctance.[23] The following day (July 17), when the Security Council received the second interim report of UNOGIL (also unfavorable to Lebanon's claim), the reservations and misgivings of the Japanese delegate became much more emphatic. He expressed the view that "it is inappropriate and regrettable indeed that the United States has taken measures to intervene in the dispute in Lebanon by sending its armed forces to Lebanon while the Security Council is still examining Lebanon's complaint." He then argued that inasmuch as the presence of US troops in Lebanon was an accomplished fact, then "we have no other recourse than to seek a prompt withdrawal of the United States forces through the implementation of appropriate measures by the United Nations. It is for these considerations that we would support, with some misgivings, the United States draft resolution."[24]

The Swedish government, on the other hand, argued that the situation in Lebanon was improving, that the presence of the UNOGIL had contributed to this development, that the dispatch of American troops would complicate matters, that it was unjustified under Article 51 of the UN Charter, and that their presence in Lebanon would "blur the distinction between the UN Observers and United States soldiers. The continued activities of the Observers could in this new situation become a political handicap to the United Nations."[25] Mr. Jarring, the delegate of Sweden, then tabled a draft resolution which called for the suspension of the activities of UNOGIL until further notice.[26]

The UAR delegate denied the charges made against his govern-

* By the vote of the representative of the monarchical régime, before the seating of the representative of the revolutionary government.

ment. He maintained that the crises in Lebanon, Jordan and Iraq were domestic in nature and the exclusive concern of the peoples of these countries. He pointed out that the situation in Lebanon, according to official reports and the world press, was improving. He argued that the dispatch of American and British troops under Article 51 of the Charter was unjustified, and that this action constituted in actual fact "armed intervention" in the internal affairs of Lebanon and Jordan, and constituted a threat to peace and security.[27]

The most verbose of the delegates was the Soviet representative, Mr. Sobolov. His numerous speeches can be described, at best, as abusive. Following the usual communist line, they were designed to aggravate old wounds and fears in order to generate and intensify hate; to portray the Soviet Union as the friend and protector of Arab nationalism, unity and independence; and conversely, the West as the enemy of the Arabs—interested only in the exploitation of their oil; to create a war hysteria in the world and to capitalize on the difficulties of all the parties directly concerned in order to launch a world-wide propaganda campaign in favor of the Soviet Union as the promoter of peace.[28] He made known a statement by the USSR which concludes with the following paragraph:[29]

> The Soviet Government states that the Soviet Union cannot remain indifferent to the events which constitute a serious threat in an area which is adjacent to its national frontiers and it assumes freedom of action that may be dictated by the interests of the maintenance of peace and security.

On July 15, Mr. Sobolov introduced a draft resolution which accused the United States of "gross intervention in the domestic affairs of the people of Arab countries" and called for immediate withdrawal of US forces from Lebanon. After British troops landed in Jordan, the resolution was revised to include the withdrawal of British troops as well.[30]

On July 18, the Soviet, American and Swedish resolutions were voted on in succession. They all failed. The results were as follows: the Soviet resolution, one in favor (USSR), eight against, and two abstentions (Sweden and Japan); the American, nine in favor, one against (USSR), and one abstention (Sweden); the Swedish, two in favor (Sweden and the USSR), and nine against.[31]

A Japanese draft resolution, following in the path of the Swedish resolution of June 11, passed no judgments, in contrast to both the Russian and American resolutions.[32] It did not contemplate the creation of a UN emergency force in Lebanon, or a type of UN force as in Korea, or a "police force of any kind." "Within these limits," it empowered the Secretary-General to take all the steps he deemed necessary to fulfill the obligations of the Security Council undertaken in the June 11 resolution.[33]

The Japanese resolution was approved by all members of the Council as a way out of the impasse, with the exception of the Soviet Union. Even Lebanon accepted it, though with misgivings.[34] The Soviet delegate proposed several amendments, including a new paragraph calling for the immediate withdrawal of American troops from Lebanon.[35] These amendments were rejected by a vote of one in favor (USSR), eight against, and two abstentions (Sweden and Japan).[36] Consequently, when the resolution came to a vote, it was vetoed by the Soviet Union.[37]

When the Council reached a state of complete impotence, Mr. Hammarskjöld, the Secretary-General, took the initiative. He stated that since the Security Council and traditional diplomacy failed to find a solution, it is in "keeping with the philosophy of the Charter" that he take appropriate action to "help prevent a further deterioration of the situation in the Middle East and to assist in finding a road away from the dangerous point at which we now find ourselves."[38]

The Security Council, having failed completely to take any constructive action, adjourned on July 22.

* * *

During the Security Council meetings the Lebanese crisis was also being debated on a still higher level. In a series of letters to Eisenhower, Macmillan, De Gaulle and Nehru, Khrushchev demanded a summit meeting. The letters to Mr. Eisenhower and Mr. Macmillan were couched in the most provocative language. The purpose of the meeting, the letters stated, was to take "immediate steps . . . to put an end to the conflict which has broken out," to find a solution which would, "meet the vital interests of the people of the Near and Middle East, and would insure the observance of their sovereign rights, while taking into account the interests of all the states concerned with the countries of that region," and possibly to "take up the question of putting an end to the deliveries of arms to the countries of the Near and Middle East. The Soviet Union would be willing to meet any time, any place. . . . The important thing is not to waste precious time . . . for the guns have already begun to speak."[39]

It was clear from the language of the letters that Mr. Khrushchev was attempting to stampede the Western Allies, on his own terms, into a "summit meeting" without an agenda—something which they were unprepared for, and which they had been resisting for the previous eight months; to create a wave of war hysteria, and to force the West officially to recognize the Soviet Union as a great Middle Eastern power.

As it turned out, Khrushchev's letter campaign ended in ignominious failure. He failed to force the West into a summit conference. He failed to force the West into recognizing the Soviet Union as a Middle Eastern power. He failed to impress the West with his implied threat of war. Finally, and perhaps most important of all, his sudden and complete turn-about concerning a summit meeting under Security Council auspices after his visit to China made it abundantly clear that the USSR was not interested in the welfare of the "Arab people" and the "peoples of the Middle East," but rather in parceling the area into spheres of influence among the Great Powers, in the grand tradition of the 19th century diplomacy.

On August 7, the Security Council met for the third time. Both the American and Soviet delegates introduced draft resolutions calling for an emergency session of the General Assembly.[40] The American resolution would call the General Assembly in order to discuss the complaints of Lebanon and Jordan; the Russian resolution, "to consider the question of the immediate withdrawal of United States troops from Lebanon and of United Kingdom troops from Jordan." Following a lengthy debate which lasted over six hours (3-9:15 p.m.), the US resolution was unanimously adopted after certain amendments were made to render it acceptable to the Soviet Union.[41]

* * *

The General Assembly began its meetings on August 8. By that time, however, the climate of tension had eased. In Lebanon, a new President, acceptable to all factions, had been elected on July 31, and fighting had virtually ceased. The UN Observation group had been greatly augmented. The United States, just before the Assembly began its meetings, announced the withdrawal of one battalion from the country. In Iraq, the revolutionary government was in full control and had been recognized by most countries including the United States and the United Kingdom. In Jordan, though the dilemma remained, the situation had calmed down considerably. Mr. Hammarskjöld had been conducting extensive negotiations in his now famous method of "quiet diplomacy." In short, all developments seemed to disprove Soviet prophecies of impending doom, although the specter of an atomic war was still hanging over the world.

Consequently, the debates of the Security Council and those of the General Assembly turned out to be worlds apart:

Whereas the Council was restricted to eleven members, the

Assembly was a world forum of some 81 nations. Whereas the Council was hampered by the veto, the Assembly was free from this impediment. In the Council debates, permanent delegates represented their respective countries. In the Assembly, a galaxy of top diplomats—many of them foreign ministers—were present. The Council debates were characterized by anger and recriminations. In the Assembly a mellow mood and a spirit of constructive purpose prevailed. With a few exceptions, there was a surprising absence of polemics and invective. The Council debates centered almost exclusively on Lebanon and Jordan. In the Assembly, the emphasis shifted to the problems of the region as a whole, and in particular, those of the Arab countries.

The tone and direction of the debates in the Assembly were set by an unexpected statement from Mr. Hammarskjöld on the first day, before any speeches were made, in which he outlined "some basic needs for action in the region." These he constituted into a six-point program. He proposed an inter-related political and economic regional program of action which would essentially be initiated and executed by the Arabs, themselves, with the assistance of the United Nations. The Arabs were to give the assurance of non-interference in each other's affairs, and the Arabs were to initiate and execute the economic and social programs. In polite, diplomatic language, he also requested the Big Powers publicly to declare that they would not interfere in their affairs.[42]

The second meeting was held five days later (on Wednesday, August 13) to allow time to the various delegates to arrive from their respective countries. President Eisenhower addressed the Assembly that day.[43] He solemnly pledged that American assistance to Lebanon was exclusively to uphold its independence in accordance with the spirit and purpose of the United Nations Charter and of "such historic resolutions . . . as the 'Essentials for Peace' Resolution of 1949 and the 'Peace through Deeds' Resolution of 1950," and that "we have no other purpose whatsoever." He did, however, serve notice that "the United States reserves, within the spirit of the Charter, the right to answer the legitimate appeal of any nation, particularly small nations."

The President proposed to the General Assembly a six-point program for the Middle East, covering immediate and long range questions:

1. "United Nations concern for Lebanon."
2. "United Nations measures to preserve peace in Jordan."
3. "An end to the fomenting from without of civil strife."

4. "A United Nations Peace Force."
5. "A regional economic development plan to assist and accelerate improvement in the living standards of the people in these Arab nations."
6. "Steps to avoid a new arms race spiral in the area."

As can be seen, the President's proposed program was closely akin to that of the Secretary-General. In terms of the immediate problem, both indicated the need for UN concern for Lebanon and Jordan. Both proposed measures for stability in the area, and both suggested the establishment of an Arab regional economic development program with heavy emphasis on initiative by the Arabs themselves.

The Issues

The issues discussed by the Assembly ranged over the whole spectrum of political and economic life in the area. They covered such subjects as the withdrawal of foreign troops, the safety of Lebanon and Jordan, a UN Police Force, Big Power confrontation and disengagement in the area, neutralization of the area, indirect and direct aggression from within and without, the arms race, the Arab-Israeli conflict, the refugee question, Arab nationalism, *status quo* versus change, evolution versus revolution, economic development and a multitude of other related questions.

It was clear that, although the Assembly was concerned with the immediate problems of Lebanon and Jordan, it wanted to discuss them within the context of the broad issues of the fundamental causes of instability in the area, of which the Lebanese and Jordanian crises were only outward manifestations.

Of the mass of issues, the principal ones discussed at great length were the presence of foreign troops, the establishment of a UN Police Force, Arab nationalism, Big Power politics in the area, and economic development.

The Presence of Foreign Troops

The Assembly was divided into several blocs on the question of the presence of American and British troops in Lebanon and Jordan, respectively.

The Western Powers took the position that the dispatch of American and British troops was in accord with the spirit and purpose of the UN Charter and other UN resolutions such as the "Essentials for Peace" resolution and "Peace through Deeds" resolution; that the troops were sent at the request of the duly constituted governments;

that the inherent right of collective self-defense is guaranteed by the Charter; that, as President Eisenhower stated, "if it is made an international crime to help a small nation maintain its independence, then indeed the possibilities of conquest are unlimited;" that their troops were in Lebanon and Jordan exclusively to maintain the independence and territorial integrity of these two countries, and that the troops would be withdrawn immediately "whenever this is requested by the duly constituted government . . . or whenever through action by the United Nations or otherwise" these countries are no "longer exposed to the original danger." The Western Powers agreed that the sending of troops was not the most desirable measure, but that under the circumstances, when the Security Council was held in impotence by the Soviet veto, was a necessary one.

As might be expected, the Soviet Bloc countries took the extreme opposite position. The violent charges they made, however, were unsupported by any concrete evidence. In all probability, they were intended not to be believed by the members of the Assembly, but were rather for mass consumption across the world in the propaganda war.

Andrei Gromyko, the Foreign Minister of the Soviet Union, charged that the "military action" of the United States and Britain was "a gross violation of the Charter . . . and of other generally accepted norms of international law," that the requests of President Sham'ūn and King Ḥusayn were directly inspired by the United States and British Governments," and that the "armed intervention" was undertaken "to consolidate their domination of the area, maintaining a hold over its natural resources and compelling the peoples of the Arab countries to dwell under a colonial régime," that it was conceived "as the start of a campaign against other countries," that "oil, oil and oil again" was what prompted the United States and Britain "to undertake continuous military adventures in the area," that these two powers were "acting as conspirators in order to repress the national liberation movement in the Near and Middle East," and that in any case, the Soviet Union "cannot remain indifferent to the fact that in the immediate neighborhood of its frontier, there is a focal point of military danger."[44]

Between the diametrically opposed positions of the Western Powers and those of the Soviet Bloc, there was a wide range of views.

The Arab states, with the exception of Jordan and Lebanon, and with varying degrees of intensity, requested the immediate withdrawal of British and American forces, before any other action was undertaken. It is interesting to note that, in contrast with many other states, their statements were comparatively mild, and either skirted the whole issue of the legality of the presence of troops, or mentioned it only in passing. There were no denunciations or accusations with regard to motives. For instance, UAR Foreign Minister Fawzī, whose country was directly involved in the controversy, merely stated that his government had already made its views known on the subject and that "we welcome the announcement by the Government of the United States of its intention to withdraw its armed forces from Lebanon, and of the actual beginning of this withdrawal." Although he felt "perturbed" because the USA had not indicated when the withdrawal would be completed, yet he was "happy to be able to state here that we have more than one reason to believe that the withdrawal of United States forces . . . will be soon completed."[45]

By and large, the Arab delegates concentrated on the total picture rather than on the specific issue. Essentially, they regarded the Lebanese and Jordanian crises as a domestic issue "within the family." They argued that the Arab League was the proper organization to handle such problems; that, had the League been given adequate time, it would have solved the Lebanese crisis; and asked that the big powers not interfere in their affairs.

The other members of the Assembly were divided into three main groups: those who gave unqualified support to the American and British action, such as Australia, New Zealand, Belgium, Italy, China, most of the Latin American countries, Turkey, Iran, Pakistan, Israel, and several others; those who violently opposed it, such as India, among others; those who, while not disputing the legality of the action, or the good will of the motivation behind it, nevertheless felt either that it was politically inadvisable or that the troops should be withdrawn as quickly as possible, because their presence would tend to complicate the situation or increase tension. States who felt that way were in the majority and were represented by such countries as Japan, Greece, Afghanistan and Burma. Most of the Afro-Asian nations frowned on the action. Seven states—Canada, Columbia, Denmark, Liberia, Norway, Panama and Paraguay—tried to play the role of mediators.

It was clear from the debates that the principle of the right of a state to request assistance from another when it believes its safety is threatened by outside aggression, and the right of a state to respond to such appeal pending action by the United Nations, were recognized by virtually all members of the General Assembly.

The basic issue raised by the landing of American and British troops in Lebanon and Jordan, respectively, was that such a right might be abused, and that under pretext of direct or indirect outside aggression, foreign troops might land in a country to buttress an unpopular régime and suppress the local population. This was clearly not the case with respect to the landing of American troops in Lebanon. Free elections had already taken place without the slightest interference from the troops, and a new President, supported and accepted by all factions, was elected. Furthermore, as will be pointed out later in the book, the presence of American troops did serve a constructive purpose in Lebanon itself, and contributed to the calming of the tense atmosphere in the area.

United Nations Police Force

There was general agreement among members of the Assembly, including members of the Soviet Bloc, that some form of UN intervention or "presence" in Lebanon and Jordan was necessary. Interestingly enough, the only country which categorically rejected any form of direct UN intervention was Jordan.[46]

Mr. Eisenhower's proposal for the establishment of a United Nations force was supported by most of the Western and many of the Latin American states, in addition to those countries which had special ties with the Western Bloc, such as Iran, Turkey and Pakistan. It was, however, opposed by the Soviet Bloc countries, and the large majority of the Afro-Asian and "uncommitted" nations.

In favor of the establishment of such a force, Selwyn Lloyd, the Foreign Minister of the United Kingdom, argued that this "could make possible quick action in an emergency, quick action which would not be dependent upon the willingness of individual countries to act on their own. There could be an additional safeguard for smaller countries in that the United Nations, itself, would have an instrument ready at hand of which, with agreement, speedy use could be made."[47] The Australian delegation further pointed out that such a force along with other measures "could reduce tension and clear the way for the establishment of normal political relationships between the governments of the countries concerned. It could also help to establish a calmer and more favorable atmosphere for the examination of the immediate and long term problems of the area."[48] Portugal argued that "it would be a new and important safeguard for the preservation of the independence of small nations as well as a powerful deterrent against threats to peace in the world."[49]

Mr. Lall of India led the attack on the establishment of such a force. He argued that this would constitute interference in the internal affairs of the Arabs, and that it would be "folly" to replace foreign troops by UN armed forces "to arrest the development of Arab nationalism in each state of the area." He warned: "We must be quite clear about these matters; otherwise we shall merely be sowing such seeds of discontent in the area as will, biding their time, surely spring up in a harvest which will render ridiculous such devices as I am trying to suggest should be now totally ruled out."[50]

In other words, there was expressed and implied feeling that, by such action, the United Nations would place the Arab states under a disguised form of trusteeship and that the UN force would become an instrument for preventing political and social change in the area, and for upholding unpopular and reactionary régimes against the will of the people. It was also feared that, in addition to these dangers, the United Nations would become embroiled in the local disputes and conflicts of the area, something which in the long run, would bring it nothing but discredit.

Arab Nationalism

Arab nationalism might be said to have passed a landmark in its development during this special session of the General Assembly. For the first time, it received unequivocal international recognition from the United Nations as a corporate body, and from the individual member states. It was recognized not as an academic theory, but as the primary dynamic force from which flow both the problems and aspirations for political and social self-fulfillment in the Arab world. It was also recognized as the primary force which determines the attitude of the international community and particularly the big powers to the Arab world; and conversely, the attitude of the Arab world towards individual states or groups of states.

Ahmad Shuqairy, the representative of Saudi Arabia, in a detailed analysis of Arab nationalism, probably voiced the feeling of the majority of the Arabs on the subject. He pointed out that the Arabs "from the Atlantic to the Arabian Gulf" are one nation, and that the object of the Arab national movement is the attainment of "liberty and unity."[51] He further elucidated the practical implications of the concept of "one Arab nation" as against the concept of "Arab nations" or "Arab peoples." He said:[52]

> If you speak of the Arabs as nations or peoples, you cannot secure the preservation of peace in that part of the world. If the premise of the United Nations is that the Arabs are peoples—are nations—then all your standards for aggression, your very conception of interference will fall to the ground . . . If the Arabs are treated as peoples or nations, a set of political considerations come into play. If they are treated as one single people, one single nation, then all these considerations will have to be

reversed, and reversed without mercy. Furthermore, a plan for economic development or otherwise, based on the assumption of the so-called peoples of the Arab nations, leads to a total disappearance of Arab nationalism no matter how much goodwill and good intentions we can display.

Under this concept of one Arab nation, there can be no aggression or imperialism among the Arab states, Mr. Shuqairy argued. He said:[53]

This will explain a very important aspect, too. Within Arab life, amongst the Arabs, themselves, Arab imperialism is inconceivable . . . It is unthinkable for one to enslave himself, to capture his own land, to subdue his own people, and to conquer his own fatherland. One can conceivably conquer others, dominate others, infiltrate into the territory or others, but no Arab is an alien to an Arab, and no Arab country is foreign to any other Arab country.

In contrast to the above point of view of "one Arab nation," Mr. Davin of New Zealand pointed out that:[54]

"There may be one Arab world, but it comprises a number of independent, sovereign states. All of these states, as members of the United Nations, are bound under the Charter to practice tolerance and to respect the equal rights of their neighbors. The conclusion cannot be avoided that there are forces in the Middle East directed more to the pursuit of national aggrandizement than to genuine international cooperation and interdependence."

Big Power Politics

Numerous suggestions were put forward aiming at reducing Big Power competition in the area to a minimum. Among such suggestions were a United Nations guaranteed neutralization of the area, strongly advocated by Mr. Aiken of Ireland; and "freezing the area" urged by Mr. Palamas of Greece. Mr. Aiken, who probably made the most forthright analysis of the fundamental problems of the area, said:[55]

The second point for a settlement would be a declaration by this Assembly that the neutrality of the whole region, guaranteed by the United Nations and recognized by the great Powers, would be in the interest of world peace. In addition, members should be asked to undertake not to supply atomic weapons or long-range bombers or missiles to the region, or maintain such weapons or equipment there; and that member states in the region, itself should be asked to undertake not to acquire or manufacture such weapons or equipment.

Economic Development

Another subject which received exhaustive attention was economic development. The Assembly proceeded on the premise that political action for stabilizing the area must be accompanied by economic action. The time had come, it was felt, to discard palliatives for surgery. The initiative was taken by Mr. Hammarskjöld in his statement mentioned previously, and by President Eisenhower in his address to the Assembly. The Secretary-General pledged the United Nations to providing moral support, technical assistance and other services as may be requested by the Arabs; while President Eisenhower pledged the moral and financial support of the United States. The representatives of Italy and the United Kingdom followed suit and pledged the active support of their countries to the extent of their abilities. All members of the Assembly gave their enthusiastic approval—with the exception of the Soviet Bloc countries—to active UN participation.

The approach was novel in many respects:

1. The initiative was to be taken by the Arabs themselves.
2. An Arab development institution, composed of the Arab states, was to be created to execute economic and social programs on a regional basis, and to give aid and advice to individual countries.
3. For the first time, oil revenue was officially proposed (by Mr. Hammarskjöld) as a source of regional financing.
4. The United Nations, individual states, and private organizations were to provide moral support, technical and economic assistance, but the leadership, execution and aims of the program were to be directed by the Arabs themselves.

The ideas of both President Eisenhower and Mr. Hammarskjöld were incorporated in the Arab resolution which will be discussed later. They provided impetus for the revitalization of an Arab financial institution within the framework of the Arab League, which came into being in February 1959.

In contrast, it was indicative of Russia's real intentions in the area that the Soviet Union not only failed to offer any help to the Arabs—financial or otherwise—on a collective basis; but in addition, its Foreign Minister dubbed the proposals of both Mr. Eisenhower and Mr. Hammarskjöld as attempts to divert the attention of the Assembly from the issues.

The Soviet and Seven-Power Draft Resolutions

Immediately upon the convening of the Assembly, the Soviet Union, on August 12, tabled a draft resolution. Its preambular paragraph was in terms of the General Assembly "recognizing the necessity of adopting urgent measures for the relaxation of tension in the area of the Near and Middle East in the interests of preserving universal peace." The operative paragraphs simply stated that the General Assembly "recommends" that the Governments of the United States and Britain withdraw their troops, and "instructs" the Secretary-General to strengthen the Observation Group in Lebanon, and to send another observation group to Lebanon and Jordan to supervise the withdrawal of foreign troops and "the situation along the frontiers of those countries."[56]

Compared to the Soviet draft resolution which was voted down in the Security Council, this was indeed mildly-worded. It was, however, unacceptable to the United States and Britain, the two countries directly involved, and to most members of the Assembly. For one thing, the preambular paragraph implied that the presence of US and British troops in Lebanon and Jordan had created tension and was a threat to world peace. It also, by implication, accused them of being there illegally. Finally, it recommended the immediate withdrawal of foreign troops without the necessary guarantee that the UN would take concrete action—something which the two countries insisted on.

It was quite evident that the Soviet Union's resolution was not only unacceptable but also did not have the slightest chance of being adopted if it were put to a vote. In the meantime, John Foster Dulles and Selwyn Lloyd, on behalf of the US and British Governments, sent identical letters, dated August 18, 1958, to the President of the General Assembly, stating that their troops would be withdrawn "whenever this is requested by the duly constituted government . . . or whenever, as a result of further action of the United Nations or otherwise, their presence is no longer required."[57] This was a further reaffirmation of their former statements to the same effect, thus leaving no doubt of their intention to withdraw their troops as soon as it became clear that they were no longer needed or wanted.

Seven states — Canada, Colombia, Denmark, Liberia, Norway, Panama and Paraguay—under the leadership of Norway, moved onto the scene as mediators, and submitted a draft resolution on the same day.[58] The resolution tried to steer a middle course. It noted that the American and British Governments had declared their intention of withdrawing their troops. It asked all governments to reaffirm by word and deed the principles of the Charter and other resolutions of the Assembly and of the Bandung Conference. Its instructions to the Secretary-General were couched in vague terms so as to leave him room to maneuver, and in the words of its expounder, Mr. Egan of Norway, it was also designed so as not to place the Secretary-General in "untenable positions."

The resolution, however, was rejected by the Soviet Bloc countries. Certain parts of it also were unacceptable to the Arab countries whose active cooperation was necessary for its implementation and to other countries, primarily among the Afro-Asian nations.

The Arab Resolution

The Assembly, like the Security Council before it, had reached a deadlock with the unacceptability of the Soviet and Seven-Power resolutions.

In the midst of considerable anxiety in the Assembly, the Arab delegates on August 20, through the mediation of Foreign Minister Maḥjūb of the Sudan, met in private conference. It is not known exactly what transpired at that meeting but apparently it was clear to all present that it would be greatly desirable if the Arabs were to agree on a resolution among themselves. This would have the advantage of presenting them as a united front before the world, particularly since considerable stress had been laid on Arab nationalism, on the Arabs as one family, and the stand that their disputes were family squabbles. A draft resolution was agreed upon and the delegates contacted their respective governments and obtained their approval.

In the afternoon of August 21, Maḥjūb spoke on behalf of ten Arab states: Iraq, Jordan, Lebanon, Libya, Morocco, Saudi Arabia, Sudan, Tunisia, the United Arab Republic and Yemen. He explained the resolution which was sponsored by the above ten states and submitted it to the Assembly for its consideration.[59]

In spirit, the Arab resolution was more or less similar to the Seven-Power resolution. Yet there were subtle and important differences in emphasis:

1. The preambular paragraphs of the Seven-Power resolution noted the declarations of the United States and Britain to the President of the Assembly on August 18th. The Arab resolution made no reference to them.
2. The Arab resolution followed the suggestion of Mr. Hammarskjöld, and noted that the Arab states had bound themselves in the Pact of the Arab League, to respect each other, etc. The Seven-Power resolution made no reference to the Arab League Pact.
3. In the operative paragraphs of the Seven-Power resolution I(1), the frame of reference was the UN Charter and General

Assembly resolutions. In the Arab resolution I(1), the frame of reference was article 8 of the Pact of the Arab League.

4. Section I(2) of the Seven-Power resolution "calls upon all states" to strictly observe these obligations "in relation to the general area of the Near East." The corresponding Section I(2) of the Arab resolution was more explicit as to what obligations states should observe, and made no reference to the Near East. In other words, where the Seven-Power resolution might be interpreted as being referred to the Arab states indirectly, the Arab resolution explicitly included all states in all areas.
5. Section II of the Seven-Power resolution requested the Secretary-General to take measures to uphold the principles and objectives of the Charter "in relation to Lebanon and Jordan," but made no reference to troop withdrawal. Section II of the Arab resolution, after requesting the same measures, added "and thereby facilitate the early withdrawal of foreign troops." In other words, it tied the measures to early troop withdrawal, as matters of cause and result.
6. Section III(1) of the Seven-Power resolution "notes" that the Secretary-General had under study, for consideration by the 13th session of the General Assembly, the feasibility of establishing a standby UN peace force. The Arab resolution made no reference to this at all.

The Arab resolution was met with a spirit of jubilation by all members of the Assembly, with the exception of the Soviet Bloc and Israel, which had reservations. The particularly interesting aspect of the resolution is that it reconciled what seemed to be irreconcilable. With compromise, it satisfied the positions and objectives of all parties directly concerned with the exception of the Soviet Union.

The resolution was a blow to the whole Russian position. In the first place, both the accuser and the accused sponsored the resolution, thus leaving the Soviets out of the picture. Second, by not insisting on a withdrawal date, the resolution was a moral victory for the United States, for it implicitly expressed the confidence of the Arab in the integrity and goodwill of the United States. Third, in the light of the spirit and words of the resolution, and within the context of the discussions that had taken place in the Assembly, Soviet charges of aggression, imperialism, etc., now looked particularly absurd.

Although the resolution was quite evidently a compromise which did not meet the full desires of those directly concerned, it was nevertheless, as has been shown, met with great satisfaction in the

Assembly. It was adopted by a unanimous vote on August 21 and the special emergency session of the General Assembly was declared ended on the same day.

The End of the Crisis

In accordance with his mandate under the Arab resolution, Mr. Hammarskjöld went to the Middle East on August 25 and consulted with the governments of Amman, Baghdad, Beirut and Cairo. After his return in mid-September, he submitted a report in which he detailed the principles which guided him, gave a summary of his consultations and the actions taken by him.[60]

With regard to intentions, Mr. Hammarskjöld pointed out that "the basis for consideration was the need to provide . . . both for keeping current developments . . . under purview and for proper diplomatic arrangements for any subsequent action by the United Nations which might be rendered necessary by the findings made." With the above in mind, Mr. Hammarskjöld made the following arrangements:

He appointed a representative of the Secretary-General to be located in ʿAmmān with liaison offices in Damascus and Beirut. The function of this representative was to keep "under purview" current developments. He is to be in contact with the "Government of Jordan as host government and with the Secretary-General, but not directly with any other government in the area."

He also planned to appoint a diplomatic representative of the Secretary-General to be stationed at headquarters in New York. His function would be to carry out "such direct contacts of a diplomatic nature with the Governments concerned as the Secretary-General may find called for in the light of the findings of the representative charged with the purview." He would be "entitled to take up discussions with those other Governments on behalf of the Secretary-General, but would not be in direct contact with the Government of Jordan."

The reports of the representative stationed in Amman would not be made public and would not be circulated as United Nations documents, unless the Secretary-General saw fit.

With respect to Lebanon, Mr. Hammarskjöld found that the UN Observation Group, as it was enlarged, "adequately helps in upholding the purposes of the Charter in relation to Lebanon."

On November 10, Mr. Hammarskjöld reported to the Assembly[61] that American forces in Lebanon and British forces in Jordan completed their withdrawal from the two countries on October 25 and November 2, respectively.

In the meantime, the situation in Lebanon was returning to normal. Fighting had stopped except for occasional gunfire of a private nature, and infiltration of men or smuggling of arms had, to all practical purposes, ceased. On November 17, the Observation Group reported that "its task . . . may now be regarded as completed."[62] By the early part of December the withdrawal of all Observation Group personnel was completed.

The Lebanese crisis died down as suddenly as it had appeared on the international scene. Like a Shakespearean drama with a happy ending, it seemed at some points about to engulf the whole region in the flames of war, but, on each occasion, destiny intervened to avert the impending disaster.

NOTES

1. *Mideast Mirror,* May 18, 1958, p. 5.
2. *Ibid,* p. 9.
3. *UN Doc. S/PV 818,* May 27, 1958.
4. *Mideast Mirror,* June, 15, 1958, p. 9.
5. Karāmī, *op. cit.,* pp. 106-114.
6. *Mideast Mirror,* June 8, 1958, p. 3.
7. *Ibid.,* June 15, 1958, p. 9.
8. *Ibid.,* p. 9.
9. Karāmī, *op. cit.,* p. 107.
10. *Mideast Mirror,* June 8, 1958, p. 3, and June 15, 1958, p. 9. For conflicting versions as to what transpired at Banghazi, se Appendices I(B) and II(A).
11. *UN Doc. S/PV. 823,* 6 June 1959, pp. 52-53.
12. For details of the reasons for the rejection see Karāmī, *op. cit.,* pp. 111-112.
13. *Mideast Mirror,* June 15, 1958, p. 9.
14. *Mideast Mirror,* June 8, 1958, p. 3.
15. *Ibid.,* p. 3.
16. The Security Council was then composed of the five permanent members (USA, USSR, UK, France, China), and Canada, Columbia, Iraq, Japan, Panama, and Sweden. The UAR and Lebanon were invited to participate in the discussions.
17. See text of their speeches in the following documents: Mr. de Vaucelles (France), *UN Doc. S/PV. 824,* 10 June 1958, pp. 106-115; Mr. Lodge (USA), *Ibid.,* pp. 116-120; Sir Pierson Dixon (UK), *Ibid.,* 121-132; Mr. Tsiang (China), *UN Doc. S/PV. 825,* 11 June 1958, pp. 17-21; Mr. Jamalī (Iraq), *UN Doc. S/PV. 824,* 10 June 1958, pp. 81-105.
18. See the text of Mr. Sobolov's speech in *Ibid.,* pp. 64-80.
19. For text see Appendix IV(A).
20. American troops were landing while Mr. Lodge was informing the Council.
21. For full text of his speech see *UN Doc. S/PV. 827,* 15 July 1958, pp. 21-35.
22. *UN Doc. S/4050/Corr. 1,* 16 July 1958.
23. *UN Doc. S/PV. 829,* 16 July 1958, pp. 37-40.
24. *UN Doc. S/PV. 832,* 17 July 1958, pp. 11-16.
25. For full texts of the speeches of Mr. Jarring, the representative of Sweden, on the subject, see the following UN Documents: *S/PV. 830,* 16 July 1958, pp. 21-25; *S/PV. 832,* 17 July 1958, p. 11; and *S/PV. 835,* 21 July 1958, pp. 36-40.
26. For full text see *UN Doc. S/4054,* 17 July 1958.
27. For full texts of the main speeches of Mr. Lutfī, the U.A.R. delegate on the subject, see the following UN Documents: *S/PV. 828,* 15 July 1958, pp. 16-22; *S/PV.*

830, 16 July 1958, pp. 2-6; *S/PV. 831,* 17 July 1958, pp. 54-59; *S/PV. 833,* 18 July 1958, pp. 16-17.

28. For a representative sample of Mr. Sobolov's speeches see the following UN Documents: *S/PV. 827,* 15 July 1958, pp. 47-61; *S/PV. 829,* 16 July 1958, pp. 16-31; *S/PV. 830,* 16 July 1958, pp. 6-15; *S/PV. 831,* 17 July 1958, pp. 31-50.

29. *UN Doc. S/PV. 830,* 16 July 1958, pp. 12-15.

30. *UN Doc. S/4047/Rev. 1,* 15 July 1958.

31. *UN Doc. S/PV. 834,* 18 July 1958, p. 46.

32. For text see *UN Doc. S/4055/Rev. 1,* 21 July 1958.

33. *UN Doc. S/PV. 835,* 21 July 1958, p. 6.

34. For full text of the statement of the representative of Lebanon on this point, see *UN Doc. S/PV. 836,* 22 July 1958, pp. 2-10.

35. For full text of the Soviet amendments see *ibid.,* pp. 7-15.

36. *UN Doc. S/PV. 837,* 22 July 1958, p. 6.

37. *Ibid.,* pp. 7-10.

38. *Ibid.,* p. 11.

39. For texts of Khrushchev's letters see the following: For letters of July 19 and July 23, 1958, to Eisenhower, Macmillan, De Gaulle and Nehru, see respectively, *UN Doc. S/4059,* 20 July 1958, *UN Doc. S/4064,* 23 July 1958; for his letters to Eisenhower of July 28 and August 5, 1958, see respectively, *US State Department, Bulletin,* August 18, 1958, pp. 275-277, and *Ibid.,* Sept. 1, 1958, pp. 342-46. For Eisenhower's replies of July 22, July 25 and August 1, 1958, see respectively, *Bulletin,* August 11, 1958, pp. 229-231, *Ibid.,* pp. 233-34; *Ibid.,* August 18, 1958, pp. 274-75.

40. For texts of the US and Soviet revised draft resolutions see respectively, UN Documents, *S/4056/Rev. 1,* August 7, 1958; and *S/4057/Rev. 1,* 6 August 1958.

41. For text of the final resolution, see *UN Doc. S/4083,* 7 August 1958.

42. For full text see Appendix V(A).

43. For full text see Appendix V(B).

44. For full text of Gromyko's speech see, *UN Doc. A/PV. 733,* 13 August 1958, pp. 21-46.

45. *Ibid.,* pp. 50-51.

46. *UN Doc. A/PV. 735,* 14 August 1958, p. 26.

47. *UN Doc. A/PV. 734,* 14 August 1958, p. 20.

48. *UN Doc. A/PV. 735,* 14 August 1958, p. 28.

49. *UN Doc. A/PV. 744,* 20 August 1958, p. 77.

50. *UN Doc. A/PV. 738,* 18 August 1958, pp. 48-51.

51. *UN Doc. A/PV. 736,* 15 August 1958, pp. 26-27.

52. *Ibid.,* p. 27.

53. *Ibid.,* pp. 28-30.

54. *UN Doc. A/PV. 737,* 15 August 1958, p. 51.

55. *UN Doc. A/PV. 735,* 14 August 1958, p. 30.

56. For full text see *UN Doc. A/3870,* 12 August 1958.

57. For texts of their letters see respectively, UN Documents, *A/3876,* 18 August 1958, and *A/3877,* 18 August 1958.

58. For full text see Appendix IV(B).

59. For full text see Appendix IV(C).

60. For full text see *UN Doc. A/3934/Rev. 1,* 29 September 1958.

61. *UN Doc. A/3986,* 10 November 1958.

62. *UN Doc. S/4114,* 17 November 1958, p. 7.

CHAPTER VII

The American Commitment

CORDIAL RELATIONS between the United States and Lebanon are of long standing. In 1823 the missionary Pliny Fisk arrived in Beirut beginning a tradition of ever-expanding American philanthropic and cultural activity in the country. The crowning achievement of this activity was the establishment of the American University in 1866, which since then has been not only an institution of higher learning for the entire area, but also in part, the home in which ideas of Arab nationalism were nurtured, and the *alma mater* of many of the political and intellectual leaders of the area.

Conversely, there are about half a million Americans of Lebanese origin in the United States today. In the latter part of the 19th century and the first quarter of the 20th century, their thriving Arabic press was one of the chief stimuli which brought about what has come to be known as the Arab Renaissance. In addition, until recent years, the financial contributions of Lebanese immigrants in the United States to their relatives was one of the main sources of the national income of Lebanon.

Negatively, Lebanese immigrants have tended to carry over and perpetuate in their new habitat, the attitudes, feuds and prejudices of their former homeland. Since the majority are Maronite Christians, and many of them descendants of Lebanese who immigrated to the United States after the 1860 disturbances, by and large, they subscribe to the two central ideas of the Phalange Party in Lebanon itself: love for an independent Christian Lebanon and Lebanon's cultural and political dissociation from the Arab world. This for instance, is clearly reflected on the pages of the New York Maronite newspaper *al-Huda,* the largest Arabic daily in the Western Hemisphere, and other Maronite publications such as the *Middle East Press Review,* a monthly mimeographed sheet which used to be published in New York in English by a Maronite priest. As in the case with all minority pressure groups, Americans of Lebanese origin exercise some influence on the United States government with respect to Lebanon. During the 1958 Lebanese crisis, Maronite papers and Lebanese clubs in the United States campaigned for the military intervention of the United States. In addition to their actions as corporate bodies, they exhorted their readers and members to write and wire the President and members of Congress pleading for such action—which many of them did.

Up until the end of the Second World War, United States relations with Lebanon were largely cultural. Immediately after however, a second level of relationships began to emerge—the commercial. This was due to the development of the Middle East oil industry, and the vast expansion of American business interests in the area. Today, Beirut is the center of virtually all the regional offices of American business firms, and indeed of many other foreign firms. This development was due in part to the *laissez-faire* economic policy of the Lebanese government, and its offer of attractive terms and facilities to foreign capital.

Concurrently, a third level emerged—the political. The first significant US intervention in the political affairs of Lebanon took place in November 1943 when the country was struggling for its independence from France. It was partly due to the firm position of the United States and British governments that the native government was returned to power in 1943, and the country gained its full independence in 1946, with the withdrawal of all foreign troops.

Since 1945, US political relationships with Lebanon and the Middle East have increased by leaps and bounds. This has been due to American involvement in the Palestine controversy, the speedy decline of European colonial hegemony over the area, and the assumption by the United States the mantle of leadership of the free world in its global struggle with the Communist-Soviet Bloc.

Under the Sham'ūn administration, Lebanon's friendly relations with the United States became even closer than before. In 1954, Lebanon accepted the Point Four Program, and from 1952 to May 1958 received 38 million dollars in technical and/or economic assistance over and above military aid. In 1957, Lebanon was the first, and only, Arab country to accept the Eisenhower Doctrine. In addition, while most of the Arab countries tended before 1958 to veer further and further away from the United States, the contrary was true in Lebanon.

Thus, American relations with Lebanon today rest on expanding cultural, commercial and political interests. This is reflected in the vast increase in the number of American citizens living there. Whereas, before the War, the number of Americans—mostly educators—probably did not exceed 200 in the entire country, today some three thousands live in Beirut alone. This is also reflected in the size of the American Embassy—the largest in the Middle East—

which employs a staff of nearly 800 persons, Lebanese as well as Americans. American influence in Lebanon ranges from permanent cultural achievements as in the field of education, to business and business practices, and down the line to the more mundane, such as the names of hotels, restaurants, bars and to student clothes.

* * *

When the Lebanese crisis broke out in May 1958, and the Lebanese government openly accused the UAR of intervention in its internal affairs, there were three possible avenues open to the American government: (1) not to take any action at all; (2) to give moral and limited material support to the Lebanese government and (3) to take military action.

At the beginning, the US government chose the second course, despite repeated requests by President Sham'ūn for military intervention.[1] Apparently, the American government had hoped that the crisis would be solved either on a local or a regional basis—among the Arabs themselves through the intervention of the Arab League; or at worst, through the UN intervention. In line with this approach, on May 14, the United States decided, at the request of the Lebanese Government, to airlift such police weapons as tear gas and small arms ammunition. On the same day, Mr. Robert McClintock, the American Ambassador, declared in this connection, that "We are determined to help this government to maintain internal security" while the US Navy Department announced that American amphibious forces in the Mediterranean were being doubled temporarily, although it denied that this had any connection with the crisis in Lebanon.[2] The State Department declared on May 17 that US tanks, requested months ago by Lebanon, would be sent soon and, on the 18th, that the United States was considering whether to send American troops.[3]

A study of official statements made by the United States Government between the latter part of May and July, together with the military buildup that was taking place during this period, shows that a decision for direct military intervention in Lebanon—if it became necessary—had been taken. The primary questions that remained to be answered were an evaluation of the seriousness of the situation in Lebanon itself and in neighboring countries, and second, within what framework such an intervention would take place. Intervention thus would take place only as a last resort and if all other avenues for solving the problem had failed.

During this period, the Sixth Fleet was reinforced and some of its elements moved to the Eastern Mediterranean, while American forces in Europe, particularly those in Germany and Turkey, were put on the alert. In addition, the British fleet in the Mediterranean was also reinforced and British troops, particularly parachute battalions, were moved from the United Kingdom and Malta to Cyprus. On July 1, General Nathan Twining, Chairman of the US Joint Chiefs of Staff, said that the United States was prepared to send troops to Lebanon if the situation warranted this. He added, "We are prepared for any eventuality—all out war or limited war, right now."[4] In addition, in his news conferences on May 20, June 17 and July 1, Secretary of State Dulles left little doubt that the United States would intervene directly, if in his judgment, this became necessary.[5] In his speech before the Security Council on June 10, 1958, Mr. Lodge, the American representative, said, in part:

> The record of the United States in the United Nations in defense of the territorial integrity and political independence of States is consistent and clear. We supported fully United Nations action in defense of the territorial integrity of Egypt in 1956. Now, having in mind the same Charter principles, the United States Government is concerned about the present situation in Lebanon. There should be no doubt of the firm determination of the United States to continue to support the integrity and independence of that country.[6]

When the Lebanese case came before the Security Council, and the Swedish resolution establishing the UN Observation Group was proposed, the US representative was the first to support it. Apparently it was hoped that, although the resolution was a token gesture expressing UN concern, it would still, through the moral influence of the United Nations, be helpful. This point of view was expressed by Secretary Dulles in his press conference on July 1st. In reply to a question on the authority of the Observation Group, he said, in part: "They are there to observe and report. It is believed that the very fact that they are there in that capacity will have a practical effect in stopping movements across the border."[7]

The United States soon became disillusioned with the Observation Group, either as a moral deterrent or as an effective instrument. In the first place, during the month of June, after the arrival of the Observation Group, fighting between government and opposition forces became more frequent, more violent, and more extensive. Second, as the days went by, it became progressively clear that the Observation Group, as it was composed and under the powers granted to it by the Security Council, was in no position to observe, let alone to forbid. Third, while the reports of the Observation Group at least implied that the infiltration of men and materials from Syria into Lebanon was negligible, the reports of the intelligence services of the United States government indicated that such infiltration was on the increase. Finally, although the attitude of the US Government towards the Observation Group was formally correct, and indeed mild praise was usually included in official statements related to the Group, it is a fact that the American government questioned the competency of the Group.

The fateful decision—the step of last resort—took place on July 15. In the early hours of July 14, a revolution overthrew the monarchy in Iraq, the entire royal family was killed, and the body of one of its members was dragged in the streets and dismembered. The repercussions in Beirut were immediate. Jubilation in opposition-held areas was almost hysterical and was accompanied by displays of gun fire. At the same time, opposition radio stations gleefully announced that the government of the "traitor" Nūrī al-Sa'īd had been destroyed, that of Sham'ūn was next, and the day of reckoning had come.

Haunted by what happened to the royal family in Iraq, Sham'ūn called in the American, British and French ambassadors separately during the morning of the 14th. He demanded immediate intervention, insisting that unless this took place within 48 hours, he would be a dead man, and Lebanon would become an Egyptian satellite. The American Ambassador notified Washington. In the early hours of the 15th, he received the reply: American warships, the cable said, were on their way, and marines are scheduled to strike the beaches near Beirut at three in the afternoon.

* * *

At three o'clock in the afternoon of July 15, 1958, a hot summer day, about 2,000 marines in full battle gear landed on Lebanese soil, some five miles south of Beirut. There was no opposition. In the days that followed, more marine and army formations were landed, bringing the total strength of American forces in Lebanon to some 15,000 men, all concentrated in the vicinity of Beirut. In support of these troops, the entire Sixth Fleet, consisting of about 70 ships with 40,000 men, moved to the east Mediterranean. The ships included the "heavy cruiser *Des Moines,* the guided missile ship *Boston,* the supercarrier *Saratoga,* the carrier *Essex,* 28 destroyers, some oilers and transports, and a submarine hunter-killer group. This group, consisting of a carrier and six destroyers, has thrown a screen round the area roughly from Lebanon to Cyprus."[8] American troops remained in Lebanon three months and ten days, and the last American soldier left the country on October 27, 1958.

The first two days of the landing proved to be the most critical period for American troops. The dispatch of these troops was made at the request of President Sham'ūn with the approval of the cabinet. No one else knew about the request until it was made public.

As soon as McClintock received the message informing him of the impending landing, he went to tell Sham'ūn, who was jubilant. At about noon, McClintock also went to General Shihāb at the Ministry of Defense. Shihāb was highly and visibly disturbed. He told McClintock that this could very easily provoke the Lebanese army to join opposition forces and both to resist the American landing with force. He suggested that the ambassador try to hold the marines offshore, until he made certain that his troops were under control. McClintock agreed to forward the suggestion to the admiral of the fleet, but due to radio silence usually imposed on the fleet during such military movements, he was unable to do so.

When the marines landed, the entire group moved towards the Beirut International Airport and occupied it. During the night and early the following day, more marines with tanks and heavy equipment poured in, so that by mid-day of July 16 the number of US marines ashore was estimated around 5,000 battle-ready men. Admiral James L. Holloway, CIC Eastern Atlantic and Mediterranean, arrived at dawn from London to take command of forces in Lebanon.

On July 16, had it not been for the foresight of both Lebanese and US military authorities, and a particularly high order of political vision demonstrated by the American Ambassador, there is little doubt that American and Lebanese troops would have clashed, and the landing turned into a political disaster.

It will be recalled that the Lebanese military authorities were neither consulted nor informed of Sham'ūn's request. Moreover, the Lebanese army regarded its primary function as the defense of the country against foreign invasion. In line with this concept, it did not fully support the government, and had tried to remain neutral in a conflict which it regarded as primarily domestic in nature. In addition, the practical intentions and functions of the American forces were not clear then. Would they take military control of the country? Would they fight against the opposition? Were they in Lebanon to bolster the Sham'ūn régime? These were questions which no one could answer at that time. But, since Sham'ūn requested the landing and since UAR and Soviet propaganda had been forecasting an Anglo-American invasion since the crisis began, the tendency was to answer such questions in the affirmative.

Thus, initially, there was a feeling of a loss of pride among many Lebanese army officers, a tendency to regard the landing as an invasion and to be extremely sensitive. For instance, the officer who was in charge of the defense of the airport, 'Azīz al-Aḥdab, happened to be away when American troops occupied it and cordoned it off. When he returned, the American guard prevented him from entering. He then drew out his gun and said "I will enter by force"—after which he was allowed to proceed.[9]

Around 11:00 o'clock in the morning of the 16th, a marine battalion supported by six Patton tanks with 90 mm guns and 12 amphibious-tracked vehicles, began to move along the airport road towards Beirut.

At the same time, with the knowledge of General Shihāb, Col. Yusuf Shamīṭ at Lebanese army headquarters issued orders to the Lebanese army to open fire on US troops if they attempted to enter Beirut, and dispatched a Lebanese army force under the command of Major Jamīl I'īd, supported by tanks and armored cars to cut off the airport road, with specific instructions to fire if American troops advanced.

In the meantime, McClintock was urgently summoned to the Presidential Palace. There, Sham'ūn told him that the army and the opposition were planning to seize him and resist the entry of the marines into Beirut. General Shihāb arrived a few minutes later:

> In no uncertain terms Chehab told the Ambassador that if the marines advanced, Lebanese tanks, already deployed along the airport road, would open fire. If they did not advance, Chamoun told him emphatically, the rebels would debauch from the Basta and kidnap him leaving the United States in the embarrassing situation of maintaining troops in a foreign country to protect a government which did not exist.[10]

While Sham'ūn, Shihāb and McClintock were debating the dilemma at the Palace, the situation in the field was becoming grave. A mile from the airport, the marine column was met by a Lebanese staff officer. He asked Brigadier General Sidney Wade, commander of the marines' land forces, to have the column wait, as the American Ambassador was at that moment conferring with President Sham'ūn and General Shihāb. Wade refused, stating that he had rigid orders to enter Beirut without delay. Farther down the road however, near the army school, the marines came face to face with the Lebanese force—its tanks, armored-cars, recoilless rifles and artillery, all trained on them. This left little doubt in the commander's mind that the Lebanese army was deadly serious, and that it would fight even if this meant suicide. He immediately called the Ambassador, who together with General Shihāb rushed to the scene. Separately, Admiral Holloway arrived and joined the group. By then several journalists were on the scene to witness one of the most open military negotiations in history.

Finally, a compromise plan was agreed upon, on the spot: a smaller force than originally planned was to enter Beirut. The force would be broken up into platoon groups, and these would enter Beirut with an escort of Lebanese army patrols.[11] This was satisfactory to all concerned: in the case of American marines, they were vitally interested in avoiding any clashes with any Lebanese group if at all possible, civilian or military. By adopting the compromise plan, their military objectives were served as well, the pride and honor of the Lebanese army was saved and the escort provided by it gave them both further protection against possible snipers and the appearance of cooperation between Lebanese and US forces. This cooperation, a few days later, became genuine.

When the marines entered Beirut, they were deployed with their tanks around the harbor, the US embassy, the Ambassador's residence, and other American institutions.

American troops also passed a critical period during the first few days of the landing with respect to the civilian population and political groups in the country, since no one knew what the functions of these troops were going to be. The landing was met with jubilation by government supporters and government irregulars in east Beirut celebrated the occasion with gunfire.[12]

The central command of the United National Front issued a proclamation in which it called upon the people to "kill the invader,"[13] while various political parties and influential persons in the opposition sent telegrams of protest to President Eisenhower, and/or the Security Council, Mr. Hammarskjöld, Mr. Dulles and the US Congress. The most important of these, to the extent that they represent the views of constitutional authority, are the telegrams sent by 'Adil 'Usayrān, president of the Lebanese Chamber of Deputies, to Eisenhower, Dulles, Hammarskjöld, and the Security Council. He wrote:[14]

> The sole authority which represents the will of the Lebanese people is the Chamber of Deputies. We have learned with regret that American troops have landed in Lebanon under the pretext of protecting American lives and preserving the independence and sovereignty of the Lebanese republic. Such an action is an encroachment on Lebanon's independence and sovereignty.
>
> American lives and property have not so far been exposed to danger. After 65 days of the current dispute among the Lebanese none of them has threatened American lives or property.
>
> The crisis which we are passing through is a domestic one and cannot be solved except through the Chamber of Deputies. I, therefore, on

behalf of the chamber, protest against the violation of Lebanon's independence and sovereignty, consider the landing of American troops a threat to peace and security in the Middle East and hold the United States responsible for the consequences, which might lead to a world war. I demand the evacuation of the troops forthwith lest the good relations between the Lebanese and American peoples be harmed.

The above telegram is also important because it was supported by some twenty other deputies, and because it represented the first open split between Sham'ūn and 'Usayrān. 'Usayrān started out as a Sham'ūn supporter. During the conflict, he tried to steer a neutral course, leaning, however, a little towards Sham'ūn. It was later discovered that the post office, which is a state agency in Lebanon, did not send 'Usayrān's telegrams—presumably on instructions of the government.

* * *

The major initial problem which confronted American troops in Lebanon was the confusion in the mind of the Lebanese public as to why they were there. Apparently, Sham'ūn, although the question of his remaining in office had already been decided in the negative, had hoped and probably expected that American troops would fight on his side, suppressing the opposition and giving him a decided victory over his enemies—both within and outside Lebanon. Government supporters believed that American troops came to bolster the Sham'ūn régime. The Phalanges hoped that, in addition, the landing of American troops would result in an international guarantee for the independence of Lebanon. Thus Lebanon, and by extension the Christians there, would become a perpetual trust of the international community. This hope was apparently shared by both Sham'ūn and Dr. Malik.[15]

The opposition shared most of the above beliefs, and in addition was convinced that Lebanon would be used by American troops as a base for aggression against other Arab countries.

All these speculations were soon dispelled by the exceptional conduct of American troops and the great restraint which they displayed, which indeed have no parallel in modern times. In the first place, the main body of troops remained stationed outside Beirut. Only a very small number were assigned duty inside the city. Even these were restricted mainly to guard duty at such places as the harbor, American institutions, and certain areas where American citizens lived. Areas controlled by the opposition were completely out of bounds to troops whether on or off duty. Second, at no time did Americans interfere in the internal conflict or give support to government forces against the opposition. American forces rigidly abstained from supporting one faction against another. This was clearly reflected in the changeover from the Sham'ūn to the Shihāb administration. President Shihāb was primarily the candidate of the opposition —with grudging approval from Sham'ūn and his supporters. Moreover, the first cabinet under the new administration was composed entirely of men from the opposition.

Friendly relations and cooperation between American and Lebanese forces, once the initial misunderstanding was removed, developed into a high order of excellence. On August 1, "four-men patrols, made up of two Lebanese security men and two members of the American forces" began "regular duty in Beirut to promote friendly relations and keep order in areas where American troops were posted. The American members of the joint patrols had police authority over all American troops but no authority over Lebanese citizens. The commander of the American military police said that cooperation with the members of the Lebanese security forces had been first rate."[16]

Even the opposition which, at first, was extremely suspicious of American motives, acted with restraint approximating friendship.[17] An incident which took place on July 17 is a case in point. Two marines in a jeep lost their way in Beirut, wandered into opposition held areas and were taken by opposition forces—having offered no resistance. Their captors went through the motions of questioning them, but otherwise treated them in a friendly manner, and offered them soft drinks. A few hours later, they were returned safe and sound—but minus their guns.

American troops remained confined in their barracks until August 9. On that day, 1,000 marines were given leave from noon until curfew time—eight in the evening. From there on, about a thousand soldiers entered Beirut each day on leave. It is estimated that they spent between 1.5 and 2.5 million dollars on entertainment and souvenirs during their stay in Lebanon.

Casualties among American troops were minor. The total death toll came to less than eight persons. With the exception of one, all were due to accidents. On August 2, Army Sergeant James R. Nettles was killed by a sniper's bullet while traveling through Beirut in a jeep.[18] In another case, not fatal, "an American soldier was shot and wounded on August 22 while he was walking near the fringe of the opposition barricaded area of the town. The soldier was on an authorized pass but had wandered into an out-of-bounds area. The man who shot him first beckoned him. The soldier refused to obey and was hit by two bullets as he made off."[19] In addition, during the entire period in which United States forces were in Lebanon, some 30 military aircraft were hit by snipers' bullets, but with no serious damage. Six other planes were lost in the course of normal operations. Two other points should perhaps be emphasized in this connection: (1) that on several occasions American troops, while on duty, were shot at by snipers, but in most cases, in accordance with their instructions, they did not return the fire and (2) that not a single Lebanese suffered any injury of any kind—whether in his person or property—as a result of US military action.

* * *

Three principal questions arise from these facts: first, was the landing of United States troops legal; second, what were the motivations and objectives of the United States in landing these troops; and finally, to what extent was the United States successful in achieving these objectives?

American troops landed in Lebanon at the official request of Camille Sham'ūn, then President of the Republic—made on July 14, with the support and approval of the cabinet. The Chamber of Deputies was neither informed nor consulted and no one knew of the request until it was made public. This fact raises two legal questions: did President Sham'ūn have the constitutional authority to request the military intervention of the United States and, did the United States by international usage, and with particular reference to the United Nations Charter, have the right to respond to his appeal?

According to the Lebanese constitution, the President of the Republic—in addition to his legislative powers which are numerous—is the Chief Executive. He is responsible for the execution of the laws, for the defense of the country against aggression, and for internal security. All the executive departments are subordinate and responsible to him (and in certain respects to the Chamber), and are designed to help him in the performance of his duties.

In addition, article 52 (as amended in 1943) of the Lebanese constitution explicitly authorizes the President of the Republic to negotiate and conclude treaties and executive agreements which are not binding on Lebanon for more than one year. No ratification by the Chamber of Deputies is required to make such agreements binding on Lebanon. The President is further authorized to withhold knowledge of such agreements from the Chamber as long as he believes that the "interests of the country and the security of the state" demand it. According to article 52, as amended, the only treaties and agreements which require ratification by the Chamber to make them binding are treaties of commerce and trade, treaties which contain provisions "relating to the treasury of the state," and all treaties and agreements which cannot be dissolved from year to year.

Since President Sham'ūn was responsible for the defense of the country, and since his request for and acceptance of United States military assistance was in the nature of an executive agreement not binding on Lebanon for more than one year (the American government explicitly stated on many occasions, that United States troops would withdraw whenever requested to do so by the Lebanese government), and since it did not involve the treasury of the state, then President Sham'ūn was clearly within his constitutional right to request and accept such assistance and to withhold such information from the Chamber. It can perhaps be argued—on the basis of one's personal judgment—that President Sham'ūn acted unwisely, that he acted in bad faith, but it cannot be claimed that he acted in violation of the constitution.

It may be argued that, granted Sham'ūn was within his constitutional rights, yet on such a vitally important step, he should have consulted the Chamber of Deputies. Under normal circumstances, this argument would be valid indeed. However, under the conditions existing in Lebanon at that time, it would have been impractical and probably unwise to do so. For one thing, it would have been extremely difficult—and probably impossible—to convene the Chamber on such short notice, particularly since several of its members were not in Beirut. Second, some deputies were not only in the opposition, but at that time were leading opposition forces against government troops. Warrants had been issued for their arrest, though not executed. It would have been a contradiction in terms—and indeed a spectacle—for the government to "consult and inform" persons whom it called rebels and outlaws and for whom it had issued arrest warrants. Third, and probably most important of all, was the factor of military security. Had the Chamber (composed then of 66 persons) been informed, the news would, without doubt, have leaked out within minutes. This in turn would have represented possible danger to the security of United States forces, particularly since the international political climate was extremely tense.

In the above connection, it is of interest to go one step further, and speculate on the possible outcome had the Chamber been consulted. It will be recalled that the 1957 elections brought in a Chamber composed mostly of government and, in particular, Sham'ūn supporters. If this is true—and no one challenges the fact—then it follows that the Chamber would have approved the request, had it been consulted. This speculation is supported further by material evidence after the fact. We have mentioned that Mr. 'Usayrān, then President of the Chamber, after American troops landed, sent several telegrams protesting in essence that President Sham'ūn had no authority to make the request and that American troops were in the country illegally. It was reported that 20 deputies supported him, and that 25 deputies signed a petition requesting an immediate meeting of the Chamber to consider the American landings.[20] Up till then 'Usayrān had been regarded more or less as a Sham'ūn supporter. Thus 'Usayrān and the 20 deputies who supported him probably represented the maximum possible shift in political alignment in the Chamber. But to be on the safe side, let us add nine more and assume that the total of those opposed was thirty. This would leave 36 in favor. Since voting in the Chamber is by absolute majority (i. e., 34 votes were needed in this case), then Sham'ūn's request would have been approved with two votes to spare.

Both the Lebanese and United States governments justified the landing of American troops on the basis of the inherent right of states to defend themselves individually and collectively against aggression, as provided for by article 51 of the United Nations Charter. Both stated that there was "indirect aggression from without," and that American troops would be withdrawn if and when the United Nations took effective action to safeguard the territorial integrity and independence of Lebanon. 'Azqūl, the Lebanese representative, stated in the Security Council on July 15, with respect to this point:[21]

> In the face of the danger which threatens the independence of Lebanon and to maintain international peace and security in the Middle East, pending the fulfillment of the action which it requests the Security Council to take, the Government of Lebanon has decided to implement Article 51 of the Charter of the United Nations which recognizes the right of self-defense, individual or collective, and it has requested the direct assistance of friendly countries.
>
> It is understood that this assistance is to be temporary and that it will continue only until the entry into force of the action which we request the Council to take. As soon as this action takes effect or is inaugurated, the forces of friendly countries who will have sent troops to Lebanon will immediately have to evacuate our territory.

In his statement before the Security Council on the same day, Henry Cabot Lodge, the United States representative, said in part:[22]

> Now we confront here a situation involving outside involvement in an internal revolt against the authorities of the legitimate Government of Lebanon. Under these conditions a request from the Government of Lebanon to another member of the United Nations to come to its assistance is entirely consistent with the provisions and purposes of the United Nations Charter. In this situation, therefore, we are proceeding

> in accordance with the traditional rules of international law, none of which in any way inhibit action of the character which the United States is undertaking in Lebanon. The United States is acting pursuant to what the United Nations Charter regards as an inherent right—the right of all nations to work together to preserve their independence . . . Let me emphasize again what I have said before, that these forces will remain there only until the United Nations itself is able to assume the necessary responsibilities to insure the continued independence of Lebanon.

Three questions arise in this respect: (1) did the Security Council recognize the existence of "indirect aggression" in Lebanon; (2) does indirect aggression come within the preview of Article 51 of the Charter and (3) did the Lebanese and United States governments have the right to take such action while the Security Council was seized with the Question?

As to the first question, it will be recalled that when the Lebanese case came before the Security Council in June, the members were divided — some supporting, some opposing, Lebanon's contention. The division took place on the basis of East-West power politics, rather than on the basis of facts. Finally, as a measure of the least common agreement, the Security Council adopted the Swedish resolution of June 11, which avoided the whole issue of aggression entirely. In fact, the Security Council was incapable of reaching such a conclusion because of the veto. For instance, if we assume for the sake of argument that ten members (out of eleven) of the Council genuinely believed that there was aggression and voted accordingly, there is not the slightest doubt that such a resolution would have been vetoed by the Soviet Union. Thus, officially, the Security Council reached no such conclusion. But this is immaterial to the case, since it is incapable of doing so, or taking any action whatsoever, unless there is complete agreement of views among the five permanent members. Very seldom indeed has the Soviet Union been in agreement with the Western Powers in the Security Council, and it never felt inhibited from vetoing a resolution whenever it felt inclined so to do, as has been demonstrated on some ninety-odd occasions.

As to the second question, Article 51 mentions the term "aggression" only. It does not specify the type of aggression—direct or indirect—that would apply. Thus the absence of any quantitative or qualitative adjective to the term makes it both all-inclusive and obviously leaves it up to the states vitally concerned to decide whether there is or is not aggression against them and to seek and provide help for defense. Since the United Nations is not a supra-national state and has no armed force, and since we live in a world of national states where "sovereignty," "territorial integrity" and "independence" are the by-words of political life, then it follows that the decision of aggression—any aggression, must rest with the states directly concerned—unless and until the United Nations itself takes satisfactory action for their defense.

Article 51 has, since the adoption of the Charter, been supplemented by the 1949 "Essentials of Peace" and the 1950 "Peace Through Deeds" resolutions of the General Assembly, which condemn indirect aggression and make it the concern of the United Nations. The "Peace Through Deeds" resolution states in part:

> Condemning the intervention of a State in the internal affairs of another State for the purpose of changing its legally established government by the threat or use of force,
>
> 1. Solemnly reaffirms that, whatever the weapons used, any aggression, whether committed openly, or by fomenting civil strife in the interest of a foreign Power, or otherwise, is the gravest of all crimes against peace and security throughout the world;
> 2. Determines that for the realization of lasting peace and security it is indispensable:
>   (1) That prompt united action be taken to meet aggression whenever it arises. . . .

As to the third question, it is true that the Security Council was seized with the Lebanese case. However, the resolution of June 11 which created the Observation Group represented the maximum limits to which the Security Council would go in helping Lebanon. Even the comparatively mild Japanese draft resolution was vetoed by the Soviet Union on July 22. It follows, since the Security Council was unwilling or unable to afford Lebanon aid beyond that point, and since Lebanon, rightly or wrongly, believed that its independence was in grave and imminent jeopardy, and that the existing UN help was insufficient, then, clearly, it was the inherent right of Lebanon to seek aid elsewhere, and for the United States to provide it, for the purposes of defense against aggression.

The Soviet Union accused the United States of sending its troops to Lebanon to suppress the local population and to commit aggression against the Arab countries. Even if one accepts Soviet diatribes at their face value and assumes, by stretch of the imagination, that they were made in good faith, the fact remains that not only did Lebanese citizens not suffer a single injury as a result of United States military action, but also that United States troops went to extreme lengths to insure that they would not influence the course of internal events in Lebanon, and to establish friendly relations with the local population. As for aggression against the Arab countries, it is a matter of historical record that no such thing took place, and that United States troops left Lebanon of their own free will, immediately after their presence was no longer necessary.

In conclusion, it is clearly evident that President Sham'ūn was within his constitutional rights to request US assistance; and that both the Lebanese and United States governments, by international usage and with particular reference to the UN Charter, had the inherent right to seek, accept, and provide military assistance to each other for defense purposes.

* * *

The motivations of the United States in sending its troops to Lebanon were complex and numerous. They may be divided into three categories: factors which related to Lebanon itself, factors which relate to the Middle East as a whole, and factors which relate to the East-West conflict. These factors were inter-related and complementary. Their breakdown here is intended only for purposes of identification.

1. With respect to Lebanon itself, part of the motivation stems from the national character of the American people—their instinctive sympathy for the weak, their conceptions of political morality, and their political experience, particularly during the colonial period of America. The "moral theme" is found throughout the political history of the United States, and together with sympathy for the weak, has had a great influence on the course of American foreign policy. These two factors explain in part the dispatch of American troops to Lebanon in 1958, and go a long way in explaining the position of the United States in 1956 with regard to the Suez War—a position which bewildered and seemed incomprehensible to its allies, Britain and France. In the American mind the two positions were identical.

2. Of all the Middle Eastern countries, Lebanon has had the longest history of continuous friendly association with the United States. Since the 19th century, Lebanon had held a special sentimental position in America. Since 1950 this association has become even closer. Lebanon became the regional center of American business; it received United States economic and military assistance and, in 1957, it accepted the Eisenhower Doctrine.

3. The United States was sincerely convinced that men, arms and money were flowing into Lebanon from Syria in considerable quantities[23] and that this inflow, together with UAR broadcasts, were in

part responsible for the continuation of the civil strife and for aggravating it.

4. It was apparently hoped that the mere presence of United States troops—in contradistinction to the presence of United Nations Observers who had no police powers, would assure all, and particularly those who had such fears, that the independence of Lebanon was no longer in danger and, together with political mediation, calm the tense political atmosphere in the country, save the face of the leaders with uncompromising positions (foreign troops can always be blamed), and bring the various factions into closer positions. In this, the United States was indeed highly successful.

5. The Lebanese government was the only Arab state in the Eastern Mediterranean which openly and without reservation accepted the Eisenhower Doctrine. Although the Doctrine obligates the United States to defend Lebanon only in case of overt communist aggression, the friendly relations between the two governments imposed on the United States at least an implicit commitment and a moral obligation to support and defend Lebanon, if the latter believed its security to be in danger.

In addition to the factors which relate to Lebanon as such, there were others which concerned the entire region, three of which are listed below:

1. Between 1945 and 1958, the United States developed extensive political relations with many countries in the area. These involved explicit and implicit political and military alliances. If the United States had not honored its commitment to Lebanon, implied in the Eisenhower Doctrine, then no country in the area with whom the United States is implicitly or explicitly in alliance could any longer feel secure, or be reasonably sure that the United States would come to its support in time of actual need. This could eventually lead to the weakening and possible destruction of the entire political and military position of the United States in the area.

The United States was subjected to intensive pressure for intervention by Pakistan, Turkey, Iran, Iraq and Jordan. In particular, the last two named believed the Lebanese crisis to have been essentially instigated by the UAR, regarded the possible success of the opposition in Lebanon as a threat to their own security and an encouragement for the further spread of radical and subversive movements in the area.[24] The United States could not but give the views of these states some consideration, since, *de facto,* or by solemn obligation, they were their allies.

3. The Iraqi revolt of July 14 was certainly the incident which

brought all other considerations into focus and induced the American government to respond to Sham'ūn's request. The American government was shocked not only because of the downfall of a friendly government, but also because of the brutal manner in which the members of the royal family and some ministers were killed and their bodies dragged through the streets of Baghdad and dismembered. There are very strong indications that, had the Iraqi revolt not taken place, the United States would not have dispatched its troops to Lebanon.

The reaction to the Iraqi revolt must be considered within the context of the Middle East political environment. Since 1956, the Arab countries have been in a constant state of turmoil. Shooting on the Arab-Israeli borders was (and still is) almost a daily occurrence. Plots and counterplots to overthrow established governments, accompanied by conspiracy trials, became the general pattern in Syria, Jordan, Iraq, Egypt, Saudi Arabia, the Sudan and Tunisia. Closing and opening the border between Syria and Jordan, and between Syria and Lebanon, developed into a virtual game. Syria itself was saved from a communist takeover by a union with Egypt, and the Lebanese were murdering each other.

In addition, there was considerable unrest in the Persian Gulf: disputes and shooting over Muscat and Oman, the Buraimi Oasis, and the Aden Proctectorate. It seemed as if the entire area was drifting into a state of anarchy.

Thus, when the Iraqi revolt occurred, no one knew who was behind it or whether it would overflow into neighboring countries and possibly generate a local or a world war. It will be recalled that, during the 14th and 15th of July, very little news, and most of that rumor, came out of Baghdad. The dispatch of American troops, in addition to serving the local needs of Lebanon itself, was also designed to serve two other regional purposes: (1) to enable the United States to be prepared to meet all eventualities and contingencies—including war; (2) to help calm the atmosphere if the circumstances allowed and (3) to allay the fears of those states who felt that their security was in jeopardy. This was particularly the case with Iran and Jordan.

Finally, as a factor which doubtless played an important part in the decision to dispatch United States troops related to the East-West cold war and the concerted Russian-Communist attempt to penetrate the area. Between 1948 and 1958, the United States, and the West in general, lost ground in the area at an ever increasing momentum, particularly among the Arab states. Conversely, the Soviet Union began to gain—gradually at first, but increasingly so after the death of Stalin. The first major breakthrough was the Egyptian arms deal in 1955. From that time on the Middle East became a major target area for the Soviet Union. The Soviet Union not only posed—and became accepted—as a friend of the Arabs, but also supported them in their numerous quarrels with the West—including the sending of an ultimatum to Britain and France in the Suez crisis, and extended economic and technical assistance "with no strings attached" to those countries among them which had "liberated" themselves from the West. Not only did Soviet influence vastly increase in the area, but communist parties also flourished and developed to become a major source of unrest and subversion in the area. By 1958, within the span of three years, the communist party, financially supported and directed by Moscow, became the second strongest party in the Arab world, with the Ba'thists—the Pan-Arab socialists—holding first place. Until 1958, the protestations of the West to the Arabs that the seemingly altruistic friendship of the Soviet Union was only a mirage, not only went unheeded, but was also met with derision and contempt.

By early 1958, the Soviet Union was insisting that the West recognize it as a Middle Eastern Power. When the Lebanese crisis began, it commenced a vicious campaign against the Lebanese government, and local communists throughout the Arab world were active —although uninvited and undesirable allies of the opposition. Even before American troops were sent, the Soviet Union accused the United States of intending to "invade" Lebanon and enslave the Arab people. Using the same tactics of the Suez crisis, it threatened the United States with war.

In this respect, therefore, the dispatch of US troops had three objectives: (1) to serve notice on the Soviet Union that the United States is willing to go to war to defend the Middle East if this became necessary; (2) to "call the Russian bluff"; and (3) to demonstrate to the Arabs conclusively that the Soviet Union would not go to war to defend them, and that its threats were intended only to win it friends among them. To be sure, in view of the Soviet threats, this involved a great risk, but in army jargon, it was a "calculated risk," for both the Pentagon and the State Department were reasonably certain that Soviet threats were what they proved to be—threats for propaganda purposes.

* * *

The American commitment in Lebanon was unique in several respects:

1. Except once during the heyday of the Barbary pirates, this was

the first time the United States had taken unilateral military action in the area. This reflected the increasing involvement of the United States in the Middle East, and the eminent position which the Middle East had assumed in US foreign policy.

2. It was the first time in modern history that foreign troops entered a country in the Middle East under war conditions but employed no force whatever, and made no attempt either to perpetuate an existing régime or effect internal political changes in their favor.

3. It was the first time that foreign troops entered Lebanon and withdrew not only voluntarily but promptly. To be sure, there was some pressure in the United Nations, but it should be noted that no resolution to that effect was made; and second, that the United States declared repeatedly that its troops would leave Lebanon immediately either at the request of the Lebanese government, or when their presence was no longer necessary. These declarations were honored without any procrastination.

The American involvement in Lebanon was a good example of a limited war to achieve political objectives. In the case of Lebanon, the presence of American troops, without question, helped in calming the tense political climate, and together with political mediation, in the solution of the crisis on a "no victor, no vanquished" basis. In addition, it allayed the fears of those who believed that the independence of Lebanon was in immediate danger.

In all probability, with respect to Lebanon, the most lasting effect of the American involvement was in the sphere of its effect on the Christians, and particularly the Maronites. Their political and cultural thinking is still dominated to a considerable degree by the Christian versus Muslim theme, and by reliance on the "Christian West" for protection. It was therefore not surprising that in order to exploit this mentality Sham'ūn, the Arab nationalist of former years, turned into the "Christian" leader of 1958 and made desperate efforts to give the crisis the coloration of a Christian-Muslim conflict.

When American troops landed, the majority of the Maronites at first interpreted the action as another Christian incursion to protect them. Both they and Sham'ūn were soon to be disillusioned. American troops completely avoided involvement in the internal conflict, and the American government did not support one faction against another. For the first time, the Maronites came to the realization that they can no longer depend on foreign protection, Christian or otherwise; that the era of foreign protection is irrevocably past. Towards the end, the initial positions were reversed. The Maronites came to resent American troops, while the opposition began to display some friendliness towards them.

With respect to the Middle East, the United States was thus able to demonstrate to a friendly government in the area that it would come to their aid in time of need; and to the Arabs, that Russian threats on their behalf were intended, not for implementation, but for propaganda. Conversely, the exemplary conduct of US troops in Lebanon and the extreme restraint with which the United States government used its commanding position in the country, were a demonstration of the falsity of Soviet charges against the United States, and a glaring contrast to the conduct of Soviet troops and the Soviet government under similar circumstances.

With respect to the Soviet Union, the American government was thus able to serve notice on the Soviets, in no uncertain terms, that it is willing to go to war to defend the Middle East.

NOTES

1. This writer was informed by a highly authoritative Western source, who asked that his name be withheld, that President Sham'ūn made two such requests to the American Ambassador in Beirut, McClintock. The first request was made during a meeting between the two at the Presidential Palace. Sham'ūn wrote out the request, but after a lengthy discussion, McClintock was able to persuade him to tear it up. The second request was verbal. Sham'ūn sent a trusted emissary with the communication. Mr. McClintock replied that in order for him to be able to communicate such an important message to his government, he would have to have the request in writing. The emissary departed but did not return.

The above is in addition to the efforts of Dr. Charles Malik in Washington, who exerted every influence in favor of such action.

2. *Mideast Mirror,* May 18, 1958, pp. 21-22.

3. *Ibid.,* p. 23, and May 25, 1958, p. 23.

4. *Ibid.,* July 6, 1958, p. 15.

5. For texts, see *US Dept. of State Bulletin,* June 9, 1958, pp. 945, 947-48; July 7, 1958, p. 8; July 21, 1958, pp. 104-106.

6. *UN Doc. S/PV. 824,* June 10, 1958, p. 118.

7. *US Dept. of State Bulletin,* July 21, 1958, p. 105.

8. *Mideast Mirror,* July 20, 1958, pp. 19-20.

9. Karāmī, *op. cit.,* p. 285.

10. Charles Thayer, *Diplomat,* New York: Harper, 1959, p. 33.

11. For a version somewhat different in the details of the whole incident, see Karāmī, *op. cit.,* p. 286.

12. *Mideast Mirror,* July 20, 1958, p. 15.

13. For full text, see Karāmī, *op. cit.,* pp. 290-291.

14. *Mideast Mirror,* July 20, 1958, p. 17.

15. When Dr. Malik returned to New York for the meeting of the General Assembly in August, he took with him a plan—to be proposed to the Assembly—calling for the neutralization of Lebanon to be guaranteed by the United Nations. See *Mideast Mirror,* August 17, 1958, p. 4.

16. *Ibid.,* August 3, 1958, p. 7.

17. The irony is that most members of the opposition had been, and still are today, close friends of the United States.

18. *Mideast Mirror,* August 3, 1958, p. 16 and *Ibid.,* August 10, 1958, p. 24.

19. *Ibid.,* August 31, 1958, p. 4.

20. Thirty-four signatures were required to make the petition officially effective.

21. *UN Doc. S/PV. 827,* July 15, 1958, pp. 43-45.

22. *US State Department Bulletin,* August 4, 1958, pp. 187-88. See also President Eisenhower's message to Congress of July 15, *Ibid.,* pp. 182-84.

23. See the examples cited by Mr. Lodge, the US representative, before the Security Council on July 16. *Ibid.,* August 4, 1958, p. 192.

24. State documents and State expenditure vouchers (the authenticity of which has not been challenged) revealed at the People's Court in Baghdad, show that before and during the crisis, both Iraq and Jordan supplied Sham'ūn and the PPS with arms and money, and that they were seriously considering military intervention in Lebanon in support of the Sham'ūn government.

CHAPTER VIII

Intervention or Internal Revolt?

THE FULL STORY of the Lebanese crisis will probably not be known for many years to come. It is buried in the secret files of the foreign offices and defense ministries of Lebanon, the United Arab Republic, the Soviet Union, the United States, the United Kingdom, France and other governments, such as those of the Baghdad Pact countries. Thus the discussion of this question at this time has obvious limitations. All the facts—and perhaps the most important facts—are not available. The best that can be done here is the gathering and reconstruction of external evidence, the evaluation of public documents and the piecing together of statements made by individuals who were involved in the crisis.

The discussion below will be divided into three main parts: (1) complaints of the opposition; (2) complaints of the Lebanese government and (3) evaluation of the UNOGIL reports.

Complaints of the Opposition

The opposition claimed that the Lebanese crisis was an internal affair due to internal causes and one supported entirely by internal forces. They further declared that Lebanon's independence was not the issue at stake, and that there was no intention of their joining the UAR. This declaration was made in a letter by Ṣā'ib Salām to the American Ambassador in Beirut on May 15, 1958, and in numerous statements before and after that date by the United National Front and various other opposition groups. The opposition made two principal complaints of its own: (1) that the government was arming its supporters among the Maronites, the PPS and others; (2) that in addition to legal military aid the government was receiving from the United States, it was also receiving secret and illegal military and financial aid from Britain, Turkey and Iraq, and in particular the last named.

With regard to the PPS, the evidence is overwhelming that the opposition's claim was true. It should be noted that the PPS was an unlicensed political organization in Lebanon. And yet, it openly had offices in Beirut, Tripoli, Sidon, Tyre, Zaḥlah, Ba'lbak, and other towns, and published its own newspaper. Its leader then, As'ad al-Ashqar, became a member of parliament as a government candidate in the 1957 elections. This was the first time that the PPS had a representative in parliament. The party openly operated several training camps near the Syrian border. With no apparent reason given, nine of its members who had been serving life sentences (eight since 1949 and one since 1950) were pardoned and released on September 11, 1957. Finally, one of the last acts of the Sham'ūn administration was to legalize the party. On September 18, 1958, just three days before he was due to retire from office, the PPS was granted a license to operate. It is rather difficult to explain how an unlicensed party could conduct all these activities so openly, and be on such friendly terms with the leaders of the government unless the assumption is that some form of collaboration existed between the two. This assumption is further reinforced by the fact that during the crisis it was found that the party had been operating a radio transmitter (demolished by opposition forces) at the village of Nabi 'Uthmān, only a few miles from the Syrian border. The transmitter had been broadcasting to Syria, as the *Voice of Reform,* attacking Syrian and Egyptian leaders. Since the transmitter was located near a gendarmerie post, one can hardly escape the conclusion that the Lebanese government knew of its existence.

As to active cooperation with the government, sources close and friendly to the opposition claim that Sham'ūn, on May 12, 1958, told three of his close associates—Sāmī al-Ṣulḥ, Pierre Eddé and Albert Mukhaybar, that:

> he depends on about 4,700 armed PPS members: 1,500 in Tripoli; 2,000 in the Biqā'; 1,000 in the south, and 200 in the Shūf area; and that he believed that this number in addition to the security forces will be sufficient to quell any disturbances in any area. Particularly, in view of the fact that they [i.e. the PPS] are militarily well-trained, and receive respectable salaries, in addition to the large sums which their leaders have been receiving since 1955 from the department of propaganda and publication of the Baghdad Pact.[1]

But even if we ignore statements of opposition sources, collaboration between the PPS and government security forces (but not the army) is clearly evident from the daily files of Western news agencies during the months of May, June and July, 1958, which reported various operations of government forces in conjunction with PPS and other irregulars. In the Shūf area, for instance, they operated along with other irregulars under Na'īm Mughabghab,[2] and with government regulars against Kamāl Junblāṭ's forces.

It is true that the PPS is a para-military organization, and that its members were fairly well-armed long before the crisis. However, there is sufficient evidence to show that the government, either directly or indirectly, was also supplying them with the necessary equipment. First, since PPS members were fighting side by side with government forces, it is therefore not unreasonable to assume that theye were given sufficient arms to fight with. Second, there is factual evidence: Captain ʿAbd al-Karīm Zayn of the gendarmerie resigned and issued a statement on May 27, 1958 to the effect that he had resigned in protest because he was an eye witness to government distribution of arms to loyalist civilians from its depots. Finally, on May 25, the government issued a decree creating a militia of national volunteers "without pay." Although it was officially stated that the volunteers could be used only to guard and protect public establishments such as waterworks, electricity plants, bridges and other public places vulnerable to dynamiters and bomb-throwers, it was more probable that the decree was an attempt on the part of the government to give legal character to the distribution of arms among its followers such as the PPS, the Phalanges, and other civilians. In addition to the opposition, the decree was denounced by the religious head of the various communities. On May 29, the Mufti of Lebanon, Shaykh ʿAlāyā; Shaykh ʿAql Muḥammad Abū Shaqrā of the Druze and Shaykh al-Taqī al-Sadīq of the Shiʿa sent a joint letter to General Shihāb, the Army Commander, in which it was stated that persistence in this course of action would endanger the country. The arming of one section of the population would prompt others to appeal to foreign countries for volunteers to defend themselves and their freedom. On May 27, the Maronite Patriarch denounced the decree in even stronger terms.

In addition to the above, at the public trials in Baghdad after the revolution of July 14, state documents and expenditure vouchers were revealed showing that the PPS had, since 1955, been receiving funds and arms from the Iraqi government.

The question arises, why did the PPS collaborate with the Lebanese government since, according to its doctrine, it was against the concept of an independent Lebanon? The answer lies in the realm of practical politics. The party was suppressed in Syria and a large number of its leaders were under death sentence there, while many others were languishing in Syrian prisons. The party was (and still is) also outlawed in all other Arab countries, leaving Lebanon as its last refuge. Hence, if Lebanon joined the UAR in some form of union or federation, or was controlled by a government favorable to the UAR, this last refuge would disappear; its leading members would presumably be handed over to the Syrian authorities and the party and its activities would be suppressed in Lebanon. The collaboration of the PPS with the Lebanese government was not a question of principle but rather, in a real sense, a matter of life or death.

The opposition also claimed that the government was secretly receiving financial aid and military equipment from various sources including Turkey, Iraq, Britain and even Jordan. A United National Front press statement (undated, mimeographed in English) gives the following illustrations of arms shipments:

(a) A certain Mr. Arman has in the last few weeks sent by air several cargoes of arms to Beirut from Zurich in the name of Mr. Camille Chamoun.

(b) A cargo of arms arrived in Beirut on the 11th of August, 1958 in the name of Mr. Nicolas Rizkallah, the Administrator of Beirut.

(c) The following arms shipments were handed over to the gendarmerie forces at the International Airport of Beirut:

Date	*No. of Boxes*	*Weight in Kgs.*
16/5/58	130	7,000
16/5/58	350	7,000
16/5/58	732	14,000
18/5/58	150	——
23/5/58	350	8,000
24/5/58	400	16,000
27/5/58	135	615
14/6/58	15	1,300
21/6/58	48	1,300

(d) 339 boxes containing 16,611 pounds of cartridges, shipped from the United Kingdom on 11/7/58 to the British military attaché in Beirut.[3]

(e) Several shipments of arms from the former Iraqi government reached Beirut by air. The Iraqi planes carrying the arms declared themselves to be enroute to Libya and asked permission to land in Beirut in transit. The planes were unloaded at night and in secrecy by civilian supporters of Mr. Camille Chamoun. The arms were then transported to the Presidential palace where they were distributed generally to the right-wing Syrian Party and the Lebanese Phalangists. One such load of arms arrived on the 14th of June, 1958, and consisted of 150 rifles, 150 sub-machine guns and 20 bren guns. On most occasions, the Popular Syrian's liaison officers with the Presidential Palace and the Iraqi Embassy in Beirut were Dr. Sami Khoury and Mr. Salameh Issa.

In addition to the above, documents and official receipts revealed at the public trials in Baghdad after the revolution showed that President Sham'ūn and several of his associates had been receiving extensive sums of money from the Iraqi government.

Since there is no material evidence (except statements and allegations) the opposition's claim that the Lebanese government was receiving secret financial and military aid, is at best inconclusive. The only substantial evidence available in this respect is the documents revealed at the Baghdad trials and the testimony of the accused there.

The Lebanese Case

In its complaint to the Security Council, the Lebanese government accused the UAR of: (1) massive intervention in the affairs of Lebanon, and (2) the fact that this intervention aimed at undermining and did, in fact, threaten the independence of Lebanon.

Essentially, Lebanon alleged that intervention took the following forms:

(a) press and radio attacks by the UAR

(b) supply of arms "on a large scale" to subversive elements in Lebanon (i.e. the opposition)

(c) participation of UAR nationals in subversive and terrorist activities in Lebanon

(d) participation of UAR governmental elements in subversive and terrorist activities and in directing the rebellion in Lebanon.[4]

We shall first examine each of the alleged causes of intervention and then discuss the second part of the complaint, namely, that the alleged intervention aimed at undermining the independence of Lebanon.

Press and Radio Attacks

A review of the Egyptian and Syrian press and *Radio Cairo,* the *Voice of the Arabs,* and *Radio Damascus,* conclusively support the allegations of the Lebanese government in this respect (see Appendix III).

It should be noted that most of the quotations in Appendix III are taken from newspaper editorials. As such, the UAR government might disclaim (as it did) responsibility for them. Such an argument, however, is not valid for two reasons: (1) all the above press quotations were broadcast over the state-controlled radio stations in "reviews of the press" and (2) the press in the UAR, as in all Arab countries with the exception of Lebanon, is controlled. Even in Lebanon, the Utopian freedom of the press, which Charles Malik tried to paint before the Security Council, was a little less than the truth. Nevertheless, in essence, he was right. In Lebanon, some 25 newspapers and magazines took the Egyptian viewpoint, and attacked the policies of their government.[5] In contrast from early 1957 until the end of the crisis in late 1958, not a single Egyptian newspaper of any considerable circulation had anything good to say about the Lebanese government. Such 100 per cent unanimity, to say the least, is rather suspicious. In his presentation of the Lebanese case at the Security Council, Dr. Malik gave a number of illustrations from UAR press and radio attacks.[6]

The UAR representative, 'Umār Lutfī, in addition to showing that many of Dr. Malik's quotations were in actual fact reports from news agencies and not editorial comments, countercharged that Lebanese papers also attacked leaders of the United Arab Republic.[7] In reply, Dr. Malik made the following remarks:

> . . . It may well be true that in some instances where I quoted from Egyptian and Syrian newspapers, they were themselves printing material that originated first in Lebanon. That may well be true, but what is significant is that they print only that kind of material, they print no other kind of material. That is the most significant thing . . . It is the selectivity of the Egyptian press, from whatever emanates from Lebanon, which is most significant. That selectivity can be shown to have taken only those parts of the news which comes out from Lebanon that inflames and encourages and foments rebellion and anti-government activity in Lebanon. That seems to me to be most significant.
>
> The second point is this: the representative of the United Arab Republic spoke about our press having published certain material to which he takes exception. That may well be. Again, we have a press that criticizes not only Egypt and Syria, but pre-eminently ourselves. But now—and this is the significant thing—we have a press in Lebanon which defends the point of view of Egypt. They have nothing like that in Egypt. In fact, when we want to publish an official governmental denial, it is never allowed to appear in Egyptian papers. We have done that many times. We have sent in official governmental denials to our Embassy in Cairo and asked them to have them published in the Egyptian press, and they never appeared there. Whereas every morning you can find in at least six newspapers in Beirut—and we like that and welcome it—articles and accounts defending the Egyptian point of view and presenting the Egyptian point of view . . . In fact, I will make a fair bet with my friend, Mr. Lutfi, a very fair bet. If you can produce one sentence during the last year, from any paper in Egypt or Syria, that is appreciative of or kind to the Government of Lebanon—one sentence—I will withdraw this complaint. This is a fair bet.

Supply of Arms

In his presentation of the Lebanese case, Dr. Malik cited various instances of supply of arms from the UAR—allegedly by UAR authorities. He concluded his recital with the following statement:

> There are several thousand armed men engaged in subversive activities in Lebanon today. Most of these men operate near the Syrian borders in the north of Lebanon, in the Bekaa Valley and in the south. We have no doubt at all, from all the evidence that we have gathered, that all the arms

> that these men use were supplied from Syria. I have given above only a limited selection of the evidence in our possession that there is a considerable flow or arms coming from across our borders from Syria. The Government of Lebanon therefore believes that all men engaged in subversive activities in Lebanon today are supplied with arms from the United Arab Republic.

The evidence presented by Dr. Malik, and other evidence revealed before and after, is at best somewhat inconclusive. It only establishes the fact that there was a substantial flow of arms from Syria into Lebanon. It does not follow from this that the UAR authorities, themselves, were involved—although this may have been the case. Furthermore, the above statement by Dr. Malik that "all men engaged in subversive activities . . . are supplied with arms from the UAR" was so patently untrue that it is suprising that Dr. Malik should make it at all. The evidence is inconclusive for the following reasons:

The Lebanese, particularly the mountain people among them, do carry arms most of the time.

It is a well-known fact that Beirut is a smuggler's paradise. It is a smuggling center and a transit route for virtually any commodity that cannot be obtained or transferred from one country to another by legal means—gold, narcotics, arms, currency, and so on, down the line. For instance, on December 6, 1957, 1000 revolvers were smuggled in from Italy by a "member of an Arab ruling family." Three days later, December 9, an Italian with a diplomatic passport was caught smuggling 280 pistols from the same country.[8] In other words, smuggling for purely monetary gain has been going on for a long time in Lebanon.

With regard to Egypt and Syria, three facts should be taken into account:

(a) During the Sinai campaign in 1956, the Israelis captured a large quantity of Egyptian arms and ammunition. Some of these eventually found their way to the smugglers' markets of the Middle East. This is confirmed by a Beirut report from the British-owned Arab News Agency, which reads in part as follows:[9]

> Arms captured by the Israelis in the Sinai campaign last year are helping to pay for Lebanese hashish smoked by Egyptian addicts, it is learned at the Ministry of Interior here.
>
> Some of the captured weapons and ammunition have fallen into the hands of smugglers who barter them for hashish which goes by devious routes to Egypt. This is one feature of the revival of arms smuggling which came to light this week when the authorities announced that within three days they had confiscated 30 automatic rifles, 25 ordinary

military rifles, 15 pistols, and 46,000 rounds of ammunition which had been smuggled into Lebanon from across the Syrian border. Most of the arms bore Egyptian markings. Thirteen suspects have been arrested, including two Syrians and a girl in red trousers who were passengers in a car that was searched after coming in from Syria. The bulk of the arms and ammunition arrived by car, being hidden inside the doors and other parts, but some were seized in houses during a countrywide check. The smuggling gang is believed to number about 25 persons.

Up to 1950 arms smuggling was common in Lebanon, where French and allied forces had, sometimes by design and more often by accident, left large quantities after the second world war. Then there was a lull, and because the demand was so small the smugglers sought other markets, but towards the end of last year arms of various kinds began to pour into Lebanon, some of them in diplomatic bags.

The above report, based on information from the Lebanese Ministry of Interior, hardly suggests the complicity of the Egyptian government.

(b) Syria, particularly in 1957, had gone through one severe crisis after another. During these crises, when it was believed that the security of the state was threatened by external danger, the Syrian government distributed arms to civilians—the so-called popular resistance forces. As is usual in such cases, some of these arms were never returned to the government. For instance, the Syrian government distributed arms among civilians during the Suez War in 1956, and several times during 1957. It is therefore reasonable to conclude that many of these arms found their way to the smugglers' market, or were used by private individuals to fight their own private wars. In addition, it should be noted that the tradition of going about well-armed is as strongly entrenched in Syria as it is in Lebanon.

(c) In Syria, where military service is compulsory, every man who had received military training is required by law to carry an identity card to that effect at all times. Thus a man who had been released from service, say in 1955, would still be carrying such a card in 1959—which, however, would give neither the date of his enlistment, nor the date of his discharge.

Of course, the fact that the evidence is inconclusive does not in itself preclude the possibility that the UAR authorities did in fact supply arms to opposition forces. The allegation in itself is of such a nature as to make the production of concrete physical evidence that could stand in a court of law next to impossible. It can be suggestive, as the evidence revealed was, but not conclusive.

Information gathered by this writer from various sources in Lebanon, the evidence presented at the United Nations and news reports, would seem to lead to the following conclusions:

1. Between 1957 and 1958, considerable quantities of arms and ammunition were smuggled from Syria into Lebanon—although not to the extent claimed by the Lebanese government. Part of these arms, at least, were brought in by professional smugglers for purely monetary gain.

2. There is some reason to believe that the Syrian authorities may have been involved in the supply of some of these arms to opposition forces in two ways: (a) by premeditated lack of vigilance of their guards and police patrols on the Syrian-Lebanese border, and (b) by directly supplying opposition forces. This conclusion is accepted as fact by virtually everyone in Lebanon, including followers of the opposition. In addition, one opposition leader admitted to this writer receiving some arms from both Syria and the Syrian authorities.

Participation of UAR Nationals

The Lebanese government also accused UAR nationals of participation in subversive activities in Lebanon. Guided by this belief, the authorities deported between the spring of 1957 and May 1958, about 15,000 UAR nationals—most of them Syrians, some of whom had been fairly long-term residents in Lebanon. In May and June of 1958, these deportations reached mass proportions.

In this respect, Lebanese allegations can be divided into two main parts: (1) that Syrians and Palestinians participated in terrorist activities, primarily upon instructions of the Syrian authorities—in particular the Syrian *Deuxième Bureau*; and (2) that Syrians, either on ther own, or on the instructions of the Syrian authorities, crossed the border and joined opposition forces operating in the country side.

With regard to part (1), the Lebanese authorities seemed to imply that most of the bombings and other acts of sabotage and terrorism were conducted by Syrians and Palestinians. Both the Prime Minister, Sāmī al-Ṣulḥ, and the Foreign Minister, Charles Malik, made several press statements to that effect at various times. Hundreds of such persons, it was stated, had been arrested and had "confessed" to the police. Yet of these alleged hundreds, very few were ever brought to trial and of those who were brought to trial, only a comparatively small number were actually convicted by the Lebanese courts. Most of them were Palestinians. For instance, of these hundreds only thirty-eight were brought to trial *en masse* on January 3, 1958, and charged with terrorist activities, distributing subversive literature and sending threatening letters to Lebanese personalities.[10] Thirty-four of these were Palestinians. Some were indirectly accused of being agents of Syrian Intelligence. Of the thirty-eight, the charges against fifteen were dismissed for insufficient evidence, while twenty-three —most of whom were Palestinians, were convicted on February 24, 1958. The sentences ranged from three months to 15 years imprisonment.[11] It is interesting to note that, in support of his arguments, Dr. Malik in his statement before the Security Council on June 6, 1958, could only cite the names of five persons convicted in this mass trial as examples of agents working for Syrian Intelligence.

It should not be concluded from the above discussion that the statements of the Lebanese governments in this connection were completely unfounded. They were, however, exaggerated. It is quite true—and this is open knowledge in Lebanon—that most Syrians and Palestinians living in Lebanon sympathized with the opposition, and many of them probably did participate in demonstrations and carry out acts of sabotage and bombing. This is a far cry from the imputation that all, or nearly all, acts of sabotage and bombings were conducted by Syrians and Palestinians and were to be traced to a planned conspiracy against Lebanon by the Syrian *Deuxième Bureau.* In fact, President Sham'ūn and Dr. Malik developed a virtual obsession about the Syrian Intelligence Service and saw its hand in almost everything that happened to Lebanon.

With regard to part (2), that Syrians crossed the border and joined opposition forces fighting in the countryside, the evidence is fairly conclusive with two reservations. The number of Syrians operating with opposition forces was greatly exaggerated and it is not definite that they were there at the instigation and active approval of the Syrian authorities, though certainly they were there with their tacit approval.

Dr. Malik gave several illustrations in this respect. However, in this case, sufficient evidence is available from opposition sources. We shall take Kamāl Junblāṭ's forces which operated in the Shūf area, and which bore the main brunt of the fighting in the mountains, as an example. The commander of Junblāṭ's forces was Shawqat Shuqayr, retired Commander in Chief of the Syrian Army.

According to Nawwaf Karāmī—who was one of Junblāṭ's lieutenants in the Shūf area, witnessed and knew the details of both the fighting and organization of the forces—Sulṭān Pasha al-Aṭrash, leader of the Druze in Syria, organized a unit of experienced fighters which were called "The Sulṭān Group" *(Majmū'at Sulṭān).* It was commanded by First Lieutenant Ghālib Sayf, with 2nd Lieut. Ḥasan Raslān as second in command. Both were of the Syrian army. The number of men in this group is not given, but from the description, it could not have been composed of less than 500 men. It reached al-Mukhtārah in Lebanon on May 27, 1958.[12]

Two points should be noted about this group: its organization was publicly announced by Sulṭān Pasha al-Aṭrash sometime before May 27, so that the Syrian authorities must have known about it. Second, from the description given, a good number of its men, including the officers, were members of the Syrian army. Finally, one must stretch the imagination to the point of absurdity to believe that a group of some 500 men were publicly organized and were able to march into Lebanon, without the knowledge of, and at least, the tacit approval of the Syrian authorities.

Participation of UAR Government Authorities

Malik also charged that UAR governmental elements participated "in subversive and terrorist activities and in the direction of the rebellion." He gave illustrations of such activities.[13]

It is probable that most of the incidents cited did actually take place, that the details of the circumstances are correct, at least in their essentials, and that the "confessions" obtained were true. However, it should be noted that, except in one case, no convictions by Lebanese courts were mentioned. Moreover, some doubt was thrown on the validity of these confessions by the first and second reports of the United Nations Observation Group in Lebanon. In one instance, the Lebanese Government claimed to have arrested "two Syrian subjects belonging to the Syrian armed forces" who had participated in terrorist activities. When UNOGIL interrogated them, however, it came to the conclusion that "the complicity of these two persons in terrorist activities and their participation in acts of rebellion as members of an organized foreign terrorist group has not been established beyond reasonable doubt."[14] Following the interrogation of the above two prisoners by UNOGIL and the publication of the first report, the Lebanese government refused to allow UNOGIL to investigate such cases.[15]

Evaluation of the UNOGIL Reports

On June 11, 1958, the Security Council adopted a Swedish compromise resolution, which created a United Nations Observation Group in Lebanon (UNOGIL).[16]

The mandate and authority of UNOGIL were fixed by the above resolution. Its function was to observe and report present and future illegal infiltration of personnel and supply of arms or other material across the Lebanese border. It was not to investigate any such past occurrences except as they related to its present duties. It had no authority to stop any such infiltration or supply of arms—merely to observe and report. It had no police powers. Its authority and the smoothness of its operations rested exclusively on the cooperation of the parties concerned, and on the moral authority of the United Nations.

In implementing the resolution, Mr. Hammarskjöld appointed Ex-President Galo Plaza of Ecuador, Mr. Rajeshwar Dayal of India, and Major General Odd Bull of Norway, as the three members of the Group. The Group held its first formal meeting in Beirut on June 19. It elected Mr. Plaza as Chairman and designated General Bull as "Executive Member in charge of military observers."

During its five months of existence, UNOGIL submitted five reports to the Security Council, the first on July 3, and the fifth and last on November 17, 1958.

Generally speaking, the reports were all unfavorable to the contention of Lebanon concerning massive intervention by the UAR. In the first report, after giving a detailed account of its activities and observations, the Group came to the following conclusions:[17]

> The arms seen consisted of mostly a varied assortment of rifles of British, French and Italian makes. Some hand grenades were also seen at various places. Occasionally, opposition elements have been found armed with machine guns. Mines seen near the Baalbek area were of British and French makes. It had not been possible to establish from where these arms were acquired but in this connection the remarks continued in paragraph 11 of this report should also be borne in mind. Nor was it possible to establish if any of the armed men observed had infiltrated from outside; there is little doubt, however, that the vast majority was in any case composed of Lebanese.

In its second report, submitted on July 30, the Observation Group came to the following conclusions:[18]

> The extent of the infiltration of arms which may be taking place has been indicated in the report. It is clear that it cannot be on anything more than a limited scale, and is largely confined to small arms and ammunition. In conditions of civil conflict, when the frontier is practically throughout its length, open and unguarded, some movement of this kind may well be expected.
>
> As regards the question of illegal infiltration of personnel, the nature of the frontier, the existence of traditional tribal and other bonds on both sides of it, the free movement of produce in both directions, are among the factors which must be taken into account in making an evaluation. It must, however, be said that in no case have UN Observers, who have been vigilantly patrolling the opposition-held areas and have frequently observed the armed bands there, been able to detect the presence

of persons who have indubitably entered from across the border for the purpose of fighting.

In one of its concluding paragraphs, the third report, submitted on August 14, stated the following:[19]

> As will be seen from the observations made in the report, the situation in regard to the possible infiltration of personnel and the smuggling of arms from across the border is that, while there may have been a limited importation of arms into some areas prior to the Presidential elections on July 31, any such movement has since markedly diminished. A virtual truce has prevailed since about that time in most of the disturbed areas.

In the fourth report, submitted on September 29, the Observation Group concluded:[20]

> It will be noted from the preceding observations that no cases of infiltration have been detected and that if any infiltration is still taking place, its extent must be regarded as insignificant.

In its fifth and final report, submitted on November 17, the Observation Group came to the following conclusion:[21]

> In view of the absence for some time of any reports of infiltration of personnel or smuggling of arms and of the recent marked improvement in the general security situation in Lebanon, and the relations between Lebanon and its eastern neighbor, the Group has come to the conclusion that its task under the June 11 resolution may now be regarded as completed.

In summation, although the reports did not deny the existence of infiltration of men and the smuggling of arms, they concluded that such infiltration and smuggling were conducted on a comparatively small scale. Moreover, they never established that such activities were sponsored or directed by foreign authorities (i.e., the UAR). On the contrary, they seemed to take the view that such activities were to be expected in times of civil strife, particularly in border areas where members of the same tribe lived on both sides of the frontier. In addition, although this was not stated in so many words, the Observation Group seemed to have come to the conclusion that the rebellion was largely domestic in both origin and leadership.

A close examination of the reports and the circumstances under which the Observation Group operated would seem to indicate, nevertheless, that the conclusions arrived at by UNOGIL were not warranted by the evidence.

We are here concerned with the first three reports, since they cover the really critical period of the crisis and in the operations of UNOGIL—up to the election of a new President on July 31, 1958. Once a new President was elected, a major source of difficulty was removed and the country began to return to normal. Hence, the fourth and fifth reports, covering the period from August 11 to November 14, are essentially irrelevant except to show the expansion of the activities of the Observation Group.

The first report covers the period from June 12 to July 3. By June 26 UNOGIL had 94 military observers, 74 vehicles, two helicopters, and a fully operating radio communications system.[22] By June 30, it had established four observation stations and six sub-stations. The six sub-stations, however, were established only after June 25.[23] Thus, *only during the latter part* of the period covered by the first report was UNOGIL able to establish even a skeleton organization.

During the period, this skeleton organization had to contend with the following:

1. Out of the "total land frontier with Syria, of some 324 kms. in length, only 18, lying on either side of the main Beirut-Damascus road, remained under the control of the Government forces."[24] The rest was held by opposition forces. It should be noted that this was the primary area from which men and arms were supposed to enter Lebanon.

2. On the eastern frontier (i.e., the frontier with Syria), the nature of the terrain and of the road system made virtually impossible the use of motorized surface transport, thus restricting the movement of UNOGIL patrols.

> The eastern frontier runs roughly from north-north-east to south-south-west along the mountainous formations of the Anti-Liban and the Hermon, which attain heights of 2,400 to 2,800 meters, respectively. Main roads of communications on the Lebanese side of this chain of mountains run parallel to it in the Bekaa Valley, the sole exception being the Beirut-Damascus road . . . thus physical accessibility to the border by road is considerably restricted in the area lying between the frontier itself, and the main roads running the length of the Bekaa Valley. This is an area which ranges from approximately 10 to 25 kms. in width.[25]

3. As to the northern and coastal frontiers, the first report stated the following:[26]

> The northern frontier lies in a broad plain. However, access by land from the Lebanese side is by the coastal highway running northeast from Tripoli towards Homs. There are no roads connecting this northern border area with the north Bekaa Valley. Thus, the northern border can be reached only through the area north of Tripoli, an area now under the control of the opposition forces.
>
> The remaining frontier of concern to the Observation Group is the sea coast of some 220 kms., along the full length of which runs a main highway from Harida in the north to Nakoura in the south. It will be seen,

> therefore, that the areas of primary concern to the Observation Group are those where the problems of accessibility are the greatest, both from the standpoint of topography and of obtaining freedom and security of movement.

The Observation Group had no safe and secure access to opposition-held areas—the areas of primary importance through which arms and men were supposed to be entering Lebanon. Free access was not granted to UNOGIL by the opposition until July 15.

UNOGIL patrols and observation posts during this period operated only during daylight hours, a time when the smuggling of arms and infiltration of men would presumably be at a minimum.

In certain cases, UNOGIL observation teams were allowed to visit opposition-held areas to "observe." However, such visits followed negotiations with and the consent of the local opposition leader, during which the time of the visit was set in advance. The observation team would be conducted and shown around by men from the opposition. In other words, the components which would have made such visits meaningful were absent—the elements of surprise and full freedom of movement and access.

It is rather difficult to arrive at any conclusion other than that, because of the lack of adequate number of observers and equipment and because of the extremely difficult circumstances under which it operated, UNOGIL was, during this period, hardly in a position to be able to detect infiltration of men and smuggling of arms, if indeed they were taking place. The first report must be understood as reflecting what the Observation Group was able to see—nothing more. It cannot be interpreted as evidence as to whether smuggling of arms and infiltration of men were actually taking place.

The above is not intended as a criticism of the Observation Group. It should be remembered that the report covered a period of some 20 days only. It is not a simple matter to assemble and organize a staff of some 100 men in addition to clerical personnel and equipment in such a short period of time. Second, since UNOGIL had no police powers, it could enter opposition-held areas only by suffrance and under conditions imposed by opposition forces.

The second report covers the period from July 2 to July 15, 1958. By July 15, the UNOGIL had a total strength of 113 observers including 14 at headquarters in Beirut, and a total of 15 outstations, sub-stations and permanently manned observation posts. Also, up to July 15, 82 missions had been flown in air reconaissance, totalling 150 flying hours.[27]

It was not until the 15th of July that UNOGIL was able to obtain full freedom of access to opposition-held areas. Its activities in this respect remained until then essentially as they were during the period covered by the first report. Second, patrols of the Observation Group, during this period, continued to operate only during daylight hours. The only basic improvements consisted of the addition of 19 observers, the increase of observation stations from 10 to 15, and the increased use of air patrols. Perhaps an intangible should also be added: the increased familiarity of the Observation Group with the problem.

The futile use of air patrols during the night—which under different circumstances would have been of immense value, is graphically illustrated by the following account of night flying over the Akkār plain—typical of many others detailed in the second report:[28]

> Between 2 and 15 July 1958, thirty-nine reconnaissance sorties were flown, sixteen of which were by helicopter. The Akkar area was thus observed on thirty-five occasions, twenty times during the night.
>
> The first air patrols by day revealed only sporadic traffic along the three roads crossing the frontier. At night, the traffic movements observed on the Arida-Tripoli road, as well as the Aziziye-Abde-Tripoli road, were insignificant. However, eight vehicles were observed actually crossing the border into Lebanon at 2000 hours on July 9. The greatest amount of traffic was observed on the Braghite-Halba road. On the nights of July 5-11, 50, 5, 20, 10 and 25 headlights respectively, were seen moving southwards in what appeared to be convoys at various times between 2100 hours and 2400 hours LT (Lebanon Time).
>
> It cannot be assumed that all the existing traffic has been observed by air. The traffic along the above three roads has proved to be heavier at night than during the daytime. A large majority of the vehicles observed were moving southwards and westwards.
>
> It has been observed that after the second night of aerial reconnaissance the lights of vehicles have been switched off or dimmed when an aircraft is in the vicinity. What appeared to be a strong flashing light was observed on a hill-top, presumably to warn the vehicles on the Braghite-Helba road of the approach of aircraft. Up to 6 July, the villages in this area were well illuminated at night. On successive nights, however, aerial observations have established that the villages along this road have been blacked out, except for a few odd lights.

The report then proceeds to speculate in the following manner:[29]

> This may perhaps be a normal reaction since the area has been subject to air attack in the past and even now the government air forces have been attacking the Jabal Tarbol area. The people of the area have complained particularly against strafing and against shelling from the sea by government gun-boats at Abde. The natural reaction of villages on hearing the sound of an aircraft in the air, would be to black out as many

lights as possible. The convoys returning from Syria might well have arranged a system of warning lights for their safety.

> Every effort was made to ascertain on the ground the nature of the traffic seen at night from the air, but since permission to establish permanent stations in the area had not been secured, no direct ground observation of it was possible . . .

It would seem that, had the Observation Group been adequately organized to cope with its task, had these air patrols had ground support which could proceed immediately to the spot and give a final and conclusive answer as to the nature and purpose of these night convoys, all this speculation, of which the above quotation is a typical example, would have been unnecessary. As it turned out, all the night air-patrolling did not give any answer one way or the other.

From the above, the conclusion is inescapable that, during the period covered by the second report, no basic change from the situation existing during the period covered by the first report took place. Similarly, the observations and conclusions of the second report cannot be regarded as more conclusive than those of the first report.

The third report covered the period from July 14 to August 11, during which two important events took place: On July 15 American troops landed in Lebanon and on July 31 General Fu'ād Shihāb was elected President of the Republic—an event which brought the crisis essentially to an end, at least in its internal aspects.

Between July 15 and August 11, the number of ground observers increased from 113 to 166, and of air personnel from 20 to 24.[30] The total of all types of observation posts reached 26 (five stations, 14 sub-stations and seven observation posts).[31] In addition, 12 Cessnas, four Harvard aircraft and two helicopters were in operation.[32] During the latter period covered by the report, some night patrolling by ground observers was instituted and radio communications between air and ground patrols were established.

It will be recalled that permission to the Observation Group for full access to opposition-held areas was granted on July 15. For various reasons, among them the landing of American troops, the Observation Group was unable to take advantage of this permission until the end of the period covered by the report. For instance, of the 26 observation posts reported in existence during this period, ten posts —all in the opposition-held areas—were established either a few days before the election of the new President, or after. They are listed below:

Sub-Station	*Date Established*
Halba (first opened on July 15, closed down because of opposition, re-opened on July 22, then replaced by Beino on August 4)	
Mechta Hammud (replaced later by Chedra)	July 22
El-Kah	July 26
Hermel	July 27
Koussair	July 27
Baalbeck	July 29
Notre Dame de Fort	July 31
Tell Abbas	August 4
Arida	August 11
Aziziye	August 11

From the above, it is clear that the Observation Group did not have full and free access to opposition-held areas, nor did it begin to have the necessary organization, observation network and equipment until the election of the new President on July 31. By then the internal part of the crisis was essentially over. This is confirmed by the report. It is stated that, about one week before the election of the new President, a virtual state of truce existed in the country, except for sporadic fighting between government and opposition forces, and individual acts of lawlessness, such as stealing and so forth.[33] Presumably there was no longer any acute need for the smuggling of arms and infiltration of men.

Conclusion

A study of the Security Council debates on the Lebanese question clearly shows that the establishment of the Observation Group was a gesture intended as a compromise solution to avert a deadlock and the paralysis of the Security Council.

If we assume, for the sake of argument, that there was extensive infiltration of men and arms, then it is clearly evident that the Observation Group possessed neither the men, nor the equipment, nor the powers, to enable it to "observe," let alone "check" and "prevent." Given the virtually inaccessible nature of the terrain where smuggling and infiltration was allegedly taking place; given the fact that the local people in the frontier areas knew every inch of this terrain and could travel at night using animal, in addition to motorized, transport; given the fact that the whole length of the land frontier with Syria, with the exception of some 18 kilometers was held by the opposition, it would seem that a much larger number of fully-equipped observers, with perhaps some 60 fully-manned observation posts, and complete freedom of access and movement to all parts of the country, would have been needed to achieve the task.

The above thesis is confirmed by the experience of the French during the mandate period in similar terrain and against similar people in Syria. Thousands of well-armed French soldiers could not fully suppress the successive armed rebellions or prevent the smuggling of arms. It is difficult to see how some 150 unarmed men, with little or no access to the areas where smuggling and infiltration were supposed to be taking place, were to be able to observe and render independent judgment on the question.

In addition, there were strong rumors—the truth of which this writer can neither confirm nor deny—that the Observation Group did not take its task seriously. In any case, the second and third reports show that the Observation Group did not get along too well with the Lebanese government. Also, the pro-government press in Lebanon attacked the Group severely—reflecting perhaps the attitude of the government. President Sham'ūn, himself, was reported by the London *Daily Mail* to have said that he was disappointed with both Mr. Hammarskjöld and the Observation Group and that the observers seemed to be doing absolutely nothing. He said they spent their time in clubs, on the beaches, and at the Cedars. They had asked rebels about infiltration and taken it for granted that the information they received was true.[34] Sham'ūn later denied that he made this statement. But, whether he made it or not, there is little doubt that it substantially reflected his feelings and belief with regard to the Observation Group.

Whether or not the Observation Group did take its mission seriously, it should be noted that real life began to be pumped into it only after the threat of international war became dangerously real —with the landing of American troops in Lebanon, the landing of British troops in Jordan, the *coup* in Iraq and the threats of the Soviet Union. Only then did men and materials begin to flow in large numbers. This is clearly indicated from the following data:

	August 10	*September 20*	*November 14*
Number of Observers (including air personnel)	190	287	591
Number of permanently manned stations (all types)	22	33	49
Number of vehicles	n.a.	173	290

The same increase took place in air patrolling from August on, as illustrated by the following figures.

	Number of Sorties in month	*Total flying hours in month*
June (6 days only)	15	23
July	160	360
August	210	494
September	317	775
October	305	767

It is, of course, possible that the correlation of the above increases with the increase in international tension, may have simply been a statistical incident. Yet the rather sudden decision of the Observation Group in its fourth report that it needed more than fifty permanently-manned observation stations in order to achieve full capacity,[35] as compared with its former slow build-up, is highly suggestive.

NOTES

1. Karāmī, *op. cit.,* p. 54.
2. Mughabghab was a deputy and a close associate of Sham'ūn. He was the main leader of irregular forces which fought Junblāṭ's forces in the Mountain. He was assassinated on July 27, 1959.
3. The opposition has a photostat of the alleged cargo manifest, which gives the following information: Owner or operator: Air Charter, Ltd., 21 Wigmore Street, London, W.1; Aircraft: G-AOFW (British); Flight No.: ACL/474; Date: 11.7.58; Point of Lading: Stansted U.K.; Point of Unlading: Beirut, Lebanon. (The manifest then describes the contents of the cargo.)
4. For full text of the complaint, see Appendices I(A) and I(B).
5. Some of the papers and magazines are as follows: *al-Siyāsah, Al-Talagrāph, Beirut al-Masā, al Hudā, Al-Kifāḥ, al-Sharq, al-Ṭayyār, al-Ḥawādith, al-Ṣayyād, al-Aḥad, al-Dabbūr, al-Ṣafā,* among several others.
6. See Appendices I(A) and I(B).
7. See Appendices II(A) and II(B).
8. *Mideast Mirror,* Dec. 8, 1957, p. 25; *Ibid,* Dec. 15, 1957, p. 21.
9. *Ibid.,* Sept. 8, 1957, p. 14.
10. *Ibid.,* January 5, 1958, p. 24.
11. *Ibid.,* March, 2, 1958, p. 12.
12. Karāmī, *op. cit.,* pp. 152-154.
13. See Appendix I(A).
14. *UN Doc. S/4040,* 3 July 1958, pp. 11-12.
15. *UN Doc. S/4069,* 30 July 1958, pp. 5-6.
16. For text see Appendix III(A).
17. *UN Doc. S/4040,* 3 July 1958, p. 9.
18. *UN Doc. S/4069,* 30 July 1958, p. 21.
19. *UN Doc. S/4085,* 14 August 1958, p. 15.
20. *UN Doc. S/4100,* 29 September 1958, p. 19.
21. *UN Doc. S/4114,* 17 November 1958, p. 7.
22. *UN Doc. S/4038,* 28 June 1958, p. 2.

23. *UN Doc. S/4040,* 3 July 1958, Annex "A".
24. *Ibid.*, p. 2 and *S/4040/Corr. 1,* 7 July 1958.
25. *S/4040,* 3 July 1958, p. 2.
26. *Ibid.*, pp. 2-3.
27. *UN Doc. S/4052,* 17 July 1958, pp. 2-4.
28. *UN Doc. S/4069,* 30 July 1958, pp. 7-8.
29. *Ibid.*, p. 8.
30. *UN Doc. S/4085,* 14 August 1958, p. 4.
31. *Ibid.*, Annex (map).
32. *UN Doc. S/4100,* 29 September 1958, p. 3.
33. *UN Doc. S/4085,* 14 August 1958, p. 3.
34. *Mideast Mirror,* July 13, 1958, p. 4.
35. *UN Doc. S/4100,* 29 September 1958, p. 4.

CHAPTER IX

The Political Settlement

IT WILL BE RECALLED that one of the internal causes of the crisis was the belief that Sham'ūn intended to succeed himself after his term expired, and his refusal to state publicly that he would not attempt to do so.[1]

Before American troops landed in Lebanon, the issue of Sham'ūn's re-election had been settled. On May 27, the Prime Minister, Sāmī al-Ṣulḥ, speaking on behalf of the government, said in a broadcast to the nation that the President had not requested an amendment, and that the government's statements had never mentioned such a possibility. The government had not sought to make such an amendment, and would not do so in the future, and there was no indication that the Chamber of Deputies had any such intentions.[2] This was finally confirmed publicly by Sham'ūn himself. In interviews with the correspondents of *Newsweek* and the United Press during the first week of July, he stated that he would step down on September 23, when his term expired and visit the United States "as early as possible after I become a private citizen."[3]

Election of President Shihāb

Thus when American troops arrived, the basic issue for the solution of the crisis was the election of a new president and the appointment of a new cabinet acceptable to all. Although the opposition insisted that "Sham'ūn must resign now" before any action was taken, this in fact represented a public stand rather than a real position. This is clearly indicated by its participation both in the extensive negotiations which took place before the election of General Shihāb, and in the election itself.

Under-Secretary of State Robert Murphy arrived in Beirut on May 17 and remained there until August 5, with the exception of two days spent in 'Ammān. He immediately plunged into extensive meetings with various political blocs, including the opposition, the neutrals, the government and its supporters. In unequivocal terms, he explained the objectives of his mission and was soon able to win the confidence of the opposition in this respect. He told them that his mission was one of good offices and mediation between the various political groups in the country for the solution of the crisis and for the nomination of a presidential candidate acceptable to the majority of the Lebanese people.

By that time there were several persons who were presidential aspirants, or whose names were mentioned in that connection. Generally speaking, Sham'ūn and his supporters favored the election of a pro-government deputy from parliament; the opposition was against the nomination of any deputy, and favored—among others, either ex-president Bishārah al-Khūrī or General Shihāb. The Third Force believed that only General Shihāb could solve the crisis and save the country. Thus the following names, among several others, were considered as possible candidates: from parliament, Salīm Laḥḥūd, Raymond Eddé, and Elie Abū Jawdah. From outside, Alfred Naqqāsh, Charles Hilū, Jawād Būlus, Emile Tyān, Badrī al-Ma'ūshī, Fu'ād Shihāb, and Bishārah al-Khūrī.

Concurrently with Murphy's soundings, brisk consultations and negotiations were taking place among political leaders. The consensus seemed to favor the nomination of Shihāb. Shihāb was approached by Murphy and local leaders on the subject, but was adamant in his refusal to stand for election. He insisted that he was a military man, did not want to become involved in politics, and particularly did not want to create the impression that he had any presidential ambitions. In addition, neither Sham'ūn nor his supporters were enthusiastic about Shihāb. Consequently, the meeting of parliament which was scheduled for July 24 to elect the new president was postponed by Mr. 'Usayrān to July 31. For a day or two thereafter, the name of Bishārah al-Khūrī loomed large as a possible opposition candidate and, on July 26, the National Bloc officially announced the candidacy of its leader, Raymond Eddé.

By July 29 and 30, it became abundantly clear to everyone that the solution of the crisis lay in the election of Shihāb. Sham'ūn was finally prevailed upon to agree and he, in turn, whipped most of his supporters into line. Shihāb was persuaded to accept and the opposition, after a policy meeting at the home of Ṣā'ib Salām, announced on July 30, its endorsement of Shihāb and declared that its deputies would attend the parliamentary session. Murphy had a last meeting with Shihāb (on July 30) and immediately after left for Jordan. Thus, by July 30, two candidates remained in the field: General Shihāb, supported by the great majority, and Raymond Eddé, supported primarily by his own party and close friends.

In the meantime, on July 29, the parliamentary office granted immunity to all deputies for 48 hours after the proposed parliamentary meeting on August 31. This was to enable five opposition deputies against whom the government had previously issued warrants of arrest, to attend the session. On the 30th, the Beirut garrison announced a curfew from nightfall until further notice in the general area of the Parliament building.

In the morning of July 31, Parliament, meeting as an electoral college, was officially declared open at 11:35 a.m. with 56 deputies present (12 above the required quorum of 44). On the first ballot General Shihāb fell one vote short of winning the election. The results of the secret balloting were: 43 for Shihāb, 10 for Eddé and three blanks. On the second ballot, he won. The results were: 48 for Shihāb, 7 for Eddé, and one blank. Thus the first hurdle in the way of a solution of the crisis was cleared.

Although Shihāb was not due to assume power until September 23, his election to the office brought gradual but discernible relaxation of tension. On August 4, Rashīd Karāmī, the opposition leader in Tripoli, ordered a cease fire among his followers, and the city began gradually to return to normal. On August 9, the road betweet Tripoli and 'Akkār was opened to traffic for the first time since May. On August 7, security forces were ordered to confiscate all arms—whether licensed or not—carried by individuals in the center of Beirut. On September 3, after meetings among Shihāb, the Maronite Patriarch and the opposition, shops were allowed to open until 11 a.m. daily. On September 5, four opposition clandestine radio stations were closed down, and on the same day the Phalanges Party ordered its members to surrender their arms. On September 8, after a meeting with Shihāb, chiefs of 15 leading clans in the Ba'lbak and Hirmil areas declared their allegiance to the new government, asked that the army be sent to their areas and promised their full cooperation and support.

The Counter-Revolution

Although clashes between security forces and forces of the opposition continued to occur, they became minor and fewer. Violence began to assume a personal character for vengeance or material gain. Bombings in Beirut, acts of brigandage and theft increased. Kidnapping, torture of individuals and reprisals not only increased but reached a dangerous level, because they were in most cases carried out by followers without the consent or knowledge of leaders and because they assumed a Christian-Muslim character.

In the meantime, while the country was gradually returning to normal, a political battle was being waged concerning the composition of the cabinet under the forthcoming administration. On August 26, a delegation of opposition leaders visited General Shihāb and presented him with a statement which called for the formation of a government composed of opposition leaders and "other faithful persons" to fulfill the aims of the revolution and return the country to normal. The statement also accused "subversive" and "some foreign elements" of conspiring to prevent Shihāb from taking over his duties and of delaying the withdrawal of US troops. "Certain elements," the statement said, "were propagating false rumors in an attempt to incite communal agitation and the setting up of zones in which armed elements, loyal to the present régime, were being concentrated, in cooperation with a certain foreign power with the aim of resisting the national movement and preventing it from achieving its aspirations."[4] Shortly thereafter the opposition publicly nominated Rashīd Karāmī for the premiership.

The following day, August 27, the United Parliamentary Bloc—made up of government supporters including 23 deputies, issued a statement in reply. The signatories requested that an ultimatum be given to all armed groups in the country to surrender their arms; they declared that they would refuse to cooperate with any future government which included any leader of the opposition; they demanded that those responsible for riots, terrorism and the arming of the Lebanese people, i.e., opposition leaders, "to carry out a plan aimed at destroying political and economic conditions and Lebanon's existence," be brought to trial and they thanked Sham'ūn for having realized the aspirations of the Lebanese people and for having handled the crisis with firmness and resolution.[5] A delegation from the Bloc handed copies of the statement to both Sham'ūn and Shihāb.

The above statement represented an extreme position. Before it was issued, 20 pro-government deputies told General Shihāb on August 21 that they would support any measure he may take to restore normal life to the country and to establish law and order;[6] and on September 12 three pro-government deputies declared that they would support the nomination of Rashīd Karāmī for prime minister, provided his cabinet included moderate elements from both sides.[7]

Generally speaking, despite some acts of violence, the overall political climate continued to improve with a "wait and see" attitude on all sides, until September 19. On that day Fu'ād Ḥaddād, assistant editor of *al-'Amal* newspaper, organ of the Phalanges Party, was kidnapped. This sparked the revival of political tension and was in part responsible for what has come to be known as the counter-revolution.

On the 20th, the Phalanges party declared a general strike to start on the 22nd, in protest against the kidnapping of Ḥaddād. They began erecting barricades in their quarters of Beirut, as the United National Front had done under the Sham'ūn administration.

On September 23 General Shihāb was sworn in by the Chamber of Deputies as President of the Republic. In his policy statement before the Chamber, he declared that the immediate objectives of his administration were

> the establishment of security and law in all parts of Lebanon; the disarming of all Lebanese groups with firmness and impartiality; the revival of the Lebanese economy; the rebuilding of the country's services and utilities that had been destroyed; the removal of tension in the relations between Lebanon and some of the sister Arab states—particularly those neighboring Lebanon and, above all, the realization of the prompt withdrawal of foreign troops from the soil of the fatherland.

On September 24, Shihāb decreed the formation of a new cabinet under 37-year-old Rashīd Karāmī, leader of the opposition in Tripoli. All but one of the members of the new eight-man cabinet were drawn from the opposition: four United National Front; three Third Force and one neutral.

The formation of the new cabinet caused immediate repercussions among the Sham'ūn factions, headed by the Phalanges party. On the 25th, Pierre Jumayyil, leader of the Phalanges, declared that the composition of the new cabinet was an unjustified victory for the "rebels" and that "we cannot but oppose this government." A period (September 20-October 14) of extreme tension followed: the Phalanges and other Sham'ūn partisans continued to erect barricades in their quarters, most of them in east Beirut; the strike announced by the Phalanges on the 20th began to be more rigidly enforced and parts of Beirut and some towns, particularly in Mount Lebanon, closed down; anti-government demonstrations were conducted in Beirut, Zaḥlah and other towns; some clashes took place between security forces and the Phalanges in Beirut and other parts of Lebanon; kidnappings became frequent and the Phalanges clandestine radio station, *Voice of Lebanon,* returned to the air on October 1.

In a certain sense, the series of kidnappings were the most serious aspect of the new situation because they took an exclusively religious coloration—Christian, or rather Maronite, versus Muslim. In many cases the victims were tortured; in some cases they were killed; in others, Muslim victims were branded with the sign of the cross. In most cases, the kidnappings were carried out by irresponsibles on both sides without the consent of knowledge of the leaders. It was probably to alleviate the religious aspect of the new strife that, on October 11, Christian and Muslim religious leaders formed a "Committee of Union."

On October 8, 28 deputies (22 members of Sham'ūn's National Liberal Party,[8] 5 Biqā' deputies, and al-Ashqar, former leader of the PPS) informed 'Usayrān, then speaker of the Chamber, in writing that they would not give a vote of confidence to the new cabinet. Since a vote of confidence requires an absolute majority—assuming that there is a quorum—this meant that the cabinet would have extreme difficulty in passing its draft bills through the Chamber and that it might, at any time, be thrown out of office by a vote of no confidence.

The above impasse left four alternatives open: first, the dissolution of the Chamber, which the President of the Republic could do. This was not feasible under the tense political climate and because new parliamentary elections at that time could easily have plunged Lebanon into another civil war, given the fact that all Lebanese groups were armed to the teeth.

Second, the formation of a cabinet composed completely of neutrals. Sham'ūn loyalists headed by the Phalanges, were in favor of this as an alternative, but the former opposition were against it.

Third, the formation of a military government. The former opposition favored this as an alternative to the Karāmī cabinet, but the Phalanges opposed it. Apparently this alternative was given serious consideration by Shihāb who discarded it only at the last moment. It is reported that during a meeting at Junieh which lasted nearly four hours on October 9, between Shihāb and members of the opposition, including Karāmī, Salām, Junblāṭ, Yāfī, 'Uwaynī, Mu'awwad and Majdalānī, it was agreed that the Karāmī cabinet resign to be replaced by a military government under Nāẓim al-'Akkārī with three or four army officers as ministers. The military government would immediately declare martial law and dissolve the Chamber.[9]

Four, the formation of a coalition government with representatives from both sides. This was the solution finally accepted, to the satisfaction of all concerned.

The "No Victor, No Vanquished" Cabinet

The three-week crisis was characterized by intense political negotiations. Between September 27 and October 13, in addition to numerous meetings with his Prime Minister, Rashīd Karāmī, President Shihāb received Pierre Jumayyil seven times; Salām, Yāfī, 'Uwaynī and Junblāṭ, three times each; Ḥamādah, al-As'ad, Mu'awwad and Majdalānī, once each.

On September 29, the Phalanges declared that they had no objection to Rashīd Karāmī personally and that, if he were to form a coalition government on a 50-50 basis, they would support him. On the same day, however, before a meeting with President Shihāb, Karāmī said that adding ministers of the former régime to his cabinet was out of the question.

On October 8, Salām appealed, in a press statement, to all Lebanese to strive for conciliation, adding that "the foreigner has always worked for the creation of dissension between Christians and Muslims and has used for that purpose people and tools according to the time and place. Ex-President Sham'ūn and the English behind him are trying to create sectarian strife."[10]

On October 9, Karāmī placed the resignation of his cabinet at the disposal of President Shihāb, and persistent rumors circulated in Beirut that a military government was being formed. Later in the day, after strong rallies in his support, Karāmī, in an address to the crowds, implied that he would stay in office, and Salām told them that "Karāmī will not resign." Karāmī and Salām were followed by Junblāṭ and Far'awn who addressed the crowds in the same theme.

On the 10th, through the intervention of President Shihāb, Jumayyil visited Karāmī at his office. Their meeting which lasted for about two hours was their first in over three years. Apparently, it was then agreed that Jumayyil would join a reshuffled Karāmī cabinet. On the same day, the Phalanges announced that they were leaving the solution of the crisis to President Shihāb on the basis of a "no victor, no vanquished" policy and Jumayyil, writing in the party's newspaper, *al-'Amal,* appealed to all Lebanese to help the president and cooperate with him. On the 11th, Jumayyil met Junblāṭ, again for the first time since the crisis started in May.

Between October 10 and 14, there was considerable discussion as to the possibility of forming a 14-man coalition cabinet. This was finally rejected, probably because so many ministers on both sides of the fence would not be able to cooperate with each other, in view of the intense personal animosity among them.

On the 14th, Karāmī announced the formation of a new four-man cabinet, two from each side, composed as follows: Karāmī, prime minister and minister of economy, finance, defense, information; Ḥusayn 'Uwaynī, minister of foreign affairs, justice, planning; Pierre Jumayyil, minister of public works, education, health, agriculture; Raymond Eddé, minister of interior, social affairs, posts and telegraph. Jumayyil and Eddé had never been ministers before. On October 7, 1959, the above cabinet was enlarged to include eight ministers, Raymond Eddé resigned and five new ministers were appointed: Philippe Taqlā, 'Ali al-Bazzī, Maurice Zuwayn, Fu'ād Butrus and Fu'ād Najjār.

The new government received the approval of all sides except the PPS, and immediately the country began to return to normal. On October 14 the Phalanges called off their strike. By the end of the month, the barricades erected in Beirut by various groups had disappeared completely; the curfew imposed since May was lifted; commercial activity resumed its course and roads between Beirut and the provinces were open. On October 27, by agreement with the government, Junblāṭ began to disband his private army and his followers began to trek back to their villages. Perhaps no better indicator of the return to normal can be found than that, on November 4, custom officials arrested seven persons who were trying to smuggle 1,400 kilograms of hashish out of Lebanon.

On October 17, three days after it was formed, Karāmī's government received a unanimous vote of confidence from the Chamber. Fifty deputies out of a total of 66 attended the session. In his policy statement, Karāmī told the Chamber that his government would follow the broad lines laid down by President Shihāb in his policy speech on September 23, to wit: the withdrawal of foreign troops as soon as possible, the strengthening of relations between Lebanon and the Arab states, the revival of the economy, abiding by the National Covenant of 1943, and cooperation with all countries on the basis of friendship and equality.

The Period of Transition

The crisis ended on October 14. From October on, the new government turned its attention and efforts towards the solution of the innumerable problems which the crisis had left in its wake.

Now that a new administration had come to power, Sham'ūn appointees and supporters in top government positions began to disappear from the scene. On October 2, 1958, two weeks after he took office, Shihāb appointed three army officers as commanders of the gendarmerie, the police, and public security. Respectively, they were Col. Joseph Sim'ān to replace Simon Zuwayn, Major 'Azīz al-Aḥdab to replace Ṣalāḥ al-Labābīdī, and Captain Tawfīq Jalbūṭ to replace Fu'ād Sham'ūn—brother of the former president. Several other top officials were later either removed or transferred to minor positions. A year later, on October 24, 1959, new governors were appointed for the five provinces in Lebanon.

Supporters of the former administration began also to disappear from the political scene. In a by-election in the Jizzīn district on June 21, 1959, over a parliamentary seat vacated by the death of Farīd Quzma, the Phalanges Basīl 'Abbūd, supported by his party and the United National Front, won over Marūn Kan'ān—a Sham'ūn candidate. On July 27, 1959, one of Sham'ūn's most ardent supporters, Na'īm Mughabghab, was assassinated, leaving a vacant seat in the Chamber. In the Shūf by-election which took place on September 27, 1959, to fill the vacancy, Junblāṭ's candidate, Salīm 'Abd al-Nūr, won over In'ām Ra'd—Sham'ūn's candidate and a member of the PPS. Similarly, on October 20, 1959, Ṣabrī Ḥamādah, one of the leaders of the United National Front, was elected Speaker of the Chamber against 'Ādil 'Usayrān. 'Usayrān had been Speaker for six years. Although during the crisis he tried to steer a neutral course and maintain a friendly relationship with the opposition, he was identified with the Sham'ūn administration.

In its efforts to lead the country back to stability, the new government took various measures. It declared what amounted to a general amnesty, and most persons who were in prison or under sentence in connection with the crisis were eventually released, or the cases against them dropped. On the other hand, the penal code was amended to provide the death penalty, without the possibility of a lesser sentence, for murder; and up to hard labor for life, for bomb throwing and kidnapping. In addition, the army and the gendarmerie began to penetrate the provinces to prevent clan feuds and acts of brigandage and to reassert governmental authority. Moreover, about 200 policemen and municipal guards who had previously deserted to opposition forces were either reinstated or jobs found for them. Jobs were also eventually found for a similar number of defectors from the army and the gendarmerie.

One of the chief concerns of the new government was the revival of economic activity which had come to a virtual standstill. At the height of the crisis, the national economy was losing at the rate of about two million dollars a day in wages, production and services, tourist trade, destruction of property and flight of capital. Measures were taken to revive production, commercial activity and the tourist industry. These included work programs, development projects, exemptions to industry, contacts with Arab and foreign governments and inducements for tourists. It might be mentioned that the United States government gave Lebanon an outright, unconditional grant of 12.6 million dollars ($2.5 millions in September 1958, and $10 millions in December 1958), in addition to 65,000 tons of wheat for relief and various quantities of medical supplies from the American army. All this was in addition to other economic assistance under the Point Four Program and loans. These totalled about 10 million more dollars in 1959.

On November 12, 1958, the Chamber approved a bill submitted by the cabinet, empowering the latter to issue legislative decrees in matters of security, finance, economy, administrative reform, and the budget, for a period of six months. In other words, the bill authorized the government to rule the country by decree for six months without reference to the Chamber.

With these special powers at its disposal, the cabinet carried out some of the tasks mentioned previously in this chapter. In addition, it launched a wholesale reorganization of virtually all government departments, some decentralization of power with greater autonomy for local government, strict accounting and auditing controls over government expenditures, new regulations emphasizing competence for civil service employment and, perhaps most important of all, the establishment of a civil service board and a central inspection agency with the intention of removing patronage from government employment and insuring a reasonable standard of competence among civil servants. On June 12, 1959, the cabinet issued 162 legislative decrees in the above connection. Most of the press welcomed the decrees. *Al-Ḥayāt* said, "This reform is the first serious attempt based on the experience of an independent régime to organize an administrative machinery on the foundations of our possibilities and requirements."

The 1960 Parliamentary Elections

On April 20, 1960, the parliament approved an electoral law submitted to it by the cabinet. The new law raised the number of members in future parliaments from 66 to 99 and introduced the secret ballot.

Shortly afterwards, on May 4, the parliament itself was dissolved by President Shihāb—a year before its term was due to expire. Thus, the last visible vestige of the Sham'ūn administration was removed.

It was also officially announced that elections for a new parliament would begin Sunday, June 12 (1960), and continue by stages in different parts of the country, on each of the three succeeding Sundays (June 12, 19, 26, and July 3).

A few days later, the conciliation cabinet of Rashīd Karāmī resigned, and on May 14, a new eight-man "neutral" cabinet representing various factions took office. The prime minister was Aḥmad al-Da'ūq. The primary mandate of the new cabinet was to supervise the elections and insure their fairness and legality. It was to resign immediately after this task was completed.

Although there was some purchase of votes—a normal practice in Lebanon, and although some candidates complained of interference by the authorities,[11] it is generally agreed that the 1960 elections were the most honest elections held in Lebanon since 1943. Also, in striking contrast to the 1957 elections, the 1960 elections proceeded in comparative calm and order with only incidental violence and bloodshed.

The 1960 elections can be regarded in a real sense as marking the true end of the Lebanese crisis of 1958. In the first place, the parliament dissolved in May was generally regarded as having been elected through forgery and pressure from the Sham'ūn administration. In fact, the 1957 elections, as we have mentioned previously in this book, were one of the causes of the crisis. Secondly, many of the alliances which existed during the crisis in 1957-58 (some of which were only skin deep) broke down. In particular, mention should be made of the animosity that developed between Salām and Yāfī, and the contest between Sham'ūn and the Phalanges during the election campaign, and the end of the alliance between the Phalanges and the PPS. Thirdly, the issues in the campaign—unlike those of the 1957 elections—did not deal with fundamental questions. The primary concern of the candidates was in having themselves and their supporters elected, and they formed alliances accordingly. In other words, the norms of political practice in Lebanon began to operate again. Fourthly, because of presidential aspirations and because of the nature of Lebanese politics,[12] there has been a slight shift in the position of Maronite groups. Jumayyil's Phalanges Party [13] and Eddé's National Bloc[14]—usually the extreme Maronite groups—moved to a more moderate position on the Arab question, while Sham'ūn's National Liberals assumed the extreme Maronite position.[15] Finally, Sham'ūn and his party came out of the 1960 elections comparatively weak, and were able to elect to parliament only four to five members and supporters.

When the elections were over, of the 66 deputies in the former parliament, 34 were not returned (either because of defeat, or because they did not present themselves)—thus leaving 32 old members. Of the new 67 members, 33 faced the electorate for the first time.

The parliament elected in 1960 is a mosaic of parties and groups representing almost every point of view—none of which has a commanding majority. In a certain sense, the present parliament reflects the true spirit of the Lebanese public and the reality of Lebanese political life. Table II below shows the blocs and their comparative strength in the present parliament. The figures, however, should be regarded only as indicators and should not be taken too seriously, for often, both the members and supporters in a bloc vote independently on specific issues, and even shift loyalties. It is not unlikely that new blocs and alliances would be formed during the life of the present parliament.

TABLE II

PARTIES AND BLOCS IN 1960 PARLIAMENT

	Number of Members and Supporters
Constitutional Union Party (al-Khūrī)	4–8
National Bloc Party (Eddé)	5–6
National Liberal Party (Sham'ūn)	4–5
Phalanges Party (Jumayyil)	7–8
Progressive Socialist Party (Junblāṭ)	5–8
al-Najjādah—The Helpers—(al-Hakīm)	1–2
The National Organization (Nijā)	1–1
The National Call (al-Bazzī)	2–2
Tashnaq (Armenian right wing party)	4–4
Deputies Attached to Leaders:	
Karāmī (Tripoli)	4–6
al-As'ad (South)	6–8
'Usaryrān (South)	3 5
al-'Ali (North)	4–4
Ḥamādah (Biqā')	3–5
Skāf (Biqā')	5–6
Sub-Total	58–78
Independents	41–21
Total	99–99

The election results were in many respects surprising:

1—By and large, the extremist elements on all sides were elected, while the moderates went under.

2—The electorate manifested far greater political awareness and independence than in any other previous election. The candidates had to employ bonafide electioneering methods, such as going out to the people, more than ever before. Also, the introduction of the secret ballot gave the voters privacy and freedom which was too often absent before. Finally, the results threw some doubt on the value of buying votes. Apparently, quite a few voters took the money, but voted for a different candidate.

3—The election results indicated that the hold of traditional "feudal" leaders on the electorate is declining. For instance, two such candidates (Zuwayn and Khāzin) in the Kisrawān area lost. Also Ṣabrī Ḥamādah, a strongly entrenched Shi'a leader in the Biqā', was able to return only three candidates—including himself—out of six names on his list, thus losing four seats. Conversely, Nāyif al-Maṣrī, a Shi'a "commoner" who had been previously a constable on the police force, stood for election and won.

4—Traditional parties, or rather political groupings revolving around personal loyalty to a leader, are losing ground in favor of "ideological" parties. The elections indicated the growing strength of such parties as the Phalanges, the Progressive Socialists and the Ba'thists. Although the Ba'th candidate in Tripoli, Dr. 'Abd al-Majīd al-Rāfi'ī, failed, yet the number of votes he won (14,052 against 14,830 for his successful opponent on the Karāmī list) indicates that Rashīd Karāmī no longer enjoys the complete hold he has so far had on the Tripoli area.

The End of the Crisis

Immediately after the parliamentary elections, brisk negotiations and consultations began for the formation of a new government. This, however, was interrupted by a day of drama unique in the political annals of Lebanon. On July 20—two days after the new parliament had elected Ṣabrī Ḥamādah as its Speaker, President Shihāb announced his resignation during a meeting with the cabinet at his residence in Junieh. In a message to the nation which was broadcast over the radio, he stated that he took the office only to tide Lebanon over the period of crisis; that with the election of a new parliament, he regarded his task as having been completed; and that therefore, he has decided to resign.

The announcement stunned the country, and a heavy cloud of gloom descended on Beirut. A large number of people milled around the parliament building waiting to hear the latest developments, while a big crowd demonstrated before the President's residence in Junieh shouting "We will not accept any President but you." After several hours of remonstration and pleading by members of the cabinet, and later by members of parliament, Shihāb was finally persuaded to withdraw his resignation, and he was carried by members of parliament to the balcony on their shoulders to announce his decision to the waiting crowds. The latter responded with shouts of joy and gunfire display.

Whatever may have been the real reasons,[16] the one-day resignation crisis greatly strengthened Shihāb's position and increased his prestige. In the first place, his resignation and the consequent outpouring of public feeling in his favor, was a popular referendum which demonstrated to the politicians in no uncertain terms, that he commands popular support, and that his mandate is directly from the people. Secondly, his action demonstrated his genuine disinterest in the presidency and dislike of politics. This was at complete variance with the experience of the Lebanese people. The two men —al-Khūrī and Sham'ūn—who had assumed the presidency since Lebanon gained its independence in 1943, had to be forced out of office. In contrast, Shihāb had to be begged to stay. This enhanced further his immense public popularity, for it introduced into the political scene of Lebanon a new phenomenon: the image of a new type of president who is exclusively dedicated to the public welfare, does not manipulate the government machinery for his personal aggrandizement and to perpetuate himself in office.

After the one-day crisis negotiations for a new government resumed. On July 27, Prime Minister Aḥmad al-Da'ūq placed the resignation of his cabinet at the disposal of President Shihāb. On the following day (July 28) Shihāb requested Ṣā'ib Salām to form a new one. Salām, it will be remembered, was the leader of the opposition in Beirut, and one of the most violent in his denunciation of Sham'ūn. It is also claimed that during the parliamentary elections, the UAR favored him against his more moderate rival 'Abdallah al-Yāfī.[17]

After four days of lengthy negotiations to reconcile conflicting blocs, Salām, on August 2, announced the formation of an 18-man cabinet, the largest in the modern history of Lebanon. With the exception of one—Philippe Taqlā, every minister in the new cabinet was also a member of parliament. This was designed by Salām to insure parliamentary support for himself and his cabinet.

The composition of the new cabinet reflected the growing strength of certain parties, and the new political combinations in the country. The Progressive Socialists are represented by Junblāṭ and Majdalānī; the Phalanges, by Pierre and Maurice Jumayyil; and the Constitutionalists, by Philippe Taqlā and Ilyās al-Khūrī. This is in addition to 11 other ministers representing other blocs. Conversely, the new cabinet did not include representatives of Sham'ūn's National Liberals or Karāmī's supporters. Raymond Eddé—leader of the National Bloc—was offered a cabinet post, but he declined the offer.

Thus, with the election of a new parliament and the assumption of power by a new cabinet, the Lebanese crisis of 1958 came to a full end in so far as the visible manifestations are concerned, and the country began to direct its full attention to the future with its promise and problems.

NOTES

1. Sham'ūn had never publicly stated that he would either amend the constitution or try to succeed himself.
2. *Mideast Mirror,* June 1, 1958, p. 6.
3. *Ibid.,* July 13, 1958, p. 15.
4. *Ibid.,* August 31, 1958, p. 5.
5. *Ibid.,* p. 6.
6. *Ibid.,* August 24, 1958, p. 14.
7. *Ibid.,* September 14, 1958, p. 13.
8. Shortly before he retired from office, Sham'ūn formed the National Liberal Party.
9. Karāmī, *op. cit.,* pp. 314-15.
10. *Mideast Mirror,* October 12, 1958, p. 5.
11. The most extreme case was that of Bashīr al-'Uthmān and three of his supporters. On polling day, these four candidates withdrew from the election in protest against alleged interference by the *Deuxième Bureau* against them.
12. Any Maronite who aspires to the presidency must have wide public support—including Muslim support. So far, every Lebanese president has been elected on a platform of "friendship" to the neighboring Arab states.
13. Until recently the Phalanges did not concern themselves with day to day Lebanese politics, but regarded themselves as guardians of Lebanese independence. The party, however, emerged from the 1958 crisis as a serious contender for the presidency, hence the shift.
14. In 1943, because of the role of its founder—Emile Eddé—the National Bloc fell into public disgrace. Recently, however, the party began to recoup some of its former strength, and Raymond Eddé, son of the founder, emerged from the 1958 crisis as a contender for the presidency.
15. Although Sham'ūn is still a presidential aspirant, it is unlikely that he would be acceptable for some time to come.
16. Rumors circulating in Beirut that day were to the effect that Shihāb resigned in anger and disgust because of an alleged meeting between Salām and Sham'ūn on the latter's yacht the day before (July 19) and because of alleged interference by the Army in parliamentary elections. Personal observations of the author.
17. Yāfī lost in the elections. He claimed that his failure was due to foul play by Salām who "stabbed him in the back" in order to eliminate him as a competitor for the premiership.

CHAPTER X

Summary and Conclusion

THE EVIDENCE available indicated that the claim of the opposition that the causes of the crisis were internal and the counter claim of the Sham'ūn administration that the causes were external are both, in a sense, true. The crisis was not the result of a single set of factors, but was rather generated by a multiplicity of conflicting forces, all of which emanated from one fundamental causation, i.e., the differences in cultural and political orientation that exist among various segments of Lebanese society.

Within this broad framework, the principal internal causes of the conflict can be reduced to two. First, the attempt of Sham'ūn to eliminate important traditional leaders from political life. Only a few days after Sham'ūn assumed power he quarreled with Junblāṭ, although the latter was principally instrumental in bringing him to office. In 1957, through fraudulent elections, Sham'ūn managed to prevent most of the leaders who disagreed with him from participation in the government. By the beginning of 1958, with the exception of some few, every important political leader in the country was Sham'ūn's personal enemy. This included such a powerful combination as the Maronite Patriarch, Junblāṭ, Karāmī, Salām, Yāfī, Far'ūn, Franjiyyah, Ḥamādah, al-As'ad, and Bishārah al-Khūrī among many others. These indeed represent the core of Lebanese aristocracy. Moreover, the animosity between these and Sham'ūn assumed such a bitter and personal character that it made conciliation and compromise difficult. Such animosity is usually absent in Lebanese politics, and Lebanese politicians have been traditionally famous for their constructive ability to compromise. Usually, it is virtually impossible to pin down a Lebanese politician as to where he stands on a specific issue. This is a sixth sense which he has developed by experience, and which allows him to back out of rigid or untenable positions. The personal enmity which developed between Sham'ūn and the opposition was probably the principal immediate internal cause of the crisis. All others were either derivative from or subsidiary to this.

The second principal internal cause of the conflict was Sham'ūn's attempt to succeed himself, in contravention of the constitution.

Although Sham'ūn has constantly denied that he had such an intention, there is little question that up to May 1958 he was fully determined to do so, and that most of his political activity, particularly in 1957 and 1958, was principally geared to the achievement of this objective.

Now, given the political realities in Lebanon, where almost every political leader has his own private army or group of followers ready to do his bidding any time, and where each community is highly jealous of its rights, a combination of the above two factors could only culminate in either a crisis or an armed conflict.

But the above two factors by themselves cannot account for the violent direction which the crisis took. In 1952 a similar crisis with essentially similar factors—including corruption, faked elections, and presidential succession, was solved in a typically Lebanese manner. In a quasi-legal coup d'état, the president was quietly forced to resign and a new president was quietly elected, a process indicative of a considerable degree of political sophistication.

Regional and international factors, which were absent in the 1952 crisis, were present in the 1958 conflict. They were the principal reasons why the conflict took a violent form, and why compromise and conciliation could not operate. They can be summed up under two main headings: (1) contravention by the Sham'ūn administration of two cardinal principles of the National Covenant, and of traditional Lebanese foreign policy on the one hand; and on the other, (2) UAR intervention in the affairs of Lebanon. The second factor will be discussed later in this chapter.

By 1957, whether by design or misadventure, Lebanon, for all practical purposes, was in the Iraqi-Jordan camp, as opposed to the Egyptian-Syrian bloc—thus violating the first principle of the Covenant. In 1957 also, Lebanon accepted the Eisenhower Doctrine. During that year relations between Syria and Egypt on the one hand and the United States and Turkey on the other were very bad. Thus, no matter what the intentions of the Doctrine were, Lebanon's adoption of it at that time did constitute in effect an alignment with foreign powers (the United States and Turkey) against two Arab states—Syria and Egypt. Thus in fact Lebanon became a partisan of an American-British-Turkish-Iraqi-Jordanian bloc against an Egyptian-Syrian bloc, supported by the USSR.

Politically, Lebanon's siding with the Iraqi bloc and its adoption of the Eisenhower Doctrine split the population of Lebanon into two hostile camps. The question became no longer a matter of minor difference of views, or a feud among politicians to be settled amicably in back stage negotiations, but touched the very fundamentals upon which cooperation among the various communities was based. One segment, predominantly Muslim, opposed the government. Another segment, predominantly Christian and more particularly Maronite, supported it. Many Christians were on the opposition side, but only few Muslims on the government side. In other words, the conditions stipulated by the National Covenant were no longer operative.

UAR Intervention

Damascus has traditionally been the heartland of the Arab nationalist movement. No Arab state has been consistently more willing to lose its identity in favor of a greater Arab union than Syria. It was the first Arab state to include, as an integral part of its constitution, a clause to the effect that Syria is an Arab state and part of the Arab nation.

Syria has never reconciled itself to the separation of Lebanon. It grudgingly recognized the independence of Lebanon, and its relations with that country have always been dominated by the theme of union. After the Syrian-Egyptian merger, al-Quwwatlī repeatedly invited Lebanon to join, and Lebanese Muslim leaders who visited Damascus then replied in essence—"just give us time." In addition, in a bid to unite the Arab world, the UAR fostered revolutionary movements and coup d'états in various Arab states. All of these together greatly intensified the fear which has always existed among part of the Lebanese people, that Lebanon's existence as an independent state was in danger. This fear, whether real or imaginary in cause, was genuine. Thus, violation of the principles of the Covenant and anxiety for the independence of Lebanon were two sides of the same coin.

There is little doubt that the UAR—and more particularly, the Syrian authorities—was a principal in the Lebanese crisis, and that the UAR supplied the opposition in Lebanon, in one form or another—either directly and/or through premeditated laxity on the border—with funds, arms and men, although not on the scale claimed by the Sham'ūn administration, in addition to press and radio attacks.

From all the external evidence available, it seems that the immediate objectives of the UAR intervention were: (1) the overthrow of the Sham'ūn administration which it regarded as a threat to its own security and (2) the replacement of the Sham'ūn administration with a new government—presumably composed of the opposition—which, as a minimum, would follow the lead of the UAR in its foreign policies. A third objective may have been the hope that, in time, Lebanon could be induced to join the UAR in some form of union. This certainly was and still is the case with the Syrian authorities. It was probably not one of the immediate objectives of President 'Abd al-Nāṣir.

Thus, while the Sham'ūn administration violated the principles of the Covenant, the UAR violated the provisions of the Arab League Pact. This writer is aware that many Arabs are dissatisfied with the Pact and regard the Arab League more of an impediment than an asset to Arab unity. But the fact remains that the Pact is still on the books, and that no new formula has yet been agreed upon which would replace it in regulating the relations between the Arab states.

In summation, it must be concluded that the Lebanese crisis was both internal and external in origin.

Internationalization of the Crisis

The evidence available seems to indicate that the Sham'ūn administration did not give serious consideration to the possibility of solving the crisis on the Arab League level. This may have been owing to a lack of desire to do so, or to lack of confidence in the League. Certainly the past record of the League in this respect did not inspire confidence, particularly by a state which either believed or claimed that its very existence was in imminent and grave danger.

Apparently, by internationalizing the crisis at the United Nations level, the Sham'ūn administration had hoped to achieve three principal objectives: (1) to obtain relief from the United Nations through the possible creation of some UN emergency force; (2) to obtain some form of collective international guarantee for the independence of Lebanon—thus taking Lebanon back to its 1860 status; and (3) to strike back at Nāṣir by "exposing" him in the highest international forum. In addition, if the opposition in Lebanon were squelched by the UN, this would be a disastrous set-back to Nāṣir's position in the Arab world. Finally, there may have been some vague hope on Sham'ūn's part that either a UN intervention, or a resulting international crisis, may somehow help him to stay in office.

As things turned out, the Sham'ūn administration failed in all its objectives. The Security Council failed to condemn the UAR and was only willing to make a token gesture of assistance by creating the Observation Group.

The Observation Group was an anemic organization which in

the number of its personnel, equipment, and most important of all, its powers, lacked all the elements which would have enabled it to fulfill its mission.

The reports of the Observation Group were meticulously objective. But to the extent that the group lacked the basic elements of surprise, free access and movement, in addition to equipment and a sufficient number of men, then the reports represent only what the Group saw or was allowed to see. They are essentially worthless in determining whether there was an inflow of arms and men from Syria.

The main contribution of the Group to the settlement of the crisis was probably the moral influence of their presence. Under the extremely limited powers granted to them by the Security Council, they conducted themselves in an impartial manner and were soon able to win the confidence of the opposition. Conversely, they proved to be a liability to the Sham'ūn administration, for all their reports were substantially unfavorable to Lebanon's claim of extensive interference. As the relations between the Group and the opposition improved, their relations with the administration became strained and there is little question but that Sham'ūn was highly displeased with them. The loyalist press therefore attacked them very severely. Even Mr. Hammarskjöld was not spared. He was smeared.

The American Commitment

Early in the crisis, the American government made a decision in principle to give Lebanon support by direct military intervention. Such intervention would, however, take place only if other measures of aid or efforts to solve the crisis locally, or through the Arab League or the United Nations failed, and if the situation in Lebanon and the area grew worse.

The immediate cause of the dispatch of American troops was the Iraqi revolt, which created severe tensions and repercussions throughout the area. For a few days not only Lebanon but the entire region seemed in a state of virtual anarchy, and the threat of an international war seemed dangerously real.

There is no doubt that the military intervention of the United States in the Lebanese crisis was legal. Sham'ūn, no matter what his motivations were, had the constitutional right, in his capacity as President of Lebanon, to request the military assistance of the United States and to allow American troops to be stationed in Lebanon for a limited period of time. From an international standpoint, the Lebanese government had the right to request the military assistance of any state for defense purposes, and the United States had the right to respond to such appeal. Article 51 of the UN Charter guarantees to member states the inherent right of self-defense against aggression unless and until the United Nations takes action. The above article does not define or qualify "aggression," but leaves such determination to the states directly concerned. In the case of Lebanon, the UN Security Council, because of its structure and regulations, was incapable of affording Lebanon any effective help, with the exception of token gestures such as the establishment of the UN Observation Group.

The moral position of the United States in this respect was also impregnable. The exemplary behavior and restraint exercised by American troops in Lebanon was indeed a novel and unique experience in international affairs. More important, these troops were not used to gain direct political advantages for the United States in Lebanon, nor did they interfere in any manner in the internal conflict, such as supporting one faction against the other. On the contrary, the United States acted as a mediator between them, to bring about a solution acceptable to all. Finally, it is significant that not a single Lebanese was harmed in his person or property as a result of the actions of the United States troops—military or otherwise.

Various factors and objectives must have induced the United States to respond to the request of the Lebanese government. If the United States had failed to respond after Lebanon had adopted the Eisenhower Doctrine and both the executive and legislative branches of the United States government had approved the Doctrine to emphasize their oneness of view, then no government in the Middle East who was in alliance with the United States, could any longer have been certain that the latter would come to its assistance in times of need. This would have caused the disintegration of the entire military and political position of the United States in the area. The dispatch of the troops was designed in part to reassure Lebanon and all other states in the area that the United States will stand by its commitments. Such reassurance was particularly necessary at that time, due to the collapse of the Baghdad Pact (the name was later changed to the Central Treaty Organization) with the Iraqi revolution.

Positively, the United States sought to achieve the following principal objectives: to insure, in accordance with its implicit commitment under the Eisenhower Doctrine, that Lebanon would remain an independent and genuinely sovereign state and to attempt, through mediation between government and anti-government forces, to bring the crisis and the senseless bloodshed to an end. It was successful in both respects.

Regionally, in addition to reassuring its allies in the area, the United States sought to protect its legitimate interests there and to be prepared for any eventuality. It should be emphasized that the Iraqi revolution created such severe tensions that the entire Middle East was indeed a powder keg, liable to explode into a world war at any time.

Finally, by dispatching troops to Lebanon, along with the concentration of the Sixth Fleet in the Eastern Mediterranean and placing US forces in Europe on an alert basis, the United States served notice on the Soviet Union in the plainest language possible that it would go to war in the event of Soviet aggression in the area. This last objective must be understood within the framework of the sustained Soviet offensive in the area, and the numerous threats of atomic war which the Soviet Government and its representatives made in and outside the United Nations during the Lebanese crisis.

In conclusion, the United States military involvement in the Lebanese crisis is an excellent example of a limited war for limited objectives.

Conclusions

It is quite evident that both Sham'ūn and his supporters and the opposition violated the National Covenant, and that both sides acted with considerable irresponsibility towards their own people and towards the international community. This is particularly so, in view of the tragic havoc which the crisis created in Lebanon itself; about two to three thousand persons killed or wounded, destruction of private and public property, the flight of capital from the country and major losses to the Lebanese economy. Moreover, this irresponsibility brought the world to the brink of a world war with all the horrors that such a possibility entails. Had Lebanese politicians practiced their traditional common sense, had they only taken more moderate positions, the crisis could probably have been avoided, or at least taken a much less violent form. It must be said in conclusion that from all the evidence we now have, Sham'ūn was the most irresponsible of all.

The results of the Lebanese crisis may be divided into three categories: local, regional and international:

1. The most obvious result of the crisis was the change of government. It is possible that, had the crisis not taken place, the Sham'ūn

administration might still be in power. The composition of the new administration still represents a "no victor, no vanquished" settlement of the crisis. General Shihāb was neutral and a mediator during the crisis, while the first cabinet acceptable to all was composed of two ministers from each side.

2. Insofar as the personal conflict between Sham'ūn and the former opposition, the struggle ended in a clear victory for the latter. In the first place, Sham'ūn lost a great deal of his political power and prestige. In the present administration, he is represented in the parliament by only a few deputies, including himself. Similarly, Sham'ūn's closest associates, such as Malik and al-Ṣulḥ, have disappeared from the political scene entirely, while the activities of the PPS have been greatly curtailed. Sham'ūn's temporary allies during the conflict—Jumayyil and Eddé—are now his competitors.

Conversely, most members of the former opposition came out of the conflict with their political power greatly enhanced. Salām now is prime minister and a member of parliament. Junblāṭ and his associate Majdalānī are ministers, and are represented in parliament by several deputies, including themselves. The present cabinet is controlled essentially by members of the former opposition, while the chairman of parliament is Ḥamādah, an important former opposition leader. Also as a result of the crisis, Bishārah al-Khūrī began to win back some of his lost political prestige, and has now become again a contender for the presidency.

3. It is possible that, as a result of the crisis, no Lebanese president will attempt to succeed himself, at least for some time to come, unless he has the support of both the public and a majority of the politicians. In any case, the incumbent president, General Shihāb, is known for his distaste for politics, disinterest in office, integrity and a strong sense of moral responsibility. Unless he changes radically during his six years in office—and this seems unlikely—he will probably set the precedent for Lebanese presidents to retire peacefully from office at the end of their terms. It is also possible that, as a result of the crisis and the conduct of President Shihāb, a precedent will be set for a cleaner and better government.

4. Since the end of the crisis, the Lebanese common man has manifested a growing political awareness and some degree of political independence from the hold of traditional leaders. This is probably due to the fact that, for the first time in the modern history of Lebanon, the common man played a decisive part in a national crisis. For instance, in the crisis of 1943, Lebanon won its independence from France essentially through international pressure, and the Lebanese

suffered comparatively very little as a result of their resistance. Similarly in 1952, president al-Khūrī was ousted from office through political negotiations among the traditional leaders. In contrast, during the 1958 crisis, the major burden fell on the shoulders of the common people. It was they who fought behind the barricades and in the mountains, suffered and died. Without their sacrifice, the traditional leaders would have been powerless. This has given the people a new appreciation of their importance and a new sense of power virtually absent before, and released them somewhat from the bondage of traditional loyalties. In any case, there is discernible evidence that, as a result of the crisis, the power of the traditional leaders has undergone a relative decline. Conversely, "ideological" parties with defined programs are beginning to make some headway in the political life of the country.

5. All Lebanese groups have now returned to the spirit as well as the form of the National Covenant. In 1959, I discussed this subject with various Lebanese politicians and educators, but although they all decried the confessional structure of the government, nevertheless they all felt that for many years to come, there can be no alternative to the National Covenant formula and that, if the crisis had any fundamental positive results, they lie in the possible realization of most Lebanese that they must learn to live together in peace, and that the alternative is ruin for the country and its people.

The crisis had three principal results relating to the region and to Lebanon's relations with its neighbors:

Lebanon returned to a neutral position in her relations with the Arab states. Although friendly with all of them, and acts in concert with them on matters of interest to the Arabs as a whole, she does not take sides in intra-Arab disputes. Moreover, she has returned to her former role of a mediator between them. Just as important is that all the Arab states accept this neutrality as a fact and none of them regard the policies of Lebanon as a threat to their security. The maintenance of the policy of neutrality by Lebanon is made easier because Arab politics are not as polarized as they were in 1957-58. Although there is considerable tension between the UAR and Iraq and Jordan, inter-Arab relations are comparatively fluid.

Lebanon's relations with Turkey and Iran are not as close as they were in 1957-58. Lebanon still maintains official friendly relations with these two states; however, the policies of the government today fall more or less in line with general Arab attitude towards the two

(exceptions are Iraq, which is hostile to them, and Jordan, which is very friendly with them.)

The Lebanese crisis retarded the Arab unity movement under the leadership of President Nāṣir in two ways: first, if there were any plans or hopes by some Lebanese to bring Lebanon into a form of union with the UAR, these, as a result of the crisis, have now been abandoned; second, there is some evidence that the involvement of the UAR, and the political events which transpired in the Arab world between 1958 and 1960, seemed to have introduced a deeper questioning as to the manner and form by which unity should be achieved.

In the international field, the crisis resulted in some subtle changes in the relations of Lebanon with the great powers, particularly the United States and the Soviet Union.

The friendly relations of Lebanon with the United States today are not as close as they were in 1957-58, yet, in a real sense, they are based on more solid foundations. For in 1957-58, these close relations with the United States were the subject of severe public controversy, whereas, today, less close relations which are nevertheless strong and genuine, are supported by the majority of the population. In turn this public support is due, in part, to the steady improvement in the relations between the UAR and the United States, and the Western powers in general.

Although the relations of Lebanon with the Soviet Union are still officially correct, nevertheless, there is little doubt that Lebanon, since the crisis, has drawn even further away from the Soviet Union, but with less fanfare than was the case in 1957-58. A Lebanese foreign minister said to me in 1959, "although we must remain as neutral as possible, we cannot overlook the territorial designs of the Soviet Union on Arab lands nor close our eyes to the Communist menace which has become too real for comfort, as illustrated in Iraq." The drawing away of Lebanon from the Soviet Union is part of a general Arab trend which started in late 1958, after the Iraqi revolt, and the continued attempts of the communists there to take over control of the government. Suddenly, the Arab world awoke to find the Soviet-Communist threat in its own house and to recognize its reality, something which it was unwilling to do before 1958.

The Lebanese crisis demonstrated that the Christians in the Arab world can no longer depend on foreign protection and that their best interests now lie in identification with the aspirations and life of their co-nationals. Contrary to the expectations and hopes of some

Christians in Lebanon when American troops landed, these latter showed utter indifference to any Christian-Muslim issue and refused to be drawn into the internal struggle.

The Lessons

The principal lesson of the Lebanese crisis is obvious. It is not a new revelation, but a confirmation of the wisdom of the National Covenant. It is simply this:

The bulk of the national income of Lebanon comes from the Arab hinterland and at least a majority of the population not only regard themselves as Arabs, but have strong ties with their brethren across the borders in Syria, Jordan, Iraq, Egypt and the Arabian Peninsula. Therefore, for Lebanon to be economically and politically a viable state, it must have the confidence and support of its sister Arab states. For these reasons, Lebanon cannot enter into relations with a foreign power or adopt foreign policies, if these relations and policies are believed to be a threat to the security of the Arab states, or are not supported by a substantial majority of the vocal public. Lebanon enters into such relations, no matter how immediately attractive the terms may seem to be, only at the risk of her own political collapse. In this sense, Lebanon's independence is conditional.

The crisis has also demonstrated that Lebanon is not as yet ready for any close union with the other Arab states. This may change in the future, but it is quite evident that for the present large numbers of Maronites still view such a possibility with fear. This writer does not subscribe to the views of those who announce such mystical dogma as "There always was and there always will be an independent entity called Lebanon." Boundaries as well as ideas change, and there is nothing immutable about the attitude of the Maronites. In fact, the split which is readily visible among the Maronites on the "Arab question" clearly indicates that a change is taking place.

Finally, the crisis has shown that, for the time being at least, a neutral independent Lebanon serves the best interests of its own people, of the Arabs, and of the international community. For the Arabs, such a neutral Lebanon can and does serve as a haven for their political refugees. Owing to the revolutionary changes taking place in the Arab world today, such a function is a vital one. It reduces human suffering and allows time for tempers to cool down. Second, such a Lebanon can and does serve as a mediator between them and a meeting ground for negotiations. It is interesting to note that Arab conferences are being held in Lebanon more frequently on the basis that it is neutral ground.

As for the international community, we have argued that any

close alliance between Lebanon and a foreign power, particularly if it is believed to threaten the security of the Arab states, is at best a precarious one and, in all likelihood, will fail. Conversely, a neutral Lebanon would be an important point of contact for the international community—political, commercial and cultural—with the Arab hinterland. Such a positive function is particularly important today, since the activities of foreigners are gradually being restricted in most of the Arab states. In this connection, it is interesting to note that Beirut is the center of UN activity in the area, that embassies in Beirut, particularly those of the great powers, maintain larger staffs than anywhere else in the area, that Beirut is the regional center of foreign business, and finally that Beirut is the clearing house of ideas in the Arab world.

UNOGIL MAP

FIRST REPORT

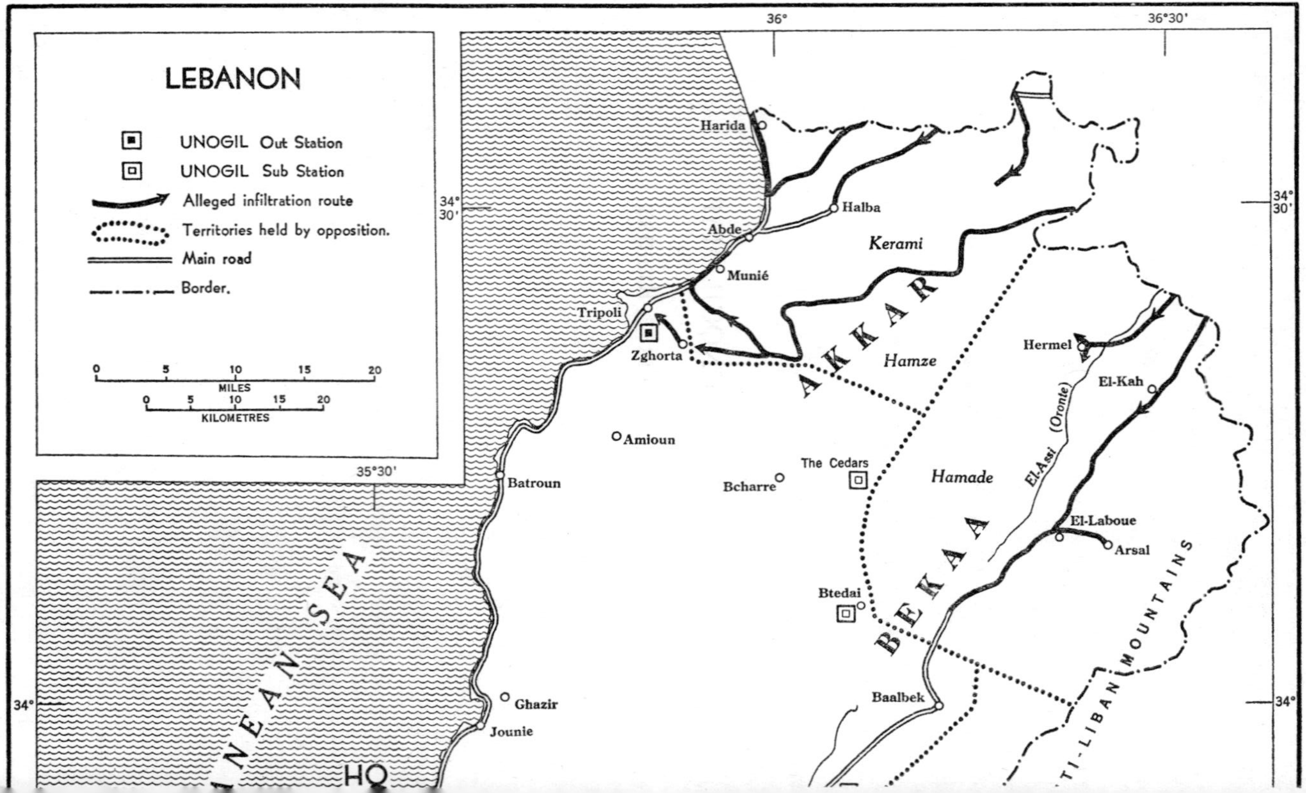
LEBANON
UNOGIL Out Station
UNOGIL Sub Station
Alleged infiltration route
Territories held by opposition.
Main road
Border.
0 5 10 15 20
MILES
0 5 10 15 20
KILOMETRES
36°
36°30'
34° 30'
35°30'
34°
Harida
Halba
Abde
Munié
Kerami
Tripoli
Zghorta
AKKAR
Hamze
Hermel
El-Kah
El-Assi (Oronte)
Amioun
The Cedars
Bcharre
Hamade
Batroun
El-Laboue
Arsal
BEKAA
Btedai
SEA
Ghazir
Jounie
Baalbek
HQ

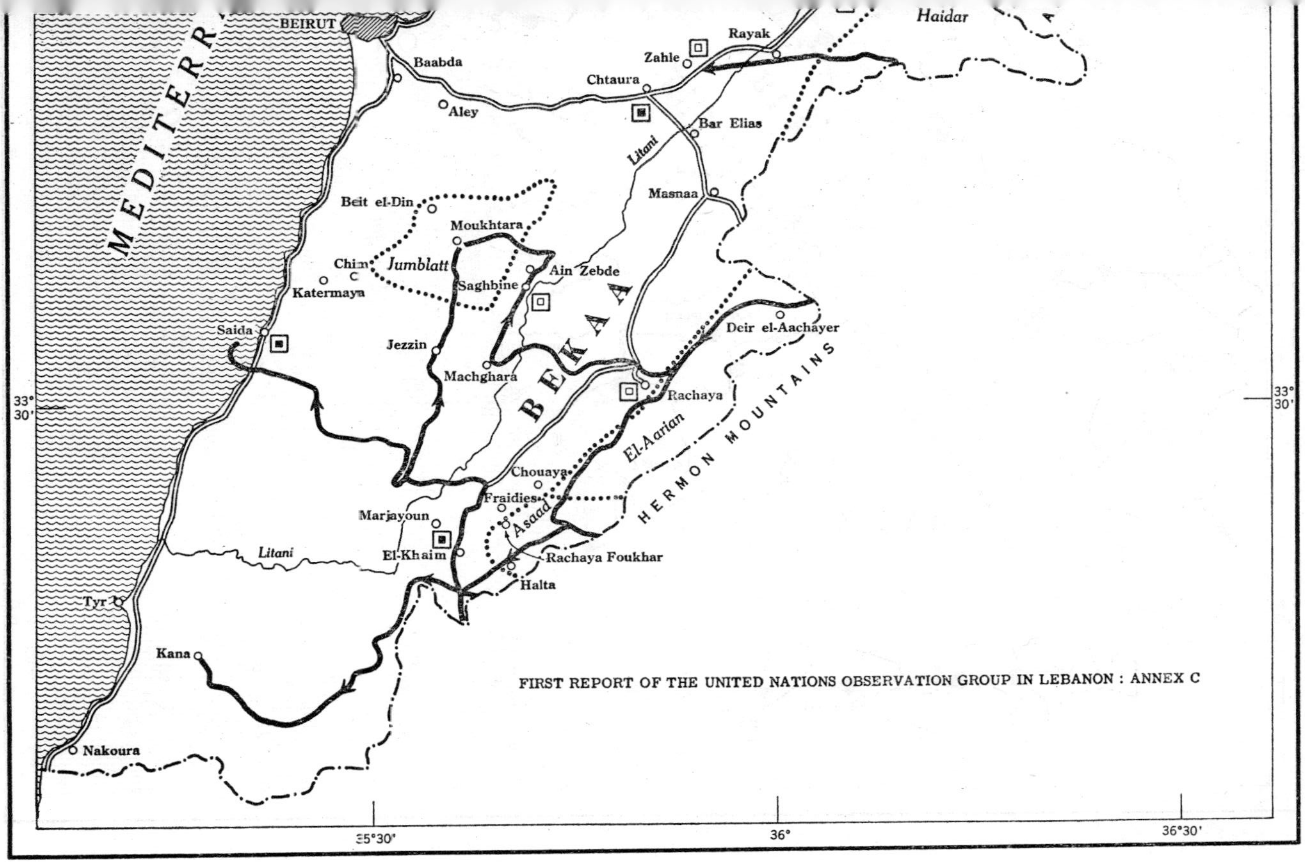

FIRST REPORT OF THE UNITED NATIONS OBSERVATION GROUP IN LEBANON : ANNEX C

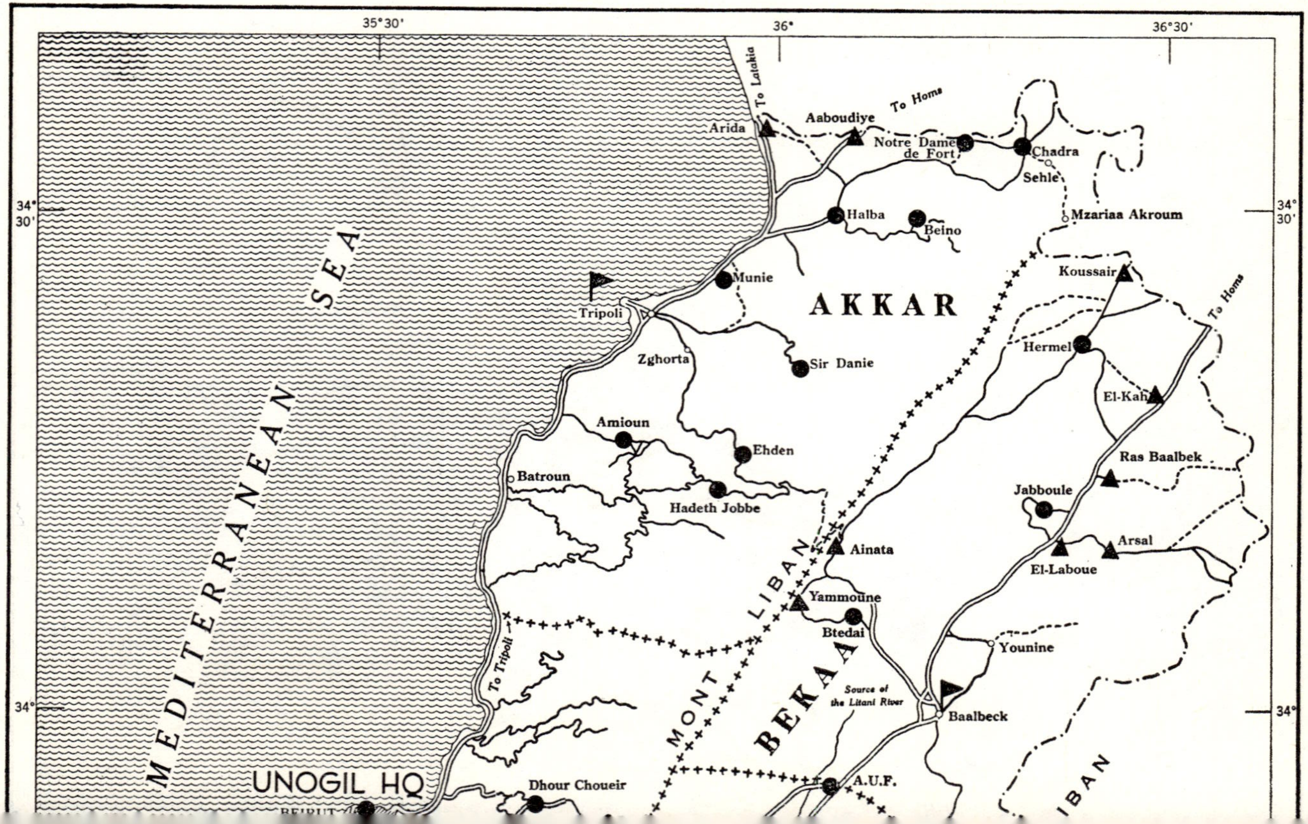

35°30'
36°
36°30'
34° 30'
34°
To Latakia
To Homs
Arida
Aabouidiye
Notre Dame de Fort
Chadra
Sehle
Mzariaa Akroum
Halba
Beino
Koussair
Munie
AKKAR
Tripoli
Hermel
Zghorta
Sir Danie
El-Kah
Amioun
Ehden
Ras Baalbek
Batroun
Hadeth Jobbe
Jabboule
Ainata
Arsal
El-Laboue
MEDITERRANEAN SEA
Yammoune
Btedai
Younine
MONT LIBAN
BEKAA
To Tripoli
Source of the Litani River
Baalbeck
UNOGIL HQ
Dhour Choueir
A.U.F.
BEIRUT

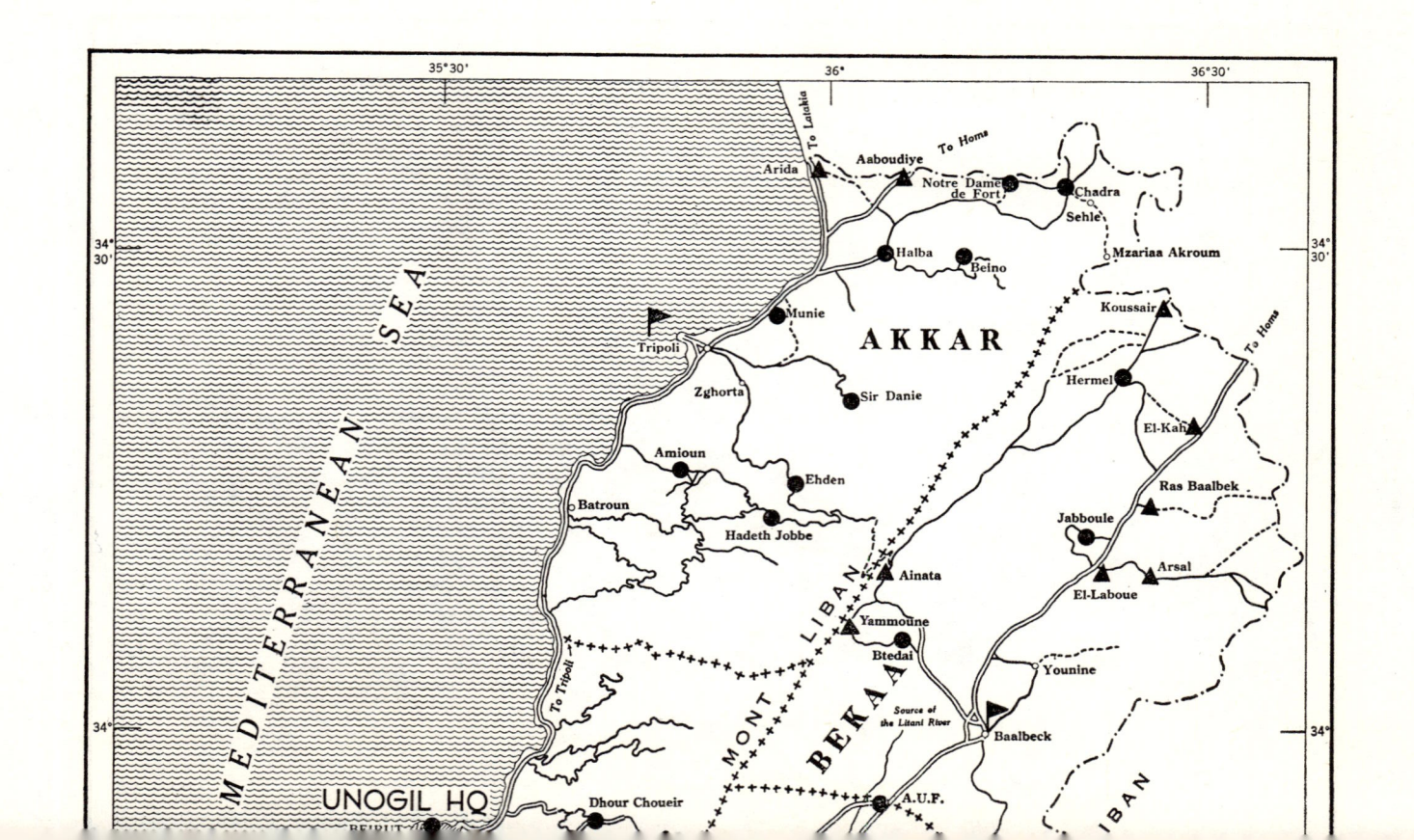

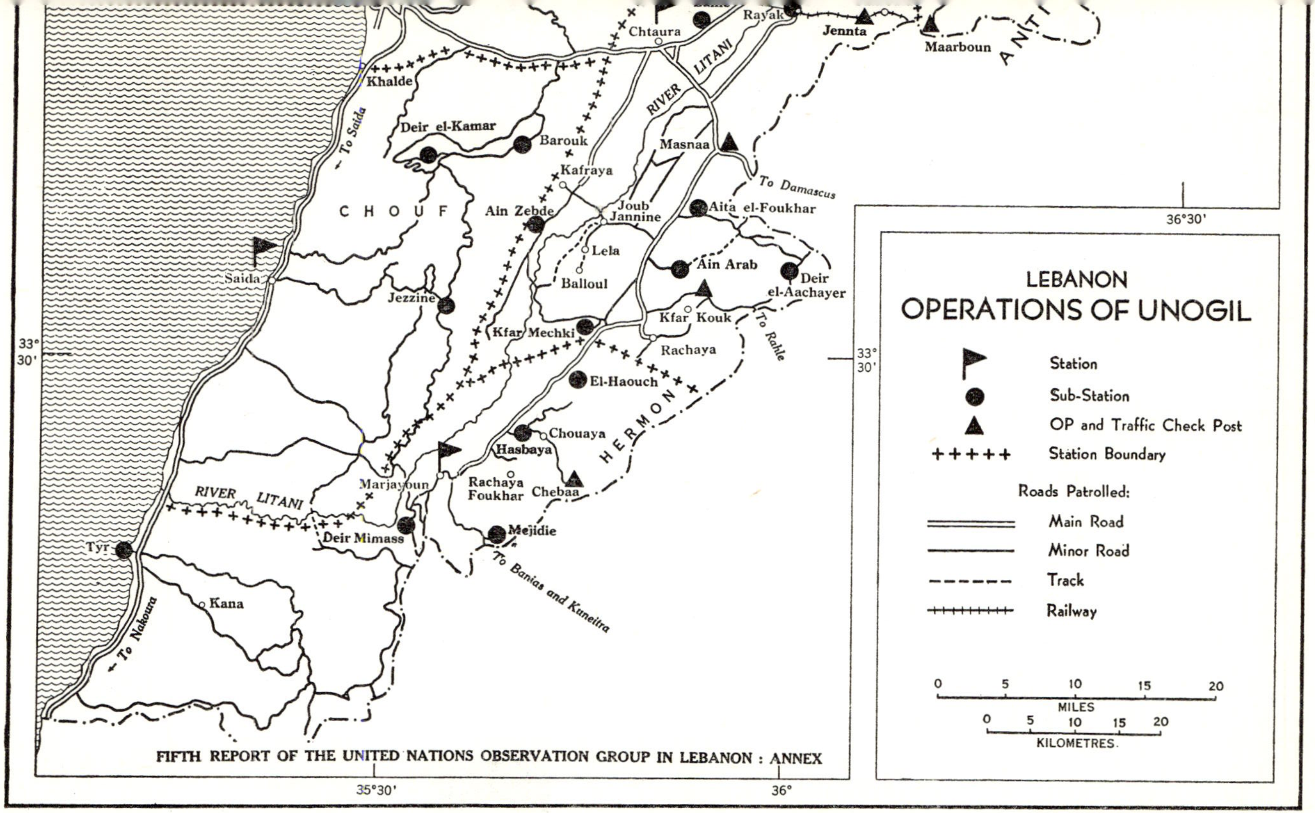

FIFTH REPORT OF THE UNITED NATIONS OBSERVATION GROUP IN LEBANON : ANNEX

Appendix I

THE LEBANESE PRESENTATION AT THE SECURITY COUNCIL

(A)

SPEECH OF DR. MALIK (LEBANON) ON JUNE 6, 1958*

Before I make my formal statement, I think I owe a word of explanation to the Security Council.

We placed our present complaint first before the League of Arab States. We are a member of that regional organization and we wanted its machinery to deal with our issue first. Then we brought it to the attention of the Security Council. The Security Council placed this item on its agenda on Tuesday, 27 May 1958. At that time, the Arab League had already called a meeting on this matter on Saturday, 31 May. The Government of Lebanon, therefore, requested the Council on 27 May only to place the item on its agenda and not to enter into a substantive examination of the issue in order that the Arab League may be given a first chance of dealing with the matter. We also asked that the Council meet again on this question one week later, namely on Tuesday of this week. The Council was good enough to accede to both these requests.

On Saturday last the Arab League began considering this matter. It became apparent on Monday that they needed a little more time for the various delegations to confer with one another and with their Governments. We therefore asked the Council at its session on Monday to postpone for forty-eight hours the meeting scheduled for the following day. The Council again kindly acceded to our request.

The Council thus was to meet yesterday to consider our question. A few minutes before the meeting we received conflicting reports about the proceedings at the Arab League, and I had at once to get in touch with Beirut by telephone. I decided, as a result, to presume once more upon your forebearance and to request one last postponement of twenty-four hours. The Council for the third time granted our request. The Government of Lebanon is grateful to the distinguished representatives here and to their Governments for their understanding.

The Arab League has been in session for six days on this question. It has taken no decision on it. Consequently, the Government of Lebanon is bound now, much to its regret, to press this issue before the Security Council. We are all the more bound to do so as the information I have just received indicates that the intervention of which we complain is increasing both in scope and in intensity.

This is the statement I wanted to make by way of explanation of the events of the last few days at the Council before I proceeded to my formal statement. I come now to the presentation of the case.

I have never before defended or pleaded for Lebanon directly in the United Nations. It is true there is always a direct bearing upon one's own country in everything one does or says at the United Nations. But Lebanon has never been the central theme of my speeches here. This central theme was often human rights, often again technical assistance, more than once the problems of development, quite often cultural subjects, several times here at this Council disarmament, again and again the diverse problems of Asia and Africa, very often indeed the great issues of freedom and totalitarianism in the tragic world of today.

Concerning the Arab world, there has not been a single issue in which I did not

---

* *UN Doc. S/PV. 823,* 6 June 1958, pp. 2-50.

take an active part. The Arab world is our world and it was my bounden duty, even apart from formal instructions from my Government, to try to elucidate its problems and defend its causes. Was it Morocco, was it Algeria, was it Tunis, was it Libya, was it Egypt in the diverse phases of its problems at the United Nations, was it Yemen, was it Saudi Arabia in its interests at the Aqaba Gulf and elsewhere, was it the other struggling Arabs in the Arabian Peninsula, was it that momentous theme Palestine with its infinite modulations since 1946 here at the United Nations and in world public opinion, was it Jordan, was it Syria—the records of the United Nations contain by now, I suppose, millions of words by me on these great Arab questions. I do not claim that this verbiage achieved much or that in any given instance it exhausted its subject; I only hold that in all these cases Lebanon tried, through its representative, to be fair, constructive, truthful and concerned not only with the rights of the Arabs, which was indeed its absolute duty, but with the fundamental interests of the world community as a whole and of peace itself. I also suggest that perhaps no single man, Arab or non-Arab, was granted what was cumulatively granted me—out of no virtue of my own but through a strange and fortuitous concatenation of circumstances—by way of massive intervention in behalf of my Arab brethren at the United Nations during the last thirteen years. I am proud of this record.

As the circle of fate must be closed, the turn of Lebanon has now come. It seems fate would not spare me this ordeal. For ordeal it certainly and painfully is to have to defend one's own country not against foreigners but against one's own friends and kinsmen. I shall rise to this task with humility and without malice, and in a spirit of absolute goodwill. The Lebanon, the peaceful and little Lebanon, the Lebanon that never harmed and can never harm anybody, the Lebanon that by its very character can only dedicate itself to the arts of peace and to the service of the human person, the Lebanon whose very existence depends upon confidence and friendship prevailing between it and the other Arab states, that this essentially good Lebanon should ever have to defend itself in the Security Council, and indeed with respect to one of its sister Arab states, would appear truly incredible. It is a great spiritual trial, and one can only pray that as he is tried he will not prove unworthy of the highest he knows.

The circle of fate has also to be closed in another sense. The Arabs have bitterly known, and are still knowing, what it means to struggle against the outside world. There is now the experience of an inner struggle. A great people achieves historic destiny by facing up not only to the challenges of the world, but especially to its own inner trials and problems. The various trends, tendencies and movements agitating and fermenting the Arab world today are bound to confront, struggle and come to terms with one another. In this way history grinds maturity and strength.

The case which we have brought to the attention of the Security Council consists of three claims. The first is that there has been, and there still is, massive, illegal and unprovoked intervention in the affairs of Lebanon by the United Arab Republic. The second is that this intervention aims at undermining and does in fact threaten the independence of Lebanon. The third is that the situation created by this intervention which threatens the independence of Lebanon is likely, if it continues, to endanger the maintenance of international peace and security. I now proceed to the proof of these three claims.

The actuality of the intervention is proven by adducing six sets of facts. (a) The supply of arms on a large scale from the United Arab Republic to subversive elements in Lebanon. (b) The training in subversion on the territory of the United Arab Republic of elements from Lebanon and the sending back of these elements to Lebanon to subvert their Government. (c) The participation of United Arab Republic civilian nationals, residing in or passing into Lebanon, in subversive and terrorist activities in Lebanon. (d) The participation of United Arab Republic governmental elements in subversive and terrorist activities and in the direction of rebellion in Lebanon. (e) The violent and utterly unprecedented press campaign conducted by the United Arab Republic against the Government of Lebanon. (f) The violent and utterly unprecedented radio campaign conducted by the United Arab Republic inciting the people of Lebanon to overthrow their Government.

These six sets of facts taken together establish conclusively the existence of a massive, illegal and unprovoked intervention in the affairs of Lebanon by the United Arab Republic. The proofs of (a), (b), (c) and (d) fall more properly under the third section of my speech below, namely, under the material aspect of the intervention.

The proofs of (e) and (f), while certainly also affording material evidence, determine more properly the formal character of the intervention, what I called above the second claim, namely, that the intervention aims at undermining and does in fact threaten the independence of Lebanon. Consequently, (e) and (f)—the press and radio campaigns—will be treated in the third section below. The third section also examines the third claim, namely, that the situation created by this intervention is likely, if continued, to endanger the maintenance of international peace and security. There will also be a necessary conclusion at the end of the argument.

I come now to the proofs of the three claims and the setting forth of the six sets of facts. The first claim is, as we have seen, that there has been and there still is massive, illegal and unprovoked intervention in the affairs of Lebanon by the United Arab Republic. The following four sets of facts determine materially the actual existence of this intervention.

The first set of facts deals with the supply of arms on a large scale from the United Arab Republic to subversive elements in Lebanon.

1. On 30 March 1958, a private vehicle with the registration number 4774 was stopped and searched at the customs post of Abboudieh, in North Lebanon. The vehicle, which was entering Lebanese territory from Syria, was found to be carrying the following: 5 semi-automatic guns, model 1949; 5 semi-automatic guns, model 1936; and 1,645 bullets. The names inscribed on these guns were names of Syrian soldiers, namely, Mohammed Abdulla, Mazhar Demian, Zakaria Mle 121971 and Ahmed El-Sheikh Mle 39593.

2. The Lebanese State Police, on 9 April 1958, intercepted and attacked a group of 110 outlaws who entered Lebanon from Syria, carrying arms. The battle between the police and the outlaws lasted several hours, and resulted in the death of three Lebanese and several rebels. Brought to court, the arrested rebels declared as follows:

> "Some hundred Lebanese followers of Kamal Jumblatt were convoked to a meeting in Damascus by the leadership of their party on Monday, 7 April 1958. On that day, Jumblatt followers were met in a café in Damascus by a certain officer of the Syrian army who asked them to stay overnight and return the next day. The next day two Syrian army officers presented themselves in the café, put the followers of Jumblatt on an army truck and drove them to the Lebanese frontiers. Before arriving there the truck left the main road, drove into the fields and stopped at an isolated spot. The Syrian officers told the Lebanese to leave the truck, called them up by name and distributed to every one of them a machine gun, 370 bullets and one grenade, while explaining to them how to use these weapons. Then the officers told them to walk into the Lebanese territory and to disperse themselves as soon as possible in order to avoid being pursued by Lebanese security officers."

3. In a report by the State Police of North Lebanon dated 10 April 1958, information was received that four Syrian officers, two of the rank of major and one captain, entered early in April 1958 the Lebanese border villages, Kora-Hawik and Moaisra. They met with members of the Jaafar tribe, now in rebellion, and handed them 25 army guns. Other arms were distributed at the same period among the tribe of Arab El Oteik in the Wadi-Khaled region. These were subsequently seen around carrying military weapons.

4. In a report by the General Security Department of the Bekan district dated 17 April 1958, members of Hamada, Jaafar and Haj-Hassan tribes had fired about 1,000

bullets on the State Police post at Hermel during the night of 7 April 1958. On the evening of 12 April 1958, the same rebels were met by a certain Mahdi Hamada who arrived from Syria carrying with him two cases of dynamite. During the night of the same day the same rebels threw dynamite at the headquarters of the Social-Nationalist party at Hermel and made an attempt to destroy the bridge at Dawra.

5. In the early days of May 1958, it was communicated by the State Police at Bekaa district that Sabri Hamadi, a leader of the opposition, was distributing arms to his followers immediately after his return from Syria in a Syrian army jeep.

6. On 16 May 1958, according to report No. 2413/12 by the State Police in the Bekaa Valley, a group of armed men penetrated into Lebanon from Syria. They had with them mules carrying arms. When intercepted by the State Police and attacked in the fields of the Bekaa by military planes, they fled, leaving several dead who were carrying weapons and ammunition.

7. During the first week of the present disturbances two sailboats were captured at sea off the Lebanese coast. In the first sailboat there were eleven Palestinians of the Egyptian region of Gaza. They carried with them two machineguns, one revolver, 740 hand grenades and 4,363 Egyptian pounds. One of them had been convicted of belonging to a terrorist group. This sailboat was captured in front of Saddiyat in the vicinity of a private house belonging to the President of the Republic. The second sailboat, captured across from Tabarja, north of Beirut, similarly had on board eleven Palestinians of the same Gaza region. These latter had been convicted once by a military tribunal of having entered clandestinely into Lebanese territory. On 21 May 1958 Lebanese naval units arrested another sailboat with six passengers aboard, all Lebanese from Tripoli, who declared that they were returning from the region of Tel-Kalakh, in Syria, where they brought arms after having received training under the direction of Syrian officers for the use of these arms.

8. In a report by the Lebanese 2éme Bureau dated 26 May 1958, a meeting was held in Damascus at the office of the Syrian 2éme Bureau. Those present were three Lebanese, namely, Ghalib Yagi (Baalbeck), Mohammed Yahfufi (Nahleh), and Riad Taha, a journalist of the opposition. At this meeting the Syrian lieutenant Bourhan Adham gave them instructions to bomb army barracks and armed forces wherever they could find them. They also instructed them to keep off American property and promised them that arms would be delivered in Baalbeck by the way of Sarghaya. These arms, he said, would be enough to make them unafraid of Lebanese armed forces.

9. According to a report by the Lebanese General Security Department dated 19 May 1958, three men were arrested near Majdel-Anjar village. Upon being questioned, they confessed that they had been in Damascus by order of the Socialist Party to receive arms and ammunition and carry them back to Dair-El-Achayer for the purpose of using them against Lebanese authorities. Trucks of ammunition and arms as well as members of the Syrian armed forces were seen by security officers in the house of Khazai Aryane, a relative of a prominent opposition leader in that district.

10. In a report by the Lebanese 2éme Bureau dated 28 May 1958, the following arms and ammunition, restricted to regular army use, were confiscated on Lebanese territory on 27 and 28 May 1958:

at Baalbeck	4 anti-tank grenades Energa
at Ain-Zabdeh (Bekaa)	1 anti-aircraft gun
	4 cases of mortar shells
	Army wireless equipment
at Hirj-Ain-Zabdeh	1 case containing 10 anti-tank grenades Energa and 6 bombs, as well as one anti-tank mine.

I suggest, Mr. President, that these arms cannot be bought on the open market.

11. A report by the Lebanese 2éme Bureau dated 28 May 1958, lists various army weapons and ammunition, coming from Syria. These were of different kinds and of various makes, and used only by regular army forces. According to a certain Hisham

Naji of Tripoli who was arrested among others on 28 May 1958, these weapons were sent to Mohammed Hamzeh, a prominent opposition leader in Tripoli. Syrian and Egyptian army marks were found inscribed on them—and I have the pictures of these arms and these marks.

12. On 12 May 1958 the Consul-General of Belgium in Damascus, M. Louis de San, was arrested at the Syrian-Lebanese frontiers, and the following were seized in his car: 33 machine guns, 28 revolvers with ammunition, 35 units of gun ammunition, 31 units of revolver ammunition containing 1,500 cartridges, 15,000 cartridges and 1 bomb with automatic detonator. The Consul-General was carrying with him a letter addressed to a mysterious person in Beirut, instructing the bombing of three main streets in Beirut and the Presidential Palace. It also ordered the throwing of explosives in various sectors of the city, the setting up of barricades in the streets, and the killing of Syrian personalities living in Beirut as refugees. It is significant that at the moment of his arrest M. Louis de San refused to allow the search of his car, and requested to return to Syria without being searched, and without continuing into Lebanon. He pretended that he had been entrusted by his driver with the suitcases containing the weapons and that he was ignorant of their contents. A few minutes later his driver presented himself at the Lebanese Customs, apparently disturbed, and accompanied by the chief of the Syrian Customs to inquire about M. de San. It should be pointed out that in the following night the Lebanese customs post that arrested M. de San was the subject of an armed attack by several hundred Syrians and Lebanese coming from Syria. This attack is the subject of another document. The Government of Lebanon had from the beginning expressed its firm belief that the friendly Government of Belgium had nothing whatsoever to do with the activity of M. de San.

13. On 29 May 1958, several persons were arrested in the neighborhood of Tyre in the south of Lebanon for having taken part in subversive activities against the village of Cana. These persons had considerable quantities of arms which they confessed they had received from across the border in Syria from the villages of Al-Ghajar and Banias. They also gave the names of scores of people belonging to their villages who had shortly before crossed the frontiers and obtained arms from Syrian Army officers. Some of these men made their contacts with the Syrian Army through the opposition leader, Ahmed El-Assad. These men come from the villages of Siddikkin and Zibkin.

14. On 28 May 1958, a truck loaded with the following arms and ammunition was seized near Tripoli coming from Syria: 88 Bertha mortars; 1 Mauser rifle; 1 machine gun (Energa-British make); 1 anti-tank gun (Energa-British make); 18 bomb shells (Energa); 12 jute bags containing ammunition for the above-mentioned weapons; 60 cases containing hand grenades; 1 jute bag containing mortar shells; 12 cans containing dynamite; 60 rifles (French make) Model 1936, of which 22 were marked "Syrian Army"; 28 boxes containing large size Bertha ammunition, inscribed "the Egyptian Army—1949—made under the supervision of Technical Research Department." Again, Mr. President, I have pictures of all these arms, and again I suggest that many of these arms cannot be bought on the open market.

15. There are several thousand armed men engaged in subversive activities in Lebanon today. Most of these men operate near the Syrian borders in the north of Lebanon, in the Bekaa Valley and in the south. We have no doubt at all, from all the evidence that we have gathered, that all the arms that these men use were supplied them from Syria. The Government of Lebanon therefore believes that all men engaged in subversive activities in Lebanon today are supplied with arms from the United Arab Republic.

I come now to the second set of facts, namely, the one that deals with the training in subversion on the territory of the United Arab Republic of elements from Lebanon and the sending back of these elements to Lebanon to subvert their Government.

1. We know that measures have been taken in Syria for training Lebanese and non-Lebanese commandos under the direction of the Syrian officer, Akram Safwa, and other officers belonging to the Syrian 2ème Bureau. These training officers constitute in Syria

a unit named "Maghawyr Unit." It is to be noted that the majority of those arrested for espionage, distribution of pamphlets and letters of threat and destructive activity in Lebanon—and we have plenty of them in our prisons, I can present them to you any time you like—belong to this unit.

2. A number of persons among the followers of Kamal Jumblatt went to Syria for training with Syrian Druses in the use of quick arms and the throwing of bombs and explosives. A number of them had been seen crossing the southern border entering into Lebanese territory. Also about 150 men from Tripoli and its vicinity had been witnessed in the Syrian town of Hadbussya, near Tel-Kalakh, being trained by the Syrian army in the use of arms. We have a considerable list of persons—I have it with me here—who had been arrested and who pleaded guilty to receiving military training in Syria.

3. In May 1958, seven armed men were arrested by the police. Upon being questioned, they confessed that they, together with 150 others, had been to Syria where they were directed to Banias military barracks. There they were handed arms and ammunition as well as money and were ordered to return to Lebanon in army trucks to participate in the current uprising against the Government of Lebanon.

4. A number of armed men were arrested following their participation in an armed attack in Southern Lebanon. They confessed having received arms and ammunition from Syrian military officers who also gave them money and training.

During the last two days, I have received considerable further information on precisely this item, namely, on the training of Lebanese nationals on Syrian territory. I have not included it in this report, but the four facts which I have just set forth here under this item are enough to prove the charge dealing with training in subversion on the territory of the United Arab Republic of elements from Lebanon and the sending back of these elements to Lebanon to subvert their Government.

I come now to the third set of facts, dealing with the participation of United Arab Republic civilian nationals residing in Lebanon, or passing into Lebanon, in subversive and terrorist activities in Lebanon.

1. Early in January 1958, Lebanese security authorities reported that two Syrians, Ahmed Kassim Al-Juju and Jaafar Al-Juju, of Sirgaya in Syria, transmitted explosives and other accessory equipment to a certain Mohammed Mulhim Kassim, of Hirtaala in Lebanon. The latter revealed that these weapons were destined to be used to blow up Government premises in Baalbeck. He was also instructed to be ready for forthcoming contacts with the Syrians. Later in May, Government headquarters were in fact blown up by the rebels.

2. During the night of 12 May 1958, the military police in Beirut arrested a certain Mohammed Katmi, a Syrian national and native of Hama, Syria, who was a student at the American University of Beirut and a resident of Al-Hamra quarter in Ras-Beirut. Upon searching his house, the police found ten machine guns and a huge quantity of ammunition. Four other Syrians who were found in the house were also arrested.

3. In the course of an armed attack by rebels in Sidon on 25 May 1958, 22 Syrians were arrested among those who were attacking, 13 of whom carried Syrian army identity cards.

4. On 12 May 1958, the military police arrested a certain Atalla Al-Hariri, of Syrian nationality, while he was engaged in setting up roadblocks in Fuad Al-Awal Street in Beirut.

5. On 9, 10 and 11 May 1958, violent demonstrations broke out in Tripoli. Among the demonstrators arrested were nine carrying Syrian identification cards.

6. During 1958, security reports show that tens of Syrians and Palestinians from Gaza were arrested for terrorist activities. On 20 May 1958, 146 terrorists of Syrian nationality were under prosecution by Lebanese authorities.

7. According to a report by the police, No. 9426, dated May 1958, a certain

Salahdin Mardini, of Syrian nationality, was arrested at the Claridge Hotel in Beirut for insulting the Chief of State. Another person of Syrian nationality, by the name of Abdul Kader Kayouh, was also arrested for carrying a military map. Other Syrian suspects were arrested on various similar charges.

8. In the same report, it is stated that a Syrian by the name of Moustafa El-Sayed was arrested for threatening a shopkeeper in the Avenue des Francais to close his shop. Another Syrian, Mohamed Mir'i, was also brought to court for carrying arms illegally.

9. On 17 May 1958, a certain Mohamed Yunis Saleh Assfari, of Idlib, Syria, was arrested for possessing and transporting dynamite shells. Evidence was brought against him as also guilty of terrorist activities. On 30 May 1958, he was sentenced by the military court to life imprisonment at hard labor.

10. This listing of specific cases in which Syrian or Egyptian civilian nationals participated in subversive activities in Lebanon can be considerably extended. But the indicated set of facts is enough to prove that United Arab Republic civilian nationals residing in Lebanon or passing into Lebanon have participated in subversive and terrorist activities in Lebanon.

I come now to the fourth set of facts, dealing with the participation not of Lebanese civilian nationals trained in Syria, nor of Syrian or Egyptian civilian nationals, but of United Arab Republic governmental elements, in subversive and terrorist activities and in the direction of rebellion in Lebanon.

1. On 19 February 1958, a certain Ahmed Alif Akachi, of Syrian nationality, a Syrian army draftee (21 Group, No. 24560), confessed before the prosecutor of the military court that he had been sent to Lebanon by his chief, Commandant Mohammed El-Sodk, in order to meet in Beirut certain individuals who would instruct him to throw explosives at the Presidential Palace and the residence of the Premier.

2. On 13 May 1958, a certain Mohammed Abdul Rahman Jabari, of Aleppo, Syria, was arrested in Beirut. He confessed that he was a Syrian army officer attached to the First Battalion under the number 13748, and that he had been sent to Lebanon by Captain Ahmed Nagib Maarawi, head of the Deuxiéme Bureau in Aleppo, to join a group of Syrian soldiers in Beirut, where they carry out terrorist activities. He also confessed that many others like him arrived in Lebanon clandestinely and separately and then formed themselves into units of eleven members each. He said that he had received arms and money in Beirut and that he had participated in terrorist acts against public order. On 30 May 1958, he was sentenced by the Lebanese military court to serve fifteen years at hard labor.

3. On 17 May 1958, the state police in the region of Chouf arrested two men on the bridge of Nabi' El-Safa, the two men being named Turki Hassan, whose number was 7348 of the Syrian army, and Mahmoud Abdel Ghany Saab, whose number was 322. The first turned out to be a student at the Syrian Military School, and the second a member of the Eleventh Group of Armed Forces in the town of Douma, Syria.

4. A Syrian army officer was arrested on 15 May 1958 in Souk-Al-Gharb. He was carrying maps of Lebanon and the names of the American, British and French Ambassadors in Lebanon, and other pertinent information.

5. On 21 May 1958, the vegetable market in Beirut was reopened. At noon on the same day, two bombs were thrown, and the explosion caused the death of two persons and injured several others. On the following day, 22 May, a bomb exploded in a main commercial street of Beirut, Souk-Tawileh, which had always refused to close its stores. This resulted in the death of one person and the serious injury of several others. The perpetrator of these two incidents, Mohammed Rabih Bakri, is of Syrian nationality. He confessed that he had arrived in Lebanon two weeks earlier, that he had left the Syrian armed forces on order of his chief, Captain Aliwan, and that he was to come to Lebanon and contact a certain group, which instructed him to throw three bombs in

the vegetable market and the Souk-Tawileh commercial street. This is all taken from the verbatim record of the military prosecutor, dated 23 May 1958.

6. For two years now, the Syrian Deuxiéme Bureau has been conducting on Lebanese territory activities contrary to Lebanese policy. It has continuously increased the number of its agents and had thus provoked a number of incidents: terrorism, setting off of bombs, dynamiting, distribution of pamphlets, sending of anonymous threatening letters. The agents of this Bureau are for the most part Syrians or Palestinian refugees, although there are some Lebanese among them. The following agents were arrested, tried and convicted for subversive activities:

Abdul Rahim Saleh Abu-Hajala, Palestinian, twelve years' hard labor;
Jalal Mohamed Kahoush, Palestinian, four years' hard labor;
Abdel Rahman Assad Keblawi, Palestinian, four years' hard labor;
Abdel Hamid Kamel Saadeh, Palestinian, four years' hard labor;
Mohamed Ali Sayyed, Syrian, fifteen years' hard labor *in absentia;*
Mustafa Kassab, Syrian, fifteen years' hard labor *in absentia.*

Many other agents of the Syrian Deuxiéme Bureau were arrested and confessed that they engaged in espionage in Lebanon.

7. During 1957 and 1958 many terrorist and subversive activities were carried out by agents of the Governments of Syria and Egypt. These activities include bombings, assassinations and kidnappings. Worthy of special mention is the case of the Egyptian Military Attaché in Beirut, Hassan Khalil. Early in 1957, he was arrested carrying in his car a considerable quantity of arms. The investigations that followed his arrest led to the discovery of a terrorist gang responsible for previous acts of terrorism. This gang was responsible for the bombing of the Iraq Petroleum Company's installation in Tripoli, the British School of Shimlan, the SS Norman Prince, the Port of Beirut, the St. George's Club, the British Bank of the Middle East and the Banque de Syrie et du Liban.

8. On 3 May 1958 a group of about 200 Syrian Army conscripts crossed the Lebanese borders and occupied the village of Kafar-Shouba, in the district of Hasbaya. Incidentally, you will notice, Mr. President, that the importance of these things increases as I go on. I have arranged them in mounting order of importance. Those that I have left to the end of any [sic] listing are, in general, of a more serious character. These 200 Syrian Army conscripts to whom I just referred attacked the Lebanese security forces, who answered their fire and drove them out of the village. The assailants then entrenched themselves in the neighboring hills on Lebanese territory, at Janan, Hirj-Sedama, Ain-Joz, Hirj-Wistani, and began thereon to open fire day and night.

9. On 15 May 1958, another group of several hundred Syrian Army conscripts occupied the Lebanese village of Chabaa and destroyed the roads and the telephone lines connecting the district with other Lebanese villages. On 18 May 1958, the chief of the Socialist party at Hasbaya met with the Syrian leaders of Chabaa and later recommended his friends at Hasbaya not to oppose any Syrian assailant that might invade the locality. During the night of 20 May 1958, the assailants opened a continuous fire at Hasbaya, but the State Police obliged them to retreat towards Chabaa.

10. On 14 and 15 May 1958, three Syrian Army jeeps carrying troops arrived in Aboudiya from the Syrian post at Dabbousi and set fire to the documents and furniture of the General Security Officer and destroyed the posts of the State Police and the Customs. On the same day the posts of the State Police at Sebhel and Miziara were attacked and occupied by armed men coming from Syria. The same happened to the post at Soueika on 13 May 1958.

11. During the night of 12-13 May 1958, an armed band of several hundred persons, at least one hundred of whom were Syrians, attacked the Lebanese customs outpost at Masnaa—the one to which I referred in connection with the Belgian Consul-General —destroying by dynamite the customs installations and those of the security police, and massacring six Lebanese officials. The Lebanese security forces arrested a few days later

three individuals of Lebanese nationality as they were crossing the border clandestinely into Lebanon coming from Syria. The cross-examination of these three prisoners revealed the fact that the band which attacked Masnaa came from Dair-El-Achayer, situated exactly at the Lebanese-Syrian frontier. It gathered at the home of Shebli Aryane who distributed arms to its members. For several days three Syrian officers, wearing respectively three stars, two stars and one or two stars, paid frequent visits to Shebli Aryane and supplied him with guns and sub-machine guns. The same officers met with the members of the band and gave them instructions for the attack on Masnaa. It also transpired from the cross-examination of drivers who wanted to cross the frontier near Masnaa during the day of 12 May that the band of attackers had started its preparation in Syrian territory around noon during that day. The Syrian authorities at the post of Jedaydet-Yabous, facing the post of Masnaa, interrupted the traffic to conceal from the Lebanese authorities the preparations in question. According to witnesses the majority of the attackers of Masnaa infiltrated later into the Shouf and the upper Metn, while 100 Druses of Syrian nationality returned to Dair-El-Achmayer to await Syrian reinforcements.

12. Already in 1957, when the terrorist group organized by the Military Attaché of Egypt in Lebanon was active in the capital and in the other towns, a serious incident took place at the Lebanese-Syrian border, in Dair-El-Achayer. During the night of 11 and 12 September 1957, a group of 175 Lebanese State Police arrived at Dair-El-Achayer to put an end to the smuggling of arms from Syria into Lebanon that had been going on for some time in that locality.

On 12 September 1957 this group was attacked from various places situated on the neighboring Syrian mountains, while trucks of the Syrian Army went back and forth carrying men and soldiers to the assailants. The State Police returned the fire. In the course of the battle it became evident that the number of Syrians had considerably increased thanks to the reinforcements brought in by the Syrian armed forces. Consequently, the Lebanese State Police were taken prisoners by the assailants and later on declared that they had seen with Shebly Aryane, the opposition leader, at Dair-El-Achayer, a Syrian Army officer named Rifai Amin. According to the information received by the authorities, a meeting was held at Dair-El-Achayer before the incident took place between Shebly Aryane and other leaders of the Lebanese opposition on the other side, and Syrian officers on the other. These were recognized to be, Commandant Talaat Sadki, Assistant Chief of the Deuxiéme Bureau; Commandant Bourhan Adham, Chief of the Syrian Military Police; and Lieutenant Bourhan Boulos, Chief of Palestinian commandos attached to the Syrian Deuxiéme Bureau. At that meeting an agreement was reached to furnish arms and money to Lebanese ready to provoke an armed revolt against the President of the Republic and the present Lebanese authorities.

I apologize for having read so much detail to the members of the Council. I wish to assure you, Mr. President, that I could have multiplied what I have read by at least twenty in order to have exhausted all the documents that we have on this subject, but I think that I have given enough examples under the first four sets of facts to prove my point conclusively, namely, the four things which I have maintained: that arms are flowing into Lebanon from Syria; that Lebanese nationals are trained in subversion in Syria; that Syrian civilian nationals are also infiltrating into Lebanon and taking part in subversive activities; and, finally, that United Arab Republic governmental elements do direct and, in some instances, take an active part in the subversive activity that is going on in Lebanon today.

I come now to the second claim—I think that the first claim is adequately proved. The second claim is that this intervention aims at undermining, and does, in fact, threaten the independence of Lebanon.

In the context of this argument the term "subversion" is used in the broad sense of any action aimed at the overthrow of the established government by violence or by illegal means. If arms flow on a large scale from Country A to subversive elements in Country B, if subversive elements in Country B are trained in subversion in Country

A and sent back to their home country to practice their training, if civilians from Country A themselves take part in subversive acts in Country B, and if officials of Country A direct and take part in subversive activities in Country B, then, I think, it is fair to conclude immediately, even without further evidence, that this massive intervention in Country B by Country A is not something beneficent or friendly, is not aimed at supporting or strengthening or upholding the government of Country B but, on the contrary, is aimed at undermining and, to the extent it succeeds, does in fact threaten the independent existence of Country B. If, then, I have proved, as I believe I have, that the United Arab Republic as Country A has in fact done all these things to Lebanon as Country B, then it appears that my second claim is already substantially proved.

But there is further evidence of a more formal nature. Conceivably, the material evidence which I have just adduced above could be attenuated or explained away as to its significance; conceivably, one could question the truth of this or that particular fact adduced; conceivably, even assuming the truth of all that I have so far set forth, one could still hold that these were sporadic instances which do not, even in the aggregate, justify the sweeping conclusions which I have drawn from them. I, personally, do not believe that any of these "conceivably possible" attitudes is right or fair or valid, given the full impact of the material evidence. But there is further evidence of a more compelling and decisive character which I propose now to turn to. It is the evidence of the word, the printed word and the spoken words, than which there is nothing that formalizes and seals more the intent and the purpose and the state of the heart.

I turn now to the fifth set of facts, namely, the violent and utterly unprecedented press campaign conducted by the United Arab Republic against the Government of Lebanon.

It is generally considered, and I believe it to be a fact, that the Press of the United Arab Republic is a government-controlled Press. Some may deny this fact, but what no one can deny is that this Press is fairly uniform in its presentation of issues and that there is no criticism in it of the Government of the United Arab Republic or of conditions in that country. I have been constrained to make this observation in order to show that there must be some connection between the Government and the Press in the United Arab Republic with respect to what that Press says about Lebanon.

Now we have a complete file of that Press for the last two years. Great libraries—private libraries, official libraries, university libraries—in the Soviet Union, in Europe, in America and elsewhere, must also have files of the Egyptian and Syrian Press. Doubtless also the Press services of the chancelleries of the great Powers—and perhaps also of many other Powers—prepare at least adequate digests of the Press of the United Arab Republic. I make this last remark in order to express my belief that many around this table know very well what I am talking about here. A study of the Press—and it is avaliable to anybody for study; I know that it is here in the United Nations—will reveal at once the most violent campaign against the Government of Lebanon. Our Government is called by every conceivable and inconceivable name. There is no war between Lebanon and the United Arab Republic, and yet I doubt if, in the darkest hours of the Second World War, the Press of the belligerents used the same sort of unrestrained violence against each other as the Press of the United Arab Republic has been using lavishly against the Government of Lebanon.

I can quote literally thousands—tens of thousands—of articles demonstrating my point. I shall not, of course, weary the Council with that, but permit me, Mr. President, to place before you a few samples, chosen completely at random, of statements made by the United Arab Republic Press in the last few weeks.

On 17 April last *Al-Akhbar* of Cairo stated:

"The Lebanese parties are against the renewal of the presidency of Chamoun."

The same paper stated on 18 April:

"Ultimatum to Chamoun. The Lebanon is threatened by a bloody revolution" . . .

This was about three weeks before the events.

". . . The inhabitants of Lebanon are ready to carry arms for a bloody uprising. Disorders in all parts of the country."

There were no disorders at all at that time.

The following statements appeared in the same paper on 14 May, five days after the outbreak of the disorders:

"Popular forces triumphed as proved by the fact that the Security Forces in most of the Lebanese localities joined them." . . .

That is not at all true.

". . . The Lebanese people have been too patient with regard to the policies followed by their rulers without consulting them and against their will. The Lebanese people have said their word against those responsible for the reactionary pro-imperialistic policy contrary to the interests of the Arabs."

The same paper stated on 18 May:

"Definitive separation of Tripoli from Lebanon and the creation of a local government in North Lebanon."

There is no truth in this. It is as though it were insinuated that this should happen.

On the same date the same paper said:

"The Lebanese people are against Chamoun: America does not want to understand."

I have no idea what America or Chamoun has to do with the matter.

Al-Gumhouriwya of Cairo, generally regarded as the mouth-piece of the Egyptian authorities, stated on 6 April:

"Open appeal for a revolt in Beirut."

This was one month before the events took place.

In the same paper, on 12 April, one month before the disorders began, there was an open appeal for a holy war against Chamoun. If this is not intervention, I would like to know what is. This paper carried out daily the most inflammatory and insulting statements against the Government of Lebanon during the past several months.

In *Akhbar-El-Yom* of Cairo, on 12 April, again one month before the outbreak of the recent disorders:

"A revolution may break out in Lebanon, the revolution of the people of Lebanon against injustice and against the tyrant, and it will end in the victory of the people and the downfall of the tyrant much sooner than people think."

In the same paper, on 26 April:

"The struggle continues in Lebanon."—this is about two weeks before the events—"The state is at the verge of a volcano. This is the struggle of the press against the tyrant, of liberty against tyranny, a struggle which one observes in the houses, in the streets, in the palaces, in the huts. Every day from hour to hour people expect an event."

In *Al-Chaab* of Cairo, on 13 April: "Danger of civil war in Lebanon. Camille Chamoun cause of the division." That was one month before the events.

In the same paper, on 19 April:

"The situation becomes more and more grave in Lebanon. The people are preparing themselves to rise against the authorities."

In the same paper, on 14 May: "A man whom the people raised to power sells this [sic] people, sells the State and sells his conscience."

In the same paper, on 18 May: "for a year"—the same paper confesses that for a year—"we have been telling the Arabs that Camille Chamoun is a spy, a liar, a deceiver and a calumniator."

In *Al-Tarbiat* of Damascus, on 20 May: "The Lebanese people continue their revolt. Forward, heroic people of Lebanon, forward to victory and liberty."

While I can multiply these quotations by the thousands, I think what I have given is enough to prove my point. I understand the possibility of these attacks being most violent. But what I frankly do not understand is that for months now, and perhaps even for two years, not a single kind or appreciative word—I repeat, not a single kind or appreciative word—has been said by any Egyptian or Syrian paper about the Government of Lebanon, a sister Government which is certainly not hostile. This fact alone, I submit, should arrest the attention of the Security Council.

The proposition that the Egyptian and Syrian press for many months now has been waging a most unrelenting campaign of attack against and vilification of the Government of Lebanon, of open incitement of the people of Lebanon to revolt against their Government, and of open support of the subversive activities now going on in Lebanon, this proposition is absolutely indubitable. I submit that there is no instance anywhere else in the world today of a similar press campaign.

The sixth set of facts which prove my second claim, and also partially the first claim, concerns the radio, the violent and utterly unprecedented radio campaign conducted by the United Arab Republic inciting the people of Lebanon to overthrow their Government.

The radio differs from the press in two crucial respects. Not everybody can read, but, except for the deaf, everybody can hear; and in the East, in general, I think it is a fact that more people listen to the radio than read the newspapers, and the living voice is more effective in the dissemination and impression of opinion than the printed word. Secondly, whatever the relationship between the press and the government in some countries, that between the radio and the government is at least as close. Thus, while it is "conceivably possible" for some to hold that in the United Arab Republic the press is "free" no one will deny that in the United Arab Republic the radio is controlled by the Government. The evidence of the radio, then, so far as the actuality and aim of intervention are concerned, is the highest and most authentic.

There is in our library—and perhaps also in the libraries of other countries—a compilation of thousands and tens of thousands of radio broadcasts from Cairo and Damascus for the last several months. I have with me about 500 of them. The following are a few more samples chosen completely at random from the more recent broadcasts.

Cairo Radio—9 May 1958:

"The free people of Lebanon know very well how to bring about the overthrow of the Government."

Damascus Radio—10 May 1958:

"The object of the strike and the demonstrations in Lebanon following the assassination of Metni is the expression of discontent and wrath of the people against the policy"—the whole thing is political—"followed in Lebanon which in no way serves the interests of Lebanon."—This is intervention—"Imperialism has succeeded in dragging a limited number of Lebanese into accepting the Eisenhower Doctrine"—that is a point—"and has thus created a breach which imperialist collaborators believe they can hide from the people under the camouflage of economic aid. These hopes have been dissipated."

Damascus Radio—11 May 1958:

"The tyrant imperialist collaborators wanted to realize today in Lebanon some of their objectives sought by the aggression against Egypt; they wanted to divert the Arab people of Lebanon from that which is most dear to them. They wanted to make of them a centre of intrigue against liberating Arab nationalism.

The Arab people of Lebanon who have decided to struggle for their liberty, for their independence and the liberation of their country from tyrants and imperialist collaborators shall persist in the struggle until they accomplish the ideals for which they are dedicating themselves, no matter what the sacrifice."

Damascus Radio—11 May 1958:

"The people of Lebanon lead today the battle against imperialism. The Arab people of Lebanon want to liquidate imperialism. They were able in a few days to demolish all that imperialism built up in years. Wide horizons open before Lebanon."

Cairo Radio—12 May 1958.

"The situation aggravates in Lebanon. Attempted destruction of the Presidential Palace"—this is only a news summary, this is a sample of the news summary that you hear these days from Cairo and Damascus. This never happened —"News of riots in Lebanese cities. The Arab people in Tripoli are in control of the entrances of the city."—this is not true—"Destruction of bridges. Rupture of communications. Insurgents dominate Zgarta"—this is not true—"Three bombs are thrown at the Presidential Palace during a meeting of the Council of Ministers."—this never happened—"The opposition urges the resignation of the President of the Republic."

Damascus Radio—13 May 1958:

"Our people who have seized the head"—and this is significant, this is one of the more, to use a mild term, violent broadcasts—"of the dragon coming from Washington, London, Paris and Tel-Aviv, have decided not to permit the tail to wag in Beirut, Amman and Baghdad. We have decided to tie the wrists and ankles of the monster, and to clip its claws and extract its fangs. The band which gathers together all the agents, the traitors, the mercenaries and the rats of Nury-Said and Rifai, and the spies of the Americans and the English cannot stop the people from speaking and from being heard. Death to imperialism and to the agents of imperialism."

Cairo Radio—14 May 1958:

"The Lebanese authorities together with the West know henceforth that the people are on the verge of imposing themselves. They started preparing themselves for an attempt to stop the people by sparking the fire. England speaks of its anxiety and the tales of the American Sixth Fleet continue. Come what may, victory shall be for the people and the forces of evil and tyranny shall retreat, and fire shall devour those who lighted it."

Now I come to something quite interesting, namely, a broadcast with which I want to end this tale of horror. On 27 May 1958, only a few days ago, at seven o'clock in the evening, radio Damascus broadcast a short skit, a short drama, entitled "The Triumph of the Revolution in Lebanon." There are various actors in this skit, one representing the President of Lebanon, one representing the Prime Minister and several representing other government officials; then of course there is the mob, soldiers in the street, insurgent leaders and other characters. The action is very dramatic and swift. I have it with me; you can hear it any time you like. It is in Arabic. At one point the guards of the President's Palace join the demonstrators and desert the President. Then the insurgents rush into the Palace and find the President there. The leader of the insurgents, as soon as he sees the President, shouts "Death to the traitor." The President starts crying, begging him to spare his life. Then there is tumult and shouts and confusion and further cries of "Death to the traitor. Yield to the will of the people." At that point one hears a crisp shot and then we hear the statement "This is the reward of treason."

It is not pleasant to quote you this stuff. But this is what we have been living under, we and our children and our people, for months and years. I leave it to your conscience and to the conscience of your Governments to judge whether there has or has not been intervention in the affairs of Lebanon and whether the independence of Lebanon is not in deadly peril.

In connection with this radio war there has lately been sprung upon us in the Near East a strange voice entitled Radio Free Lebanon. This clandestine voice incites our people to rebellion, supports the subversion at present let loose in Lebanon, and in everyway conforms to the standards and policies of the United Arab Republic. The term "Free Lebanon" is interesting. Everybody knows that if there is freedom anywhere in the Near East it exists in Lebanon, and the discerning also know that the ultimate significance of our present struggle behind and beyond every passing accident, both internal and external, is precisely to prevent whatever genuine freedom we have been enjoying from being completely submerged and extinguished. The significance of our crisis is that Lebanon as a lamp in the Near East of real freedom, both personal and social, must be preserved and strengthened, not only for the benefit of the Near East and indeed of the whole world, but as an end in itself. To speak, therefore, of freedom coming to Lebanon from outside our borders in the Near East is one of those perversions of language in which this confused age abounds. But we have been able to determine the direction from which Radio Free Lebanon comes and it is a simple method of determination. That direction is unmistakably the territory of the United Arab Republic.

This survey of the bearing of the printed and spoken word upon our crisis appears to justify the following four conclusions:

1. The vehemence of the attack upon the Government of Lebanon by the propaganda media of the United Arab Republic is practically unparalleled. This vehement attack has been going on for two years with mounting crescendo.

2. In this unparalleled propaganda attack there is mounting incitement of the people of Lebanon to rebel against its Government. Thus, long before the present disturbances broke out on 9 May, there were unmistakable preparations for them in the press and radio of the United Arab Republic, and a mood of expectancy was sedulously cultivated whereby people were made to expect that some great "event" was about to take place, that the "uprising of the people" was just around the corner, that the fall of the "tyrant" was imminent.

3. After the outbreak of the present disturbances, the entire propaganda machinery of the United Arab Republic was geared to upholding, promoting, inflaming and even directing and guiding the subversive activities going on in Lebanon.

4. The unmistakable aim of this propaganda campaign is to overthrow the present regime in Lebanon and to replace it with one that would be more subservient to the will of the United Arab Republic. You know what the only sin of Lebanon is; the only sin of Lebanon in the eyes of the United Arab Republic is not that it has really done or is likely to do any harm to any country, let alone any Arab country, but that it is independent and follows a policy of friendship towards and co-operation with the Western world. We plead guilty on both of these counts.

The second claim of my argument is now proven. The intervention of which we are complaining aims at undermining and does in fact threaten our independence. And since our independence is very sacred to us and since the threatened independence of any Member of the United Nations by definition endangers the maintenanec of international peace and security, which is the primary responsibility of the Security Council, we have deemed it fit to bring our case to the attention of this Council. And this brings me at once to the more detailed proof of the third claim.

There is massive intervention in our affairs. Our internal problems—and who does not have internal problems—are played upon, seized upon, wilfully accentuated from outside, taken advantage of, and therefore our independence is threatened. When independence is threatened by external intervention, this is automatically a situation in which the Security Council is interested.

No region in the whole world is more sensitive than the Near East. Interference in one another's affairs in that area is certain to have international repercussions. There is the most delicate balance of forces and powers there; let this balance be but slightly upset and incalculable consequences could ensue. Therefore, a situation like ours, with such possibilities of development, is exactly one with which the Security Council should be seized. This is what we have done by calling the attention of this Council to our case.

Think of the equilibrium of interests in the Near East. Think of the convergence of forces upon our area from all over the globe: from the north, from the east, from the south, from the west. There are tremendous political, economic and strategic interests at stake in the Near East. For about a month now the attention of the whole world has been steadily fixed upon us. Not a single great Power, not a single permanent member of the Security Council, has not expressed intense concern about our affair. They are all poised watching developments, eyeing one another. This is then pre-eminently a question of the maintenance of international peace and security. And nothing is more obvious than that if this situation which inherently embodies a threat to our independence continues, then the maintenance of international peace and security is endangered.

We ask this Council then to bring its wisdom into play, to the end that the unprovoked massive intervention stop, that our independence, to which we have every right, be preserved and indeed strengthened, and that as a result the threat to international peace and security inherent in this situation be removed.

By way of conclusion—and I apologize to the Council for having taken so much of its time—may I say that Lebanon is a small country. Nobody can accuse it of harboring any designs on anybody. It has always worked for peace; it has always been a modest factor for good in the world. It never meddled with other people's business. It wished well for everybody, and above all for its sister Arab States. It deserves, therefore, a better fate at the hands of the world.

Every other country in the Middle East has its formal international agreements or connexions whereby it feels more or less safe, except Lebanon. Lebanon alone in the Middle East has no vast, formal, safety-conferring arrangement with other Powers outside the area, while every other country in the Middle East has some such vast arrangement. Certainly Lebanon is not without its friends, but its relations to them have not been excessively formal. It has trusted their sense of honour and justice; it has pinned its faith upon the spirit and not upon the letter.

Of all countries in the Middle East then, Lebanon primarily depends upon the United Nations for its safety. The Charter is our primary protection. We cannot protect ourselves alone; we are much too small and fragile for that. We require the active understanding and support of the world community.

Our case then is a test case. It is the case of every small country in the world. If intervention in the affairs of one small country should be allowed to work its way without let or hindrance, how can any other small country feel secure again? The great Powers can take care of themselves; the Charter is not primarily made for them. But the small nations cannot see a small nation, one of themselves, interfered in without themselves feeling the profoundest anxiety. What if the same one day happened to them? Are they sure that if they do not now rally around this small nation, others will rally around them if at some future date they should, God forbid, find themselves in the same predicament? The United Nations must above all protect the small nations, and the small nations themselves must co-operate with the United Nations in the protection of any one of them.

What is it then that we want? We want only that the intervention in all its aspects stop. We want the press and radio campaigns to cease. We want the flow of arms to the insurgents to come to an end. We want the infiltration of subversives to terminate. We want to solve our internal problems in peace, between ourselves, and without external interference. We want the best possible relations with the United Arab

Republic. We want to be given an opportunity to prove again to our brethren in the United Arab Republic how much we love and respect them.

We believe all this is possible, necessary and natural. We ask you to help us to achieve it. We leave it to your wisdom to decide how it can be achieved. We have tried direct contacts with the United Arab Republic, but without avail. We resorted to the Arab League and we gave it all opportunity to act, but no decision was taken, and the intervention, far from abating, has actually increased in intensity in the last day or two. Now our independence, our fate, and peace in the area and perhaps even in the world, are your responsibility. You are our last recourse. We certainly also depend upon God and ourselves.

Appendix I

(B)

SPEECH OF DR. MALIK ON JUNE 10, 1958*

Mr. President, I am grateful to you and to the Council for giving me this second opportunity to say a few words in reply to what we have just heard by the representative of the United Arab Republic.

But before I proceed to make a few comments which come to my mind in passing as I heard him speak, reserving of course my right to study his remarks very carefully later on and to prepare a more reasoned and a more responsible and a more grounded reply to all that he has said, I wish to make a statement to the Council about something that my Government communicated to me only two hours ago. At about 2 p.m. New York time, which is 8 p.m. Beirut time, I communicated by telephone with the Government of Lebanon, and I was informed by them, and I was asked by them to tell the Council, that the situation is becoming more urgent, that the infiltration is increasing, that the flow of arms into Lebanon is increasing and that, therefore, there is a seriousness about the situation as of now which did not exist before. I am therefore asked by the Government of Lebanon to tell the Council that the situation is becoming very serious. We therefore request the Council to sit in continuous session until it comes to some decision about this important matter.

We would be remiss in our duty to the United Nations and to international peace and security in our area if we did not tell the Council as of this moment that the situation during the last twenty-four hours has considerably deteriorated from the point of view of infiltration of men and the smuggling of arms into Lebanon from the United Arab Republic. I wish to strike this note of urgency because, according to the information I have received from the Government of Lebanon, the situation, as I said, has become exceedingly serious. We do request you, Mr. President, and the members of the Council to meet continuously, if you so desire, until you dispose of this item.

I should now like to say a few words only about what we have just heard from my friend, the representative of the United Arab Republic. First of all, concerning his references to the incidents and facts I adduced the other day, it is clear from what he said that he was very selective in the facts which he tried to refute. If you study all that he told us today, you will find that he did not touch on more than, at most, 15 to 20 per cent of the facts to which I referred last time. Obviously that must mean that he has very little to say, if anything, about the remaining facts which I had adduced.

But even his manner of refutation of the things which I put before this Council last Friday can be easily shown to be completely unconvincing. Obviously, a government bases itself on its own official documents; obviously it can only put forward what it knows from its own services, and that is what I did before this Council when I met here with you the last time. If there is any question about the veracity of any of these documents, it is always possible for me to go back to them and to produce them in detail for the Council and to prove their complete veracity. I wish to assure the Council that the sifting of these facts was done by me with the utmost care and that, therefore, they can stand any examination by the Council at any time.

I repeat what I said, that his very selective procedure whereby he touched only upon at most 15 to 20 per cent of these adduced facts proves that he has very little, if anything, to say against the remaining facts. For instance, under (b) *(S/PV. 823, p. 7)*, "The training in subversion on the territory of the United Arab Republic of elements from Lebanon and the sending back of these elements to Lebanon to subvert

* *UN Doc. S/PV. 824,* 10 June 1958, pp. 26-45.

their Government," it is significant that he made passing remarks upon one and two but completely said nothing about three and four. I can answer his remarks very easily about one and two when I study them carefully and find out exactly what it is in these facts that did not seem to be convincing to him.

The next group of facts, (c), he hardly touched upon at all, the one which deals with:

> "The participation of United Arab Republic civilian nationals, residing in or passing into Lebanon, in subversive and terrorist activities, in Lebanon." *(Ibid.)*

He passed over them rather quickly, with a reference to one or two of them alone. Yet I gave ten instances of these matters.

The same thing applies to the last group of facts. But again, as I said, to be perfectly fair, I will study his remarks and I will admit any error that I may have fallen into, although I did not hear from anything that he said anything that proves that there was any error. I will study very carefully what he said and later on, at some other stage in the development of this case, I will have a few words to say on what he said on them.

I come now to his remarks on the press and on the radio. Here I will make only three general observations that seem to me to be convincing to anybody and that seem to me to be completely irrefutable. The first one is that it may well be true that in some instances where I quoted from Egyptian and Syrian newspapers, they were themselves printing material that originated first in Lebanon. That may well be true, but what is significant is that they print only that kind of material, they print no other kind of material. That is the most significant thing. We have a free press which prints all sorts of things, things against our Government. We have free correspondents and free press agencies which distribute information and opinion as they like.

It is the selectivity of the Egyptian Press, from whatever emanates from Lebanon, which is most significant. That selectivity can be shown to have taken only those parts of the news which comes out from Lebanon that inflames and encourages and foments rebellion and anti-governmental activity in Lebanon. That seems to me to be most significant.

The second point is this: The representative of the United Arab Republic spoke about our Press having published certain material to which he takes exception. That may well be. Again, we have a Press that criticizes not only Egypt and Syria, but pre-eminently ourselves. But now—and this is the significant thing—we have a Press in Lebanon which defends the point of view of Egypt. They have nothing like that in Egypt. In fact, when we want to publish an official government denial, it is never allowed to appear in Egyptian papers. We have done that many times. We have sent in official governmental denials to our Embassy in Cairo and asked them to have them published in the Egyptian Press, and they never appeared there. Whereas every morning you can find in at least six newspapers in Beirut—and we like that and we welcome it—articles and accounts defending the Egyptian point of view and presenting the Egyptian point of view.

We want to live in that kind of a free, varied, multiple world, and not in a world that is uniform and completely regimented. So it may well be true that there have been articles attacking the Egyptian Government or certain aspects of life in the United Arab Republic in Lebanon, but we have other Press in Lebanon which we allow to appear, which can defend and present the point of view of our neighbors; whereas such a Press is completely non-existent in Egypt and Syria. In fact, I will make a fair bet with my friend, Mr. Loutfi, a very fair bet. If you can produce one sentence during the last year, from any paper in Egypt or Syria, that is appreciative of or kind to the Government of Lebanon—one sentence—I will withdraw this complaint. This is a fair bet.

Therefore, when it comes to the Press, we are on the strongest possible ground in Lebanon because we do have a free Press and we know what we are talking about when we say that the Press of Egypt and Syria have been mercilessly attacking the Government of Lebanon for the last several months.

Now I come to the question of the radio. The representative of the United Arab Republic spoke about their radio answering our radio. Our radio is hardly heard in Beirut itself, let alone in Egypt. Certainly it is not heard in Tripoli, which is the biggest northern city in Lebanon. So it makes absolutely no sense to say that the Egyptian Radio, whatever the unit which is used in the description of it is [sic], is answering anything that our inaudible radio says. But again, I am prepared to make a similar bold bet. I can assure you that our radio has been most careful and most appreciative and most kind—I am talking about our radio this time, although it is not heard very much outside Beirut—most positive and most brotherly towards our neighbors to the South and to the East. There is no comparison whatsoever between the Voice of the Arabs in Radio Damascus and the poor radio of Lebanon which tries to be as fair, as objective, as unprovocative as it is humanly possible to be.

I now come to the question of what really happend in the Arab League. I have many things to say on that, but I will not tire the members of the Council. I will only say that I regret that the account which the representative of the United Arab Republic gave of what happened at the meeting of the League is neither complete nor even, in what it stated, completely in accordance with the facts. And I will prove my case.

In the first instance, the very report from which he read and which is supposed to be the summary report of the proceedings of the Arab League, was not submitted to the League itself for final approval, which is always the case in these important matters. You draw up your report and then, in a formal final session, you submit it for the formal approval of the body, which is supposed to have deliberated in such and such a manner. Actually, the report was drawn up after the Council of the Arab League had adjourned. I am also told, although I cannot be 100 per cent sure of this fact, that the report itself was drawn up in Cairo and not in Benghazi. But at any rate, it certainly was not submitted for the approval of the members of the Council of the Arab League. What Mr. Jamali distributed among you, as his first document, is something that was drawn up by the officials of the Secretariat of the Arab League, without the formal approval of the League in session.

That is the first point. The second point is that it is very well to say that the draft was unanimous—and he read the names of the countries which had sponsored that draft—and that only the Government of Lebanon finally rejected it. This is not exactly what happened. The representative of the Government of Iraq can speak for his own country here and I can speak for my country. What happened exactly was that they met and discussed the problem, and finally they were bandying about all kinds of texts. Most everybody said, with the exception of the representative of the United Arab Republic, that this is a matter which primarily belongs to Lebanon, and that therefore they will withhold their views until they really find out what Lebanon wants.

Towards the end there was some urgency, so a text was prepared. The various members were asked whether they would sponsor it. There was actually no printed text which was signed by representatives or the heading of which said, "Proposal submitted by the representative of so and so." The Chairman of the Sudanese delegation read a certain text and asked if the rest agreed to it, and there was no reply to that question.

Then they put it to the representative of Lebanon. The representative of Lebanon asked important questions about clarification of the text, and he received that clarification from the Chairman of the delegation of the Sudan. The clarification was so clear as to make it plain that in the minds of those who supposedly sponsored that text there was no doubt whatsoever that there was interference in Lebanon's internal affairs by the United Arab Republic. I can read to you that part of the explanation given by the Chairman of the delegation of the Sudan which you do not find in the summary which is before you.

But what is more important than that is the fact than many of these delegates said,

"Obviously we cannot be more Royalist than the King or more Catholic than the Pope. We will withhold our opinion until we know what Lebanon really thinks of this text."

It is therefore not true to say that these gentlemen approved this text regardless of the position of Lebanon. At least some of them, and I am told most of them, said, "Our view is withheld until we hear what Lebanon itself, which is most directly concerned, thinks of this text. We can send it to Lebanon."

Therefore the text was sent to Lebanon, and Lebanon rejected it for four reasons which are very carefully set forth in the detailed proceedings which are not completely before the Security Council. As soon as Lebanon rejected the text, the others said, "We have nothing to do with the text." It is not, therefore, true to say that this text was unanimously adopted by the Governments of these various States regardless of the position of Lebanon. It was simply a trial to find out whether Lebanon would accept that kind of wording. And since they could not be more Lebanese than the Lebanese themselves, they said, "We will wait to see what Lebanon itself says."

As soon as Lebanon rejected the text, certainly three representatives, the representatives of Iraq, Jordan, and Libya, said, "We have nothing to do with this text." This is not, therefore, a unanimously adopted text which was at the end rejected only by Lebanon.

But even if it were so, such are the regulations of the Arab League that a thing like that could not pass except if adopted also by the complaining country. I think this Council knows very well the rule of unanimity and its importance especially when it comes to matters which touch the very existence of a country. The last time the representative of the Soviet Union spoke about a unanimously adopted text that was rejected by Lebanon. But I do not think there is a country in the world that believes more in the rule of unanimity than the Soviet Union. In fact, we have applied it only with respect to those matters where our very existence was at stake. But even that is on the supposition that there was such a fiction called a unanimously adopted text which was really sponsored by everybody as the point of view of their Governments. This, as I said, was not the case at all because at least three representatives—and I am told that there were even more than three—said later on when Lebanon expressed its view that their view was exactly the same as that of Lebanon. They put in their own objections to the text, and I am told that the representative of Iraq has put in those objections himself before the Council in the second document.

That is the story of this fiction that you hear about concerning what happened at the Arab League.

Then there is something interesting that will also throw light on this matter of what really happened at the Arab League, and this you do not find in the document which is before us. This can be found only in the detailed account of what really happened there, which I would like to have put before the Council. I can only summarize it briefly as follows.

The representative of the United Arab Republic, who was heading that delegation, at the League presented at one point in the argument certain amendments to the text that was to be tried on Lebanon. These were to be added to the draft proposal as one of the preambular considerata. I translate directly from the Arabic text before me. It refers to the Council of the Arab League having heard and having this and having that. Then this is the text which the head of the delegation of the United Arab Republic presented to these gentlemen who were meeting there to be added to the considerations:

> "And after having felt"—that is to say, the Council of the Arab League felt —"in the two parties to the dispute the spirit of mutual respect and certain desires not to intervene in the internal affairs of each other . . ."

There was a discussion on this text which lasted for one hour according to the internal evidence of this document, and those present rejected it. The gentleman who was the head of the delegation of Egypt pleaded with them and asked them, " Why do you reject it? Do you not trust us? Are we not telling you the truth? Do you think we are intervening in the internal affairs of Lebanon?" And they would never answer. This can only be ascertained from this text which you do not find in the report which is before you.

This incident, it seems to me, is of the utmost importance. When the representative of the United Arab Republic tries to urge upon his colleagues a certain text which shows that there was no intervention on the part of his country in the affairs of my country and his colleagues completely reject it, that seems to me to be most interesting and it should be brought out in the summary which is before the Council. One of the phrases which the leader of the Egyptian and Syrian delegation there uttered, again in the very paper that is before us, was:

> "I do not understand the secret behind this unanimity in rejecting my amendment."

These are his own words. I will read them in Arabic. *(spoke in Arabic)*

If you read this document in detail, you will find many, many other interesting things that are not reflected in the summary put before you by the representative of Iraq. You will have a different picture of what really happened in Benghazi during those meetings.

That is all I want to say on that aspect of what Mr. Loutfi has been saying about what happened at Benghazi. I only want to prove that there was no unanimity; that Lebanon stood in the way of nothing; that, when we put the complaint there and here at the same time, we put it in both places in absolutely good faith. We delayed the consideration of this matter here six days. The delaying tactics were really being carried on in Benghazi, and not here. We were perfectly prepared to wait until they were through there, and we did wait until they were through, and these are the results that I have pointed out to you.

It therefore seems to me that to say that Lebanon was joking when it brought its complaint before the Arab League because it had intended from the very beginning to press its complaint here is to say something that can easily be refuted by the facts.

I will go even further and say that we made it perfectly plain to all our friends in the Arab League and even to the representatives of the United Arab Republic themselves that at any moment in the deliberations of this Council, or prior to our deliberations here, we would withdraw any complaint brought before anybody and not press for anything, provided that this massive intervention to which I referred in my first statement, and which I described in full, were really stopped. And that stands true today. We are not interested in harming anybody—least of all, Syria and Egypt. But we are in dead earnest about the stopping of the massive intervention which is occurring in our country today.

The representative of the United Arab Republic, Mr. Loutfi, complained that Lebanon was hatching plots against the United Arab Republic through the Syrian nationalists, that we have behaved improperly toward certain United Arab Republic diplomats in Beirut, that we had expelled nationals of the United Arab Republic from Lebanon. These are the three main points that he mentioned.

As to the expulsion of these nationals to which he referred, the first point to make is that we have a lot to say about the conduct of the Government of the United Arab Republic toward our own nationals in its own country. We did not say that, because it is not part of our complaint; we are only saying that the Government of the United Arab Republic is intervening in our internal affairs.

The second point to make is that, if the representative of the United Arab Republic wants to know the detailed reasons for our having had to expel some of these brothers of ours, I can produce them for him at any time. In general, it is a reaction against the subversive activities of some of them and many of them had been suspected of having taken part in these subversive activities for a long time—and many of them, again, were people who were without identity cards in Lebanon.

In this connexion, I must add that there are fifty thousand Syrians living happily in Lebanon—fifty thousand—prospering, working in commerce, taking part in agriculture, and carrying on all kinds of activity. And we are most happy with them. We are brothers with them. It is only a very small minority—I doubt whether there are more than a thousand—that has had to leave our country during the last troubles, either because they did not have identity cards or because they were caught redhanded taking part in some of these subversive activities.

Concerning our behavior toward the United Arab Republic diplomats in our country, I can produce all the facts before this Council and I can show that our patience with the activity of the Egyptian diplomats in Lebanon—an activity which is openly anti-government and openly pro-opposition, so to speak—has been more than exemplary and that, when we had to deal with the matter in one or two instances, the situation was so flagrant that it was no longer possible for us to be patient about it.

As for the plots that are said to be hatched in Lebanon against Syria or Egypt, I can only say that it takes almost infinite credulity to believe that Lebanon some day is going to send an invading army to Cairo, or even an invading army to Damascus, or that Lebanon is now engaged in any subversive activity in Syria or in Egypt. It takes infinite credulity to believe that. Lebanon is the most peaceful little country in the whole of the Middle East. It wants nothing except to live in peace with its neighbors and it wants nothing except to have its own internal elements live in peace with each other in a model State, in which Moslems and Christians can live like brothers and in which they can co-operate in the furtherance of the arts of civilization and of life and of peace. Therefore, to say that there are plots hatched in Lebanon seems to me to be beyond credulity.

I am sorry that I have taken so much of the Council's time. I want to assure the Council of the absolute goodwill of Lebanon, and of my own personal absolute goodwill, in this whole matter. Nobody is more sorry than I am that I have to be sitting here and talking about this situation. For us, it is a very serious situation. We want to retain our independence. We want to live in peace with our neighbors. We will do anything to prove that we are a peaceful country, that we want peace for ourselves and for our neighbors. But, now that the situation has been considerably aggravated during the last twenty-four hours, we want this Council please to look into it as carefully as possible and to come to a decision about it, one way or the other. We trust your honesty and we trust your conscience in doing everything you can really to bring out the truth about this matter and to help Lebanon stand on its feet as a peaceful little Arab country in that area, trying to co-operate with all its Arab neighbours and trying to make its own modest contribution to the cause of peace.

Appendix II

THE UAR REPLY AT THE SECURITY COUNCIL

(a)

SPEECH OF MR. LOUTFI ON JUNE 6, 1958*

It is with great regret that I speak today before the Council. It is perhaps the most delicate, the most painful question which has faced me during the many years which I have been in the United Nations. I need not remind you that the United Arab Republic and Lebanon have throughout history been united by many bonds of brotherhood and friendship. Egypt and Syria have given valuable assistance to the Lebanon when that country fought for its independence at the end of the Second World War.

The peoples of the United Arab Republic have expressed on many occasions their sympathy for Lebanon and have unanimously supported the independence of Lebanon. We feel sure that any attempt to render these links null and void will be destined to failure. We feel sure that Lebanon, free and independent, will be an element of security, of stability and of peace in that part of the world.

Before going into the substance of this matter, I should like to make some remarks regarding the circumstances that have surrounded the complaint made by Lebanon, which we have before us. This complaint was only presented to you after the disturbances in Lebanon had become very serious. In order to meet the situation, the Government of Lebanon has endeavored to give an international aspect to this purely domestic problem and to divert the attention of local public opinion and of world public opinion from the situation prevailing in Lebanon. An attempt has been made to prove that if there are disturbances in Lebanon, it is because of foreign intervention and it is not due to the position of the Government itself with respect to domestic matters. An endeavor has been made to deceive world public opinion and the citizens of the country itself.

We feel that the complaint, and the tendentious propaganda which surrounds it, and which endeavors to employ the Security Council in order to solve domestic matters, can only run counter to the good name of the Council. The goodwill and co-operation of States in the international field and the efforts utilized to make the United Nations succeed are the essential factors for the good progress of our Organization.

If I make these remarks, it is not because we have no faith in the United Nations. We have proved in far more important questions that we were always prepared to co-operate with the United Nations and to settle our disputes within the framework of the Charter. I need hardly recall these questions to you. You have all had occasion to discuss them. We have never been afraid of examining any question within the United Nations.

I find myself compelled to make another remark, and that is, before the Arab League considered this question we noted that the Minister for Foreign Affairs of Lebanon, Mr. Malik, arrived in New York at the head of a very large delegation for the Security Council meeting. In the statement he made at the airport, he said that it was up to the Security Council to discuss this question. It appears that the Government of Lebanon does not take seriously the presentation of its complaint to the Arab League and that it is merely a stratagem to prove that in coming before the Council it has already exhausted every other regional recourse.

---

* *UN Doc. S/PV. 823,* 6 June 1958, pp. 50-66.

The text of the complaint of Lebanon presented to the Arab League states that there has been an intervention of the United Arab Republic in the affairs of Lebanon; this is a slander which we categorically reject.

What happened at the meeting of the Arab League corroborates what I have just put forward. I have today received information according to which the six States members of the Arab League, namely, Sudan, Saudi Arabia, Iraq, Jordan, Libya and Yemen, proposed a resolution which unhappily was not accepted by the Lebanese Government. I have before me the text of this resolution, which I shall read:

> "The Council of the League of Arab States, in its extraordinary session at Benghazi, has examined the complaint presented by the Government of the Republic of Lebanon against the United Arab Republic.
>
> "After having heard the statements by the delegations of the Lebanese Republic and the United Arab Republic, and having ascertained the desire of the two parties to settle their differences in a peaceful manner within the framework of the League of Arab States, and in accordance with the charter of the League of Arab States; and desiring to eliminate all the causes that disturb the atmosphere of harmony among the brother Arab States;
>
> "The Council decides:
>
> "1. To put an end to everything that might disturb the atmosphere of serenity among all the member States by every means;
>
> "2. To request the Government of Lebanon to withdraw the complaint which it submitted to the Security Council;
>
> "3. To address an appeal to the various Lebanese groups in order to put an end to the disturbances and to take every necessary measure to settle their domestic disputes by peaceful and constitutional means;
>
> "4. To send a committee chosen from among members of the Council in order to calm the situation and to implement the decision of the Council of the League of Arab States."

This resolution which we accepted in a spirit of compromise, seemed to us the proper solution for this problem. Unfortunately, the Government of Lebanon, for reasons which I do not know, has opposed this resolution.

Now, I should like to draw the attention of the Council today to the provisions of paragraph 2 of Article 36 of the Charter which provides that

> "The Security Council should take into consideration any procedures for the settlement of the dispute which have already been adopted by the parties."

I should not like to speak at length on this at this meeting, but I would like to explain the position of my Government.

I have listened with great interest to the statement made by the representative of Lebanon. I have noted with regret that his allegations contain many inaccuracies, allegations and accusations which cannot be proved. The representative of Lebanon has based his statements on isolated facts and individual statements which in my opinion, would be very difficult for the Council to evaluate and to decide whether these are well-founded. I have already stated that this is a purely internal Lebanese question. I shall now endeavor to prove this, but in order to do so I must consider the situation of Lebanon and the regrettable events that have taken place there.

Much has been said in the press about the leaders of the opposition, that is, opposition to the present Lebanese Government, and some newspapers call them rebels. I must stress this point and specify who these opposition leaders are and what political role they play in their country. They have all occupied responsible positions. Mr. Bichara El-Khoury held the highest post as President of the Republic. Messrs. Saeb Salam, Abdullah El-Yafi, Hussein Oueni and Rashid Karamy have all held the post of President of the Council of Ministers. Messrs. Sabri Hamada, Ahmed El-Assad are former Presidents of Parliament. Messrs. Hamid Frangiyeh, Kamal Gunbalat, Gamil Mekawi are former ministers, as well as Mr. Henry Faraon; Mr. Fouad Ammoun was for a long time secretary-general for foreign affairs in Lebanon and many of you have had the opportunity of meeting him.

I should not like to speak at great length on this and mention the eminent personalities who are part of the opposition. I wish to mention Mgr. Boulos El Maoushi, Sheikh Mohammed Abu Shakreh, Mohammed Alaiae, the Grand Mufti, who are the religious heads of the country and who, as I shall prove later, certainly do not support President Chamoun and his Government.

The disturbances that are now taking place in Lebanon are mainly due to the fact that President Chamoun wishes to renew his candidacy for the presidency, in contradiction to the provisions of the Constitution, and he proposes to revise the Constitution in order to enable him to present his candidacy for the presidency at the next elections in September.

This is the cause of the disturbances—and this is in accordance with the statements made by members of the opposition—which also occurred during the elections which took place last year in Lebanon; last year the present Government was accused of intervening in the elections in order to bring about the election of the Government candidates. Furthermore, the assassination of a well-known journalist, Mr. Nassib El Mayny who, in his newspaper, *Le Telegraphe,* supported the platform of the members of the opposition, has increased the disturbances. All that I have stated is to be found in the statements which have been made on many occasions by members of the opposition. I shall now quote some of these statements.

In a statement made in *Le Telegramme* of 18 May, the former President of the Republic, Mr. Bichara El-Khoury, recalled the events of 1952, when, being President of the Republic, he preferred to resign and not await the expiration of his term because of the opposition and in order to avoid disturbances. At that time, Mr. Camille Chamoun was a member of the opposition. He himself had signed in 1951, with other political chiefs, a declaration protesting against the presence of Mr. Bichara El-Khoury as President of the Republic. Therefore, under the same circumstances which now prevail, Mr. Bichara El-Khoury, in order to avoid bloodshed in his country, did not insist and did not remain as President of the Republic.

In the same interview, in reply to a question put to him by the same newspaper, Mr. Bichara El-Khoury declared that the allegation to the effect that he wished Mr. Chamoun to resign was true, and that the United Arab Republic would leave the door open in order to take over power was totally lacking in substance and was not confirmed by any fact; that, on the contrary, the statements made on many occasions by the President of the United Arab Republic categorically denied such accusations. Furthermore, the Moslem and Christian leaders have declared that they will at no cost sacrifice their independence and their complete sovereignty.

If we examine the text of this interview, we find on page 4 what I shall distribute to the Council.

In the *Washington Post* on 20 May, we read:

"Nasser is not the cause of Lebanon's troubles. President Chamoun is seeking to amend the Constitution to permit his election for a second six-year term; his predecessor experienced similar unrest when he tried the same thing six years ago. There appears to have been considerable nationalist dissatisfaction, quite irrespective of outside influences."

At a press conference in Beirut on 23 May, Mr. Saeb el Salam, leader of the opposition, stated:

"The present Government endeavors to slander the Lebanese patriots and accuses them of receiving assistance from the United Arab Republic, and this has nothing to do with the present crisis. The allegation that Communism and the United Arab Republic are the cause of the situation is truly incredible, and it is clear that President Chamoun has no respect for the people of Lebanon."

This interview is to be found on pages 6 and 7 of the same document.

The National Union Front, which is made up of the opposition parties, in a memorandum submitted to the Ambassador of the United States in Beirut, affirms:

> "The national movement is not inspired by a foreign doctrine but is of an entirely internal character."

This appears in *Le Monde* of 17 May 1958.

Furthermore, I would like to recall that, in setting up the National Front, the members of the opposition made a statement to the effect that the main principle of the political action was maintenance of the independence of Lebanon, its sovereignty and defense, by every means and in every circumstance.

In *Le Monde,* on 31 May 1958, there appeared a letter to the effect that the opposition in Lebanon undertakes to maintain the independence of Lebanon. They addressed a message which constitutes a solemn undertaking to maintain the present status of Lebanon. The signatories—thirteen former Ministers and five Christian personalities—proclaim that they are unalterably attached to the independence of Lebanon, its sovereignty, its character as a single country, and the feelings of brotherhood, trust and fraternity which are the very reason of the existence of the people are their main principles.

After these events in Lebanon, two members of the Cabinet resigned: the Minister of Defense, Mr. Rashid Baydoun, who stressed in his letter of resignation that continuance of the rebellion, of riots and disorders, endangered the very existence of the country; and Mr. Bashir Osman, Minister of Telegraphs and Communications, who resigned on 23 May and stated in his letter that he acted thus because he was not able to convince his colleagues of the need to resign in order to open the way for other leaders to take over power and their part of the responsibility in the critical circumstances in which merely parliamentary support has no value.

This can be seen on page 13 of our document.

I have been told that Mr. Farid Kosma, Minister of Information, has also resigned.

But what is most important is the last declaration made by His Eminence Boutros el Maoushi, Maronite Patriarch, who made some comments in the *New York Times* on 31 May, that is, a few days ago. I am sure you have all read this, but I should like to recall some points which I consider to be very important. The relevant parts of the report in the *New York Times* read as follows:

> "Today, the Patriarch said at a news conference that he feared the situation had become too grave for a compromise to work. He suggested the time would soon come for President Chamoun to 'take a trip' so that the army commander could assume full power of government. . . . The Patriarch placed the blame for Lebanon's troubles largely on the Chamoun administration. He even took exception to Government charges that Communists and supporters of President Gamal Abdel Nasser of the United Arab Republic had had a hand in the disorders here.
>
> "He said President Nasser had 'many times' disavowed any designs on Lebanon. The Patriarch added: 'It is not in the interest of either Egypt or Syria to force Lebanon into the United Arab Republic.'
>
> "He said he would like 'to see what will be done' at the Arab League conference in Benghazi, Libya, where Government leaders are joining representatives of other Arab countries to discuss the Lebanese problem. But he commented that he believed the meeting was not necessary.
>
> "What Lebanon needs, he said, is 'not to wash her laundry in public,' but a 'just, honest government looking after the interests of the people.' "

Therefore, his Eminence the Patriarch and the chiefs of the opposition all hold the same view. Therefore, it is a domestic Lebanese matter, and the United Arab Republic does not enter into it at all. It is for this reason that, when the Commission for Foreign Affairs met in order to decide whether a complaint should be submitted to the Security Council, there was a very great discussion within the Commission. The President of the Commission, Mr. Philippe Takla, declared that "the Minister for Foreign Affairs has not established the fact that the complaint to the Security Council was based on true facts or that its importance justifies presentation of the complaint," and that "presentation of such a complaint could only aggravate the present crisis in Lebanon."

Mr. Adib El Farazly, Vice-President of the Chamber, who was present at the debates, stated that he had informed the Minister of Foreign Affairs that the necessary conditions in order to inscribe the complaint on the agenda were not fulfilled, in his view, because there had been no aggression or threat of aggression by one State against another, nor had there been any threat to peace and security. Other members of the Commission upheld this point of view. This can be seen on page 15 of our document.

According to the press and the information which I have received, the political parties and Lebanese organizations, particularly the National Front, have appealed to the Secretary-General of the United Nations in order to communicate to him their approach, because such a complaint has been submitted to the Security Council. The National Front has stressed, in particular, that it considers that this conflict is an exclusively internal matter, and it has protested against having recourse to the Council and has insisted on the need for the immediate rejection of the complaint, as well as the fallacious content of the complaint, which can only hamper the relations of good-neighborliness between two brother countries, and this can only increase very dangerously the tension that now prevails in the world.

The conclusion one must arrive at, and which I draw from what I have stated previously, is that we are confronted with a problem of purely internal Lebanese politics. The Lebanese people have proved on many occasions that they have political maturity, which enables them to consider political questions with circumspection, that they are merely guided by the interests of the country, and that foreign influences do not affect them.

I apologize for having had to deal with internal Lebanese political matters. I have been compelled to do so, as you will no doubt understand, in order to reply to the accusation to which we have been subjected.

What does the present Government of Lebanon accuse us of? We note that in the complaint which it has presented, which is not even accompanied by an explanatory memorandum and which Mr. Malik has sought to develop today before the Council, we are accused of the

> "infiltration of armed bands from Syria into Lebanon, the destruction of Lebanese life and property by such bands, the participation of United Arab Republic nationals in acts of terrorism and rebellion against the established authorities in Lebanon, the supply of arms from Syria to individuals and bands in Lebanon rebelling against the established authorities." (S/4007)

I do not propose today to reply to all the questions raised by the Lebanese Foreign Minister. It would be difficult for me to do so now, but I reserve my right to do it at a future meeting of the Council, after having examined his long speech. But I can state forthwith that Mr. Malik's allegations are not supported by any concrete proof. It is not difficult to obtain arms, as representatives know. Generally, it is merely a question of paying the price. The arms traffic goes on everywhere and in all parts of the world. During revolutions, periods of unrest and civil wars the parties concerned always manage to obtain arms, particularly small arms.

In order to prove the responsibility of a Government in this connexion, it must be established clearly. We reject the accusation made by Mr. Malik. He has not produced the proofs to substantiate what he has stated.

I should like to take the liberty of quoting an extract from an article which appeared in *The Times* of London on 27 May 1958 with regard to this first part of Mr. Malik's accusation. The article says:

"In addition, in spite of the Government's claim during last year's general elections, not a single Syrian agitator arrested had ever been brought to trial. It is a fact that during the past year the Government has several times claimed to have arrested Syrian nationals engaged in subversion and has also expelled many hundreds as potential trouble-makers. Last June it was officially confirmed that two members of the Syrian Deuxième Bureau had been arrested along with an officer who was believed to be a secretary to Colonel Sarraj.

"But there is no record of any of these Syrians having been brought to trial, and it is hardly surprising that the Government's latest claims to have arrested Syrian Army men and other foreign agitators, including a boatload of fedayeen from Gaza, are ridiculed by the Opposition and treated with some reserve by others who are waiting now for the evidence to be produced in the flesh."

Again, Mr. Fouad Ammoun, former Secretary-General of the Ministry of Foreign Affairs, made a statement on 24 May 1958 on this question, which I should also like to quote:

"Already the Lebanese Courts of Justice, by their acquittal of the accused whom the Lebanese Government described as Egyptian and Syrian agents, have given a fair and just opinion on the alleged case of the arms and explosive material which the Lebanese Government put forward as evidence in its unfounded complaint. The sad, indubitable truth is that the Lebanese Government demanded foreign arms, and distributed them amongst its gangs."

Therefore, we are not the ones who arm the Lebanese. It is the Government which distributes arms to its partisans and to certain organizations, and those weapons go from one person to another.

As to the two cases mentioned, by Mr. Charles Malik today in his speech, the first refers to the fishing vessel which was going to Lebanon and which was allegedly carrying arms. But even these allegations are vague and lacking in precision, and they do not show us to be responsible. I reserve my right to speak of this at another meeting of the Council if the Council should so wish.

With regard to the Consul-General of Belgium at Damascus, personally I do not doubt that this distinguished diplomat did not know that there were weapons in his car. This question is now in the hands of the Lebanese judicial authorities, and I would not wish to comment upon it at length here. The diplomat's lawyer made a statement to the Press on this matter in the course of which he refuted the charges brought against his client. His statement appears on Page 25 and following pages of the document which we have distributed.

One question to which the representative of Lebanon referred at length was the question of the so-called radio and Press campaign. Even if this allegation were substantiated, we do not feel that it could have any influence on the events taking place in Lebanon. As a general rule, the radio and the Press give only news published by the Lebanese Press, and if representatives were to take a look at that Press they would be convinced that what I say is true. For the rest, we have already given our due reply to the radio broadcasts attacking us. I do not wish to read out any of these in order that the prestige of our Organization may be maintained, but I shall have them available for any member of the Council who may wish to see them.

I really feel that the Security Council should not take up this question, because if it concerns itself with radio broadcasts and the radio campaigns now being carried on throughout the world it will no longer be able to examine the important problems, which are brought before it and which threaten international peace and security. If we examine the purely juridical aspects of this question of the Press and radio we can only agree that these problems are not such as to threaten the maintenance of international peace and security and that, consequently, they do not fall within the competence of the Security Council. Indeed, I cannot find any provision in the Charter which authorizes the Council to consider radio and Press campaigns.

Before concluding, I find myself obliged to consider the attitude taken by the Lebanese Government and the provocations of which it has been guilty vis-a-vis the Government of the United Arab Republic. We, for our part, could also have presented a complaint against Lebanon. We did not consider it necessary to do so because we felt that this kind of difference should be capable of solution through other channels. But for some months past the Government of Lebanon has been engaged in an expulsion *en masse* of nationals of the United Arab Republic from its territory. This expulsion has taken place without any explanation and without the intervention of any juridical or administrative organ, and even without the intervention of any kind of control commission of the kind prescribed by international law. The number of those expelled runs to thousands, most of them being individuals who had lived in Lebanon for many years and who had their possessions and their business in that country. Many among them were old people or children. The expulsion took place without any exercise of humanity. Many of the victims were molested and ill-treated. Some were even tortured. It has been impossible to obtain any explanation of the accusations brought against them. They were not even given the chance to defend themselves. Through its Ambassador in Beirut, the Government of the United Arab Republic protested vainly on several occasions against these acts which were devoid of justification. It was unable even to obtain a plausible explanation.

The Council will know that Lebanese citizens in the United Arab Republic—and there are many—continue to be well-treated and that they are the object of the Government's solicitude, as in the past. Our links with the Lebanese people has [sic] prevented us from placing this question before the Security Council.

The New York Times of 21 May 1958 reported in a dispatch from Beirut that on one single day, 19 May 1958, 1,000 citizens of the United Arab Republic, who were of Syrian origin, were expelled. I shall take the liberty of reading out a few extracts from that article:

> "Lebanon deported at least 1,000 Syrian nationals today. . . . Fifty trucks and buses filled with expelled Syrian nationals were seen rolling along the Damascus road under military escort.
>
> "Large groups of Syrians also stood around the United Arab Republic's Consulate here, apparently waiting to leave the country."

Even some members of the Embassy were not spared, and we had to protest to the Lebanese Government because they received treatment which was not in accordance with diplomatic usage.

All this is very regrettable and cannot but threaten the friendly relations which should prevail between countries which belong to the same region of the world.

Before concluding, I should like to recall what the President of the United Arab Republic declared on 16 May 1958:

> "The United Arab Republic has nothing to do with these events, but all the broadcasts which I have heard during my trip have stated that the leaders of the Lebanon affirm that the United Arab Republic is the cause of the disturbances. What they seek is to transform a purely domestic affair concerning the citizens of one State into an international question."

He went on to say:

> "When I went to Damascus, all that I said in my statement with respect to Lebanon was a simple expression of our respect for its independence and its unity and of our desire that Lebanon should not be divided by a civil war and that the shedding of blood should be avoided."

Later he added:

> "In the name of the people of the United Arab Republic, I repeat what I

stated previously: we uphold and respect the independence of Lebanon; we shall not permit any interference in its affairs."

On the basis of all that I have stated and all that has been said previously, it cannot be said that the United Arab Republic has intervened in the domestic affairs of Lebanon. It is, as I have repeated on several occasions, a purely domestic question. The events in Lebanon only concern the Lebanese, and it is up to them to put an end to such events.

The international diversion which the present Government of Lebanon is seeking to create by presenting this complaint, which is without justification, cannot result in a true and adequate solution to the problem. Furthermore, this domestic question does not and cannot threaten international peace. The present situation is the result of political differences which separate the Lebanese themselves. It is for them only to find a solution.

Mr. Malik asks for protection for Lebanon because Lebanon is a small country. But nobody is threatening Lebanon. We hope that that country will continue to be independent and we wish for the prosperity, well-being and peace of the Lebanese people.

Appendix II

(B)

SPEECH OF MR. LOUṬFĪ ON JUNE 10, 1958*

I wish to thank the President for giving me the floor so that I may exercise my right of reply. I intend to supplement the statement I made last Friday and to reply to charges and allegations made by the representative of Lebanon. However, I shall stay within the framework of the question that is before us.

Mr. Malik maintained, first of all, that the United Arab Republic was furnishing arms to subversive elements in Lebanon. To establish this, he adduced certain examples. May I point out that the majority of these instances are based on police reports or reports of the Lebanese Deuxième Bureau. In my view, that does not give them any probative force. We know that the courts in all countries do not take such reports into account unless they are corroborated by conclusive evidence, which is far from being the case here. Especially do I insist on the point that what has been adduced here is far from pointing to any responsibility on the part of the United Arab Republic, and that is the most important element in the question before us.

I should like to reply to a number of the examples adduced by the representative of Lebanon. To facilitate matters, I have before me the French text of the verbatim record of the last meeting of the Security Council.

At the end of page 11 of the French text, Mr. Malik says that a private vehicle with the registration number 4774 was stopped and searched at a customs post and that arms were found in the vehicle. Mr. Malik does not even say how such information was made available to him, whether the driver was arrested, who the driver was, whether he was haled before a tribunal.

In this first example, we read that the vehicle "was stopped and searched at the customs post of Abboudieh, in North Lebanon. The vehicle, which was entering Lebanese territory from Syria, was found to be carrying the following (arms) . . ." (S/PV. 823, page 11). We also read that "the names inscribed on these guns were names of Syrian soldiers" *(Ibid.)*. This remains to be proved. There are thousands of persons in Arab countries who are called by the names cited in the first example: Mohammed Abdulla, Mazhar Demian, Zakaria, and so forth. Furthermore, I do not think that even in the Syrian army the names of soldiers are inscribed on guns.

How are we to know that these arms were not stolen or purchased? Even if it were established that the accusation regarding the transport of arms was well-founded, I do not see how the Government which I have the honor to represent here could be held responsible on the basis of the kind of data which have been given.

I turn now to the second example, which is cited on pages 11 and 12 of document S/PV. 823. It is alleged that 110 outlaws coming from Syria were carrying arms. If one reads the statements of these so-called rebels, one will immediately realize that this story is ~~simply fantastic.~~ In this second example, we read:

> "Some hundred Lebanese followers of Kamal Jumblatt were convoked to a meeting in Damascus by the leadership of their party on Monday, 7 April 1958 . . ." (S/PV. 823, page 11).

Well, I should like to see a truck which can carry 110 men at one time. Yet we are told that a single truck was able to transport all these men. And if an officer of the Syrian army wished to establish contact with his agents, he certainly would not hold a meeting with 110 men in a café in the middle of a city like Damascus. Furthermore,

* *UN Doc. S/PV. 824,* 10 June 1958, pp. 3-26.

we are told that this officer taught these men how to use the arms. It seems to me that it would be difficult to give such instruction in so short a time.

Finally, we cannot in any case be held responsible on the basis of these facts, the accuracy of which is far from being established.

The third and fourth examples, which are to be found on page 12 of document S/PV. 823, are based simply on reports of the police and the Lebanese *Deuxième Bureau.* There is no proof of any kind particularly as regards our responsibility.

Let us take the example on page 13-15 of document S/PV. 823. Here, we are presented with a report by the Lebanese *Deuxième Bureau* on a meeting held at Damascus in the office of the Syrian *Deuxième Bureau.* Thus, this example concerns a report by the Lebanese *Deuxième Bureau* on an interview which took place in Damascus in the office of the Syrian *Deuxième Bureau;* it concerns events which occurred in Damascus. We cannot here take into consideration reports of intelligence offices, which, as is well known, generally have the task of giving their Governments information. Such reports cannot be used as evidence here in the Security Council.

In example 10 on page 16 of document S/PV. 823, Mr. Malik tells us that among the confiscated arms an anti-aircraft gun was found. This seems incredible to me, because anyone using such a weapon would have to have a good deal of training and knowledge concerning arms. Furthermore, from the military point of view, what would be the use of having one anti-aircraft gun? In addition, we are not even told what mark was on this gun. This information is not given in support of the contention that the gun was provided by the United Arab Republic.

Similarly, in example 14 on page 17 of document S/PV. 823, where it is stated that the arms in question were inscribed "the Egyptian Army—1949—made under the supervision of Technical Research Department," I would observe that the United Arab Republic was not manufacturing arms before 1955 and that the inscription to which I have referred and which Mr. Malik used as evidence is not correct and is not the exact inscription found on arms of the United Arab Republic.

I do not want to enter here into a discussion of the Arabic language, but I could explain to Mr. Malik or Mr. Jamali the difference between these inscriptions.

Reference has been made to two sailboats alleged to have been seized at sea off the Lebanese coast.

As regards the first sailboat, I would ask the Security Council to take note of a statement of one of the accused persons, Mr. Itani. This statement was made to the newspaper, "El Sayad." In it the accused categorically denied the charges made against him. Furthermore, members of the opposition also rejected the accusation and held that the owner of the sailboat was trafficking in narcotic drugs. This case is still before the courts, and I do not think that in the circumstances it would be appropriate to go into any details.

I would say the following with regard to the second sailboat. Mr. Malik has told us that the sailboat was not transporting arms and the eleven persons on it were acquitted by Lebanese courts because they had committed no new criminal acts. Indeed, these eleven persons had been convicted several months earlier for having entered Lebanese territory without authorization. This indicates that the example in question has no probative value, establishes no charge against my Government and is only tendentious propaganda aimed at creating the idea of interference by my Government in Lebanon's domestic affairs.

As regards the third sailboat, we are presented with imprecise statements by Lebanese nationals, to the effect that they were transporting arms. We are not told what the arms were, whether or not they were confiscated, if the persons concerned were prosecuted, and so forth. In any case, it is impossible to maintain that we are in any way responsible with regard to this question of sailboats.

I have already dealt with the matter of the Belgian Consul-General at Damascus. Today, I would merely add that we cannot in any way be held responsible in this regard. As I have already said, this diplomat was very probably unaware of what was in his car. As for the letter which allegedly was found on him—a letter, incidentally, of which we are unaware—the diplomat's lawyer, Mr. Mohsen Selim, in a statement to the press which is before the Security Council, categorically denied the charges made against his client. This statement is to be found on page 25 of the document distributed last Friday. In any case, as I have already said, I do not want to go into any details on a question concerning a member of the diplomatic corps before a verdict has been rendered by the courts.

Furthermore, I cannot conceal my astonishment at Mr. Malik's drawing from what he calls his first series of facts the conclusion that

> "all men engaged in subversive activities in Lebanon today are supplied with arms from the United Arab Republic." *(S/PV. 823, pages 18-20)*

That is the statement made by Mr. Malik at the last meeting—that all the arms carried by these persons in Lebanon have been received from the United Arab Republic. Are we to understand, then, that there was not a single rifle in Lebanon before this unrest began? Is it we who have supplied all these arms? In putting this thesis forward it is forgotten that we are dealing here with Lebanon where, as I think it would be difficult to deny, all the mountain people are armed, as well as the other tribes, and that there always have been and always will be those who cross the frontier between Syria and Lebanon at one point or another.

I have already said that to obtain arms is not a serious problem. The legal and illegal arms traffic goes on everywhere and in all parts of all the world. We find, even after the Second World War, that during revolutions, periods of unrest and civil wars the parties have always found the means of obtaining the necessary arms. Furthermore, on the open market it is easy in most countries to obtain arms. In fact, I have in my possession catalogues showing that weapons are available to any purchaser, even here in the United States.

Therefore, Mr. Malik, I really must reject your accusations, and I regret infinitely that you should have stated that the United Arab Republic armed all those who are at present engaged in subversive activities in Lebanon, particularly since you know that the Lebanese Government has distributed arms to its partisans and to certain organizations in large quantities. Those weapons have passed from hand to hand, as happens always and in all countries when there is unrest or civil war. This has been stated by many members of the opposition, including Mr. Fouad Ammoun, the former Secretary-General of the Ministry of Foreign Affairs, and by others also who have all categorically denied that it was the United Arab Republic which provided them with arms.

With regard to what he called the second series of facts, the representative of Lebanon maintained that elements from Lebanon received subversive training on the territory of the United Arab Republic and were sent back to Lebanon with the task of overthrowing the Government there. Again, all we have is allegations which are not supported by facts.

In the first example cited, Mr. Malik tells us: "We know that measures have been taken in Syria for training Lebanese and non-Lebanese commanders." He maintains that they have many of them in their prisons but he does not give us a single name and does not ever say whether they have been tried and condemned or whether it has been clearly established that they were trained by the Syrian Deuxième Bureau.

In the second case Mr. Malik even told us that some 150 persons from Tripoli and its environments had been seen in the Syrian town of Hadbussya, where they were trained by the Syrian Army. By whom were they seen? Was this established by a court? It is not on the basis of facts of this kind that one submits a complaint to the United Nations about a friendly State. It is fortunate that Mr. Malik did not dwell at too great length on his allegations in the second series.

He went on to a third series of facts which he called facts dealing with "the participation of United Arab Republic civilian nationals residing in Lebanon, or passing into Lebanon, in subversive and terrorist activities in Lebanon" *(S/PV. 823, page 21)*. It is quite evident that it is difficult for me to discuss these question example by example. Mr. Malik has not given me facts which I could accept or refute.

In his sixth example in this series, which appears on page 22 of the verbatim record, Mr. Malik tells us that during 1958 security reports showed that tens of Syrians and Palestinians from Gaza had been arrested for terrorist activities. He did not tell us what had been the result of those arrests, whether the persons concerned had been condemned or even brought before the courts, or what charges had been preferred.

Mr. Malik spoke frequently of Syrians carrying Syrian military identity cards. Well, in Syria every person who has completed his military service is obliged to carry such a card. It does not follow, therefore, that the persons referred to by Mr. Malik actually belong to the Syrian Army.

I really do not see anything in these allegations—which for the most part comprise isolated cases—that could in any way establish the responsibility of our Government.

In his latest series of facts, Mr. Malik told us, in particular, that the Syrian Deuxième Bureau was carrying out on Lebanese territory activities directed against Lebanese policy. He mentioned the names of a few so-called agents who are, for the most part, Palestinian or Syrian refugees, and among whom there are apparently a few Lebanese. I am repeating what was stated by Mr. Malik. Some of them were condemned by the courts. Mr. Malik says that they belonged to the Deuxième Bureau, but there is nothing in the facts put forward by him to prove that this was so. They were condemned for acts from which it did not follow that they were members of the Deuxième Bureau. Furthermore, there is nothing there to establish our responsibility in any way for these acts—which, incidentally, are not proved.

In example (8), which appears on page 26 of the verbatim record of the Council's last meeting, Mr. Malik speaks of 200 Syrian Army conscripts who, it is alleged, crossed the frontier in the region of Hasbaya. Mr. Malik states this fact, but he gives us no proof. How does he know that they were Syrian conscripts? He does not say whether they have been taken prisoner or arrested or condemned. We are still in the domain of allegations unsupported by proof.

In example (7), which appears on the same page, Mr. Malik spoke to us in particular of the case of the Egyptian Military Attaché, Mr. Hassan Halil, who at the beginning of 1957, was reported to have been arrested while carrying a large quantity of arms in his car. Our embassy in Beirut published, on 6 June just a few days ago, a statement on this important question which I shall take the liberty of distributing without delay. In this explanatory statement it was mentioned that the Lebanese Government itself had published a statement in which it was denied very clearly that the Egyptian Military Attaché was in any way involved in anything relating to arms trafficking. Furthermore, it was added in this *dementi* that all the rumors about arms trafficking by Egyptian diplomats were devoid of any foundation. I am surprised that Mr. Malik should have brought up this question which had been the subject of an official *dementi* by his Government.

Mr. Malik spoke to us also of an incident which took place at Dair-El-Achayer. From information received by us and from a statement which was made by Mr. Gumboulat on 13 September 1957 and distributed in Beirut, it appears that the cause of this incident was to be found in the fact that after the elections, which had led to unrest in the region, negotiations had taken place between the Druses and certain representatives of Lebanese Government and other political personalities with a view of preserving calm when, unfortunately, the Lebanese police intervened and tried to arrest certain leaders of the Druses, Al Achebli and El Erian among them, despite the fact that an agreement had been reached that no arrests would take place. Fighting followed between some of the Druses and the Lebanese police, and the Council knows that the Druses, who are mountain people, are always armed and do not hesitate to defend themselves.

It can be seen from all that I have stated, and from what was declared at the last meeting, that the grave accusations which Mr. Malik has made against us have not produced one concrete fact and that they are not of a nature such as to render my Government responsible for the events in Lebanon. It appears besides that Mr. Malik is not quite sure that his charges are convincing, particularly as he has declared that "one could still hold that these were sporadic instances which do not, even in the aggregate, justify the sweeping conclusions which I have drawn from them." *(Ibid., p. 32)* There is no doubt that we are confronted with isolated cases, with declarations and affirmations which cannot, in my view, be established or serve as a basis for accusations against my Government.

I will show later the attitude that has been adopted regarding the United Arab Republic by the present leaders in Lebanon.

The representative of Lebanon, in his last intervention, spoke at length on the question of radio and press campaigns.

I had already informed the Council, at its meeting of 6 June, that the Egyptian press, generally, only reported what had been published by the Lebanese press and press agencies. I should like to give the Council some examples to prove what I have just stated. These examples are based on statements and quotations which were made by Mr. Malik at the last meeting of the Council.

On page 33 of the verbatim record of the last meeting Mr. Malik quoted from the newspaper *Al-Akhbar* of Cairo of 17 April last:

> "The Lebanese parties are against the renewal of the presidency of Chamoun." *(Ibid., p. 33)*

I have that paper before me and I am ready to communicate its contents to the members of the Council and to the representative of Lebanon if they wish to peruse it. In this paper it is stated that the political party El Nagada made a declaration in which it was said that any attempt to revise the Constitution by President Chamoun would meet with vigorous opposition. Therefore, *Al-Akhbar* has simply reported the statement made by that political party, and this is stated very clearly in the paper. I have the text before me and I shall be glad to circulate it.

Mr. Malik said that the same paper stated on 18 April:

> "Ultimatum to Chamoun. The Lebanon is threatened by a bloody revolution." *(Ibid.)*

Again, this is merely from an article of the Reuter Agency, and I have the clipping before me.

Mr. Malik then quoted from *Al-Akhbar* of 14 May. However, I have not been able to find that quotation. Perhaps there is an error in the date.

Mr. Malik also quoted from the paper *Al-Gumhouriyya* of 6 April where it was stated: "Open appeal for a revolt in Beirut." *(Ibid., pages 34-35)* He did not say, however, that the information published constituted criticisms voiced by Deputy Ahmed Assaad against the Lebanese Government and that it was also a report made by a press agency.

Referring to *Akhbar-El-Yom* of 12 April, Mr. Malik stated that what was said there was that a revolution could start in Lebanon any time; but he did not say that this was only an article written by a Lebanese journalist by the name of Said Freiha.

Mr. Malik also quoted from *Al-Chaab of Cairo* of 13 April 1958 as follows:

> "Danger of civil war in Lebanon . . ." *(Ibid., page 36)*

This information was published in a Beirut paper, the information having come from press agencies.

The text quoted by Mr. Malik from *Al-Chaab* of 18 May was again simply taken from an article by a Lebanese journalist named Selim Ellouzi.

On my side, I could quote extracts from Lebanese papers in which the leaders of the United Arab Republic are attacked.

On 17 May 1957 the Lebanese Press Agency stated that Egypt had assassinated Tewfik Abou El Hodah, former President of the Jordanian Council, and that he had not committed suicide.

On 24 May 1957, the newspaper *El Amal* of Beirut published an article under the following heading: "Tragedy of Freedom in Egypt" and claimed that a law had been promulgated in Egypt stipulating condemnation to death of anyone who attacked the President of the Republic.

On 27 May 1957 the same paper published, on the basis of information available to all the Arab world, information which was slanderous regarding Egypt and its policy, stating that Egypt was utilizing Arab nationalism in order to consolidate the dictatorial regime; that Egypt had betrayed the cause of Arab nationalism by the participation of a delegation in the youth festival at Moscow; that the President was giving Egypt to Communism.

On 30 August 1957 the newspaper *Le Jour* published a caricature of Mr. Dulles trying to find a vaccine for Egypt.

On March 1958 *El Nahar* published an article which characterized the Syrian and Egyptian leaders as criminals.

The attack against the United Arab Republic has not been confined to the Lebanese press and radio; it has gone to the point of forging issues of Egyptian dailies and weeklies, such as *Le Progres Egyptien* and the *Rosa El Youssef,* which contain calumnies against the responsible leaders of the United Arab Republic.

Every imaginable activity in the field of propaganda against the United Arab Republic, from any imaginable source, has been and continues to be authorized in Lebanon. As for the radio, I have already told the Council that the radio generally transmitted news published by press agencies and newspapers of Lebanon. It is obvious that sometimes the radio was obliged to respond to these accusations of which we are the object.

Mr. Malik has read to us some extracts from the Egyptian radio. I could also read extracts of this nature transmitted by a secret post called *"La Voix de la Verite,"* and, according to our information, one of the relay points was destroyed in the village of El Nabiosman.

As I have promised the Council, I shall content myself with communicating the texts of these broadcasts to the Secretary of the Council. Moreover, I shall also distribute the falsified pamphlet concerning publicity on tourism from which I am going to take the liberty of reading an extract. In the excursion programme we read the following:

"Visits to the palace of ex-King Farouk, turned into a private residence for revolutionary soldiers, and visits to the villas confiscated for the benefit of officers. Visits to the cemetery to place a wreath on the tombs of Salah Salem and his Moslem brothers."

The programme contains things of that kind. It will be distributed to the members of the Council.

In my last statement on Friday, 6 June, I touched on the question of the Arab League. There is no need for me to quote to the Council the text of the Charter which deals with regional organizations and which has been quoted here repeatedly, especially by my colleagues from Latin America. This text makes clear the importance which the Charter assigns to international organizations in their work of conciliation and of arriving at solutions of disputes which might arise between Members of this Organization. Articles 33 and 52 of the Charter are very clear on this point. In my last statement, I cited Article 36, paragraph 2, which specifies that the Security Council should take into consideration any procedures for the settlement of a dispute which have already been adopted by the parties.

As members know, the Arab League has dealt with the complaint of Lebanon, even though Lebanon had at the same time submitted a complaint to the Security Council. Members know that on 21 May 1958, the representative of Lebanon sent a letter to the Secretary-General of the United Nations advising him that the Government of Lebanon had on the same day presented a complaint against the Government of the United Arab Republic to the Arab League.

On 22 May, in other words twenty-four hours later, the representative of Lebanon sent a letter to the President of the Security Council requesting an urgent meeting of the Security Council in order to examine the complaint which the Council has before it today; that is, within twenty-four hours we were advised of a complaint filed in the Arab League and of another one, which was said to be of an emergency character, presented to the Security Council.

Three times the Government of Lebanon requested the adjournment of the meetings of the Security Council, even though it had previously described its complaint as being urgent. As I stated the other day, in arriving in New York Mr. Malik told journalists, even before the Arab League had examined the question, that this question could find a solution only in the Security Council.

The Arab League has discussed the Lebanese complaint, as I had the honor to tell the last meeting of the Council. Six States of the Arab League—Sudan, Saudi Arabia, Iraq, Jordan, Libya and Yemen—presented a joint resolution which, unfortunately, failed to obtain the support of the Lebanese Government. I have had the honor of quoting that resolution to the Council. With the Council's permission, I shall quote again only the operative part of the resolution, which reads:

"The Council decides

"1. To put an end to everything that might disturb the atmosphere of serenity among all the member States by every means at its disposal;

"2. To request the Government of Lebanon to withdraw the complaint which it submitted to the Security Council;

"3. To send an appeal to the various Lebanese groups to put an end to disturbances and to take the necessary measures to settle their internal disputes by peaceful and constitutional means;

"4. To send a committee chosen from among members of the Council to calm the situation and to implement the decision of the Council."

Had that resolution been accepted in a spirit of conciliation, there would have been a good chance of finding a solution of this dispute.

With the Council's permission, I should like to read out some extracts from the record of the Arab League meeting of 4 June 1958. It was stated that the six States supported the resolution and that the two interested Sates had accepted it implicitly subject to the reservation that the two delegations would contact their Governments. The Minister for Foreign Affairs of Sudan, Mr. Mahgoub, stated that the draft had been presented by the six States which were not parties to the dispute. At the end of the meeting, the President announced: "Gentlemen, do you approve this draft resolution subject to the reservation that the two delegations of the States concerned will enter into contact with their Governments?" Unanimous approval followed, and the meeting was adjourned.

I think the text is clear and requires no further comment.

Even an appeal for calm and tranquility addressed to the Lebanese people, which had been worked out by the Council of the Arab League in which the Director of the Political Department of the Foreign Ministry of Lebanon had taken part, and to which no objection had been forthcoming from the members, was rejected by the Lebanese delegation, even though it was an attempt to put an end to the disturbances and to restore calm and quiet.

If the Government of Lebanon had really been eager to find a solution of this dispute, surely it would have approved the resolution of the Arab League. Unfortunately, however, it seemed to be intent on getting this problem discussed in the Security Council for purposes of submitting tendentious propaganda against the United Arab Republic.

As I have already told the Council, this is merely an attempt to create an international diversion for the events that are occurring inside Lebanon, events which concern only the Lebanese themselves. It is also an attempt to use the Security Council to solve domestic questions which concern only the Lebanese themselves.

If Lebanon had accepted the recommendations contained in the resolution of the Arab League, it surely would have contributed to restoring tranquility and stability in this part of the world, it would have avoided bloodshed and it would have spared the many casualties that were claimed by the sad events which are now taking place in Lebanon.

Let us examine Lebanon's position toward the United Arab Republic. In my last statement I discussed the large expulsions of citizens of the United Arab Republic. I also told the Council that if our relations with Lebanon were not ideal, we could well have presented a complaint to the Council. But we consider that this kind of dispute between two sister peoples must be settled by other methods. These expulsions were arbitrary in nature. They took place without any explanation and without passing through the juridical or administrative channels prescribed by the rules of international law. These expulsions were inhuman. A number of those expelled were molested and even tortured. I have before me the documents which establish these charges. According to the latest information in our possession, the number of those expelled has reached 13,000 persons. Despite a number of protests, we have been unable to obtain any plausible explanation for this bizarre attitude of the Lebanese Government.

Moreover, Lebanon has for some time been the scene of plots which were hatched against the United Arab Republic. The principal instruments of these plots have been the members of a terrorist group known as Syrian nationalists. In 1949 Lebanese judicial organs convicted them of high treason. Under the present regime, they have been pardoned en masse. They were allowed to publish newspapers and, worse yet, they had training centres located in five areas of Lebanon, namely, the village of Nabi Osman near the Syrian frontier, the village of Bawachi near Baalbek, Borge el Barajna near Beirut, and others. There is no doubt that the Government has distributed weapons to them. This may be seen from the statements of the members of the opposition and from a document which we have before us and which we are prepared to distribute to the Council. It contains the resignation of Captain Abdel-Kerim El-Zaban, who resigned in protest against the supplying of arms to these terrorists. I shall read out the translation of the text of his letter of resignation.

> "As a sign of protest against certain flagrant violations of the law, such as the distribution of military weapons to civilians carried out at the post of the Commander of the Gendarmerie under the control of responsible officers, kindly accept my resignation from the Gendarmerie. I have in my possession irrefutable proof which I shall place in the hands of competent authorities if it should be necessary."

These outlawed Syrian nationalists, participated in plots against Syria in November 1956, August 1957 and December 1957. Exchanges of correspondence on these matters have taken place between Lebanon and the Syrian Republic. There was another plot against the Egyptian Government in December 1957. The guilty parties have in fact been judged by the tribunals of the United Arab Republic.

Moreover, the Government of Lebanon has treated the diplomats of the United Arab Republic in a manner contrary to the rules of international law. Thus, on 14 May 1958, the First Secretary of the Embassy, Mr. Hefri Mohamadein, was arrested and searched even though he had presented his identity card. His car, which bore diplomatic plates, was also searched. On 15 May 1958, Mr. Moustafa Ghoneim, an Embassy Secretary of the United Arab Republic in Beirut, was molested by a Lebanese officer and three soldiers. He was required to get off a taxi and was brutally searched.

Nothing was found on his person. On 28 May 1958, Mr. Ezzedine El Hoseini, an Embassy official, was arrested while visiting the central post office. He was placed in jail, chained and treated as a criminal. He was released on 31 May 1958. Needless to say, the Embassy of the United Arab Republic in Beirut has vigorously protested against this treatment.

It is clear from all that I have said that the Government of the United Arab Republic has nothing to do with the painful events which are occurring in Lebanon.

It has not been established that there has been any interference on our part in the internal affairs of Lebanon. Far from it. As I have repeatedly stated, it is a purely domestic Lebanese affair which only concerns the Lebanese. It is up to them alone to solve this problem.

Notwithstanding these facts, we have tried to solve this problem in the framework of the Arab League. Unfortunately, we ran headlong into systematic opposition on the part of the leaders of Lebanon. As I have already stated, it does not appear that the Lebanese leaders are taking their complaint to the Arab League seriously.

As the leaders of my country have repeatedly stated, we respect the independence and unity of Lebanon. We do not want Lebanon to be torn asunder by civil war. We have always considered that an independent Lebanon would be an element of stability and peace in this part of the world.

Appendix III

ILLUSTRATIVE SAMPLES OF UAR PRESS AND RADIO ATTACKS ON THE GOVERNMENT OF LEBANON

Commenting on the murder of al-Matnī under the headline "Victim in Battle of Lebanese People," *al-Sha'b* wrote on May 9th (this was broadcast by Radio Cairo) :[1]

> The sinful criminals whose hands were smeared with blood have sneaked under cover of darkness to commit their abominable and horrible crime. However, all the people of Lebanon know the real criminals. This is not their first crime, and perhaps it will not be their last.
>
> The free and struggling people well know how their rulers have committed crimes against them time after time. The people know how they rigged the elections in order to elect a Chamber of Deputies from among their supporters so that they would condone their crimes and overlook the blood which smears their hands. The people know how their rulers tied themselves to the bandwagon of imperialism to its pacts and doctrines, and how they threatened to resort to fleets and guns to protect them, and save the seats which shake under them.
>
> All this and more is known to the Lebanese people. This abominable crime is not committed against the martyr Nasib al-Matni alone. In the first place, it is committed against all the people of Lebanon. It is a challenge to the people and a mean attempt to frighten them. However, the rulers of Lebanon would be making a mistake—Camille Shamun, Sami as-Sulh, and Charles Malik would be making a mistake—if they thought that by these crimes they would destroy the will and voice of the people. Every free Lebanese citizen is merely another Nasib al-Matni. The free men of Lebanon are much greater in number than imagined by Camille Shamun and his criminal gang. These free men of Lebanon will not allow the blood of Nasib al-Matni to be shed unavenged.
>
> If the courts of Lebanon are unable to punish the real criminals, the people of Lebanon are capable of doing so. The people will inflict just punishment. The cause of the free men of Lebanon will triumph. The blood of Nasib al-Matni is the fuel which will feed the torch of freedom in Lebanon and which inflames the spirit of sacrifice in the people of Lebanon, until final victory is accomplished for these struggling people against their traitorous and assassin rulers. Bow your heads to Nasib al-Matni, the free Arab martyr. Raise your heads and await the coming victory for the free Arab people of Lebanon.

Under the headline of "The Battle has Begun," *al-Ahram* wrote on May 10th:[2]

> Lebanon is in mourning. The people there in every town and village are in turmoil. This is not only mourning for the free journalist who was assassinated by unknown bullets, but mourning for freedom of opinion—the mourning of all free men in Lebanon and indeed the mourning of Arab heroism everywhere.
>
> We wonder, does the Lebanese President wish to remain in office despite this great number of martyrs? Does he wish to renew his term of presidency over all these bodies and victims? This mourning which Lebanon wears, this blackness which crowns every head, and these tears which fill all eyes—are they the cost of the battle for the desired renewal?

1. *Radio Cairo,* May 9, 1958, 0445 GMT.
2. *Radio Cairo,* May 10, 1958, 0445 GMT.

On May 11th, *al-Sha'b* wrote:[3]

> Shamun and his government stand on one side and the people of Lebanon on the other. The two sides exchange fire. However, in such cases the result is inevitable. O President Shamun: beware of a bloodbath not for the sake of the people of Lebanon whom you antagonized and upon whom you declared war, but for your own sake. You will be the first to drown in the bloodbath.

Under the headline "The Reins Got Loose," *al-Ahram* wrote on May 12th:[4]

> The reins have been wrenched forever from the hands of those who rule the people of Lebanon with steel, fire, bullets, dynamite, and darkness. The reins have got loose from the hands of those who impose themselves on Lebanon and on the Lebanese regime, and who hatch the plots, kill free men, and arouse sedition. The people of Lebanon now reply to the government's terrorism with terrorism and to fire with fire. The people of Lebanon will not keep quiet when they see their free men, leaders, and heroes fall one after the other at the hands of this government.

On May 20th, *al-Ahram* wrote:[5]

> The Lebanese towns are still continuing their revolution. Hundreds of martyrs who fell under Shamun's and Sulh's bullets have left to the Lebanese people - - to liberate themselves from this regime, this ruler, and this oppressor. The message of the martyrs will not be lost. The ruler will go, no matter to what extent he relies on foreign support, because the people do not want him. It was not the foreign fleets which raised Shamun to the Presidency, but election by the people. Shamun and his government will fall because this is the wish of the people and because this is the era of the people and not the age of rulers and governments.

On the same day (May 20th), *al-Akhbar* wrote:[6]

> The battle of the Lebanese people started its second week yesterday. There is no sign that the people have retreated even a single step in their desire to achieve their noble goal of being ruled by a democratic regime. Shamun used the gangs of the Syrian Nationalist Party. He resorted to military aid with the consent and support of Israel. He incited the imperialist forces against his people. He threw his canon [sic], tanks, and bombs into the streets to kill men, women, and children and to destroy the towns. Beware, O Nero of 1958, beware of destiny. This free blood which is being shed will choke you to death.

On May 21st, *al-Akhbar* wrote:[7]

> The resignation of Camille Shamun is no longer sufficient to avenge the Lebanese people. A quick trial and a drastic sentence is required in such circumstances. All provisions of the constitution protecting the President of the Lebanese Republic against trial and punishment should be torn to pieces. This should be done because the people who drafted these provisions did not imagine that Lebanon would some day be ruled by a shedder of blood who would kill 120 citizens a day, hire criminals to assassinate the free people, and distribute weapons to a group of his followers for use against the people.
>
> The people who drew up the provisions of the constitution did not image that their republic would at any time be ruled by a traitor who would find it very easy to provoke the imperialists against his own people. In demanding only Shamun's resignation, the Lebanese opposition is being very merciful.

3. *Radio Cairo,* May 11, 1958, 0445 GMT.
4. *Radio Cairo,* May 12, 1958, 0445 GMT.
5. *Radio Cairo,* May 20, 1958, 0445 GMT.
6. *Radio Cairo,* May 20, 1958, 0445 GMT.
7. *Radio Cairo,* May 21, 1958, 0445 GMT.

Addressing himself to the Lebanese, the well-known Aḥmad Sa'īd of *Voice of the Arabs* broadcast the following (in part) on May 20th:[8]

> My brother in Lebanon, there was no other way before you than the revolution to achieve your hopes. Your enemies are now killing and murdering your free people. There is no other way for you but to rise and fight them with their own weapons and system with which they are fighting you.
>
> You have noticed your rulers bringing back your enemies to colonize your country and use it as a base for their attacks and a nest for their plot. You have awakened to an oppressive and pro-Western rule, a rule which is conspiring against Lebanon and against its neighbor Syria and its sister Egypt. The struggle has begun between you and your enemies.
>
> The assassination of the free journalist Nasir [sic] al-Matni by the Syrian nationalist gangs was the spark which set off this revolution throughout Christian and Moslem Lebanon. It was natural for you to carry arms, O brother, in Lebanon. Your enemies are arming the hirelings of the Syrian nationalist gangs to kill you, make you submit to their rulers, and accept their colonialism.

Commenting on the complaint of Lebanon to the Security Council, *al-Sha'b* wrote in part, on May 23rd:[9]

> Poor Camille Nimr Shamun directed his weapons and bombs against the people, but he failed. His seat has been considerably shaken and he has confined himself to his palace like a terrified mouse, while the indignation of the rebelling people strikes his ears like raging waves.
>
> Shamun, or those provoking him, has thought of another front to which he would draw attention—the UAR. Shamun has complained against us to the Arab League. Not content with this, he has complained against us to the Security Council alleging the presence of UAR interference in Lebanon's domestic affairs.
>
> Despite the fact that the Lebanese people have repeatedly declared through their free leaders that the people's revolution has emerged from within Lebanon and that there has been no interference by the UAR in Lebanon's affairs, Camille Nimr Shamun persists in pursuing the course he has laid for himself—the course which is full of spite and hatred of everything that is pure Arab, the course which he followed from the beginning, since the time he made of Beirut a traitor-plotter cell from which to concoct conspiracies against the UAR.
>
> We are not astounded by this behavior. We are not surprised when he resorts to deceit, fraud, and lies. This is not the first time he has resorted to such a thing nor will it be the last. It is not much for him to be a deceiver, liar, and impostor, he in whose happy era free struggling people were assassinated by criminals very well known to Camille Nimr Shamun. Poor Camille Nimr Shamun is bidding farewell to the last days of his rule of terrorism, but he does not wish to bid farewell until he affirms that he is himself—Camille Nimr Shamun, defender of criminals, liars, and deceivers.

On May 22nd, *Radio Damascus* made the following commentary (quoted in part):[10]

> Where are those Lebanese who made Lebanon a paradise? What would Riyad as-Sulh, who died for Lebanon, say if he saw Sami as-Sulh dying to give away the independence of Lebanon and swimming in the innocent blood of the Lebanese people? What would he say if he saw Sami as-Sulh extending his hands to the Syrian nationalist gang who assassinated Riyadh as-Sulh in Amman, and trying to instigate them to fight and kill the people of Lebanon? By God, Sami as-Sulh has blackened the face of the Arab nation. May God blacken his face. Resign and spare bloodshed and lives.

---

8. *Voice of the Arabs* (Cairo), May 20, 1958, 1700 GMT.
9. *Radio Cairo,* May 23, 1958, 0445 GMT.
10. *Radio Damascus,* May 22, 1958, 1615 GMT.

Commenting on the Lebanese complaint to the Security Council, *al-Jumhūriyah* maintained that Shamun cannot be part to the dispute because he himself is the accused. It wrote (in part) on May 25:[11]

> The blood of al-Matni proves that Shamun instigated the assassination. The blood of al-Maliki is a proof that Shamun granted refuge to assassins and criminals. The blood of the Lebanese people shed in Beirut, Sidon, Tripoli, and elsewhere in Lebanon is the greatest proof of Shamun's crimes. Shamun is accused of antagonizing [sic] the imperialists against the independence of his country. He is accused of conspiring with Israel against the Lebanese people. He is accused of converting the government into a gang to serve his purposes.
>
> In fact, Shamun has surpassed the limit of accusations. He is a criminal. The Lebanese people in Tripoli and south Lebanon have established popular courts for the trial of his stooges. In fact they are trying Shamun himself. Shamun adores everything foreign and hates everything Arab.

Commenting on the Prime Minister's announcement that his cabinet will not seek Sham'ūn's re-election, *al-Ahram* wrote on May 28th:[12]

> This is not enough. Shamun must go. He must leave the palace and the seat of rule, for he cannot stay in office with all this blood flowing and all those bomb blasts rocking Beirut. The people have decided that Shamun must resign. Peoples never back down from a cause which they have consecreated [sic] with the blood of their martyrs. The Lebanese people cannot bear the thought of Shamun being their President for another three months. They cannot trust a ruler who has sold out his country to remain in office and appealed to foreign fleets for protection from the people's wrath.
>
> The demands of the martyrs who were killed by government bullets is that Shamun must go. Therefore, those free men who still live cannot abandon a cause which hundreds of martyrs have signed with their blood. Shamun must go immediately. He has no place in Lebanon today. Sami as-Sulh, the man who has chosen to protect the people's enemy from the people's wrath, also must go. Shamun will go in spite of himself because it is the Lebanese people who are now the virtual president of the republic.

Under the headline "Tomorrow Every Shamun will fall," *al-Sha'b* wrote on May 28th:[13]

> March Forth, people of Lebanon, but keep fully awake and vigilant against all attempts to put you off guard and all plots or compromises. Continue your struggle brave people, for you have always been in the lead among the Arab peoples on the road to liberation, struggle, freedom, and democracy. May you be blessed, beloved Arab people.
>
> Your insistance [sic] on a liberated policy in which all Arab peoples believe shows your adherence to Arab nationalism and your awareness of the menace which Shamun and his gang are to this nationalism. We once said that Shamun is the first line of defense of imperialism, the Baghdad Pact, and the Eisenhower Plan. Today we declare that you, free Lebanese people, are the first line of defense of Arab nationalism, Arab independence, and the self-liberated Arab policy. The existence of Shamun or his kind means that Lebanon will remain a center for plots and a foreign base in the midst of our homeland, weaving conspiracies, engineering aggressions, and threatening peace.
>
> Shamun therefore must go. To us Shamun is not specifically Camille alone, but represents every enemy of the Arab people and peace. So strike and strike again, beloved Lebanese people. Alarm and confusion have afflicted the ranks

11. *Radio Cairo,* May 25, 1958, 0445 GMT.
12. *Radio Cairo,* May 28, 1958, 0445 GMT.
13. *Radio Cairo,* May 28, 1958, 0445 GMT.

> of reaction. Tomorrow Camille Shamun and every Shamun will fall and the Arab people will dictate their desires.

As broadcast by *Radio Cairo,* the Syrian newspaper *al Naṣr* wrote on May 27th:[14]

> The UAR will not need to deny the false claim which the authorities of David Ben Shamun have lodged. . . . Camille Shamun and Sami as-Sulh have burned all bridges which connect them with the Arab nation. Arab public opinion declares that they are criminal traitors, condemns them to national and moral death, and expects that they will soon meet their fate now that they have become the prisoners of terror and pessimism. The spears which protect them will not veil the face of the future in which the caravan of Arab nationalism will tread on the remnants of the agents and cast them into the deep abyss of the past.

---

14. *Radio Cairo,* May 27, 1958, 1430 GMT.

Appendix IV

IMPORTANT U.N. RESOLUTIONS

(A)

SECURITY COUNCIL RESOLUTION OF JUNE 11, 1958*

The Security Council,

Having heard the charges of the representatives of Lebanon concerning interference by the United Arab Republic in the internal affairs of Lebanon and the reply of the representative of the United Arab Republic,

Decides to dispatch urgently an observation group to proceed to Lebanon so as to ensure that there is no illegal infiltration of personnel or supply of arms or other material across the Lebanese borders;

Authorizes the Secretary-General to take the necessary steps to end;

Requests the observation group to keep the Security Council currently informed through the Secretary-General.

(B)

THE SEVEN POWER DRAFT RESOLUTION OF AUGUST 18, 1958†

The General Assembly,

Having considered the item "Questions discussed at the 838th meeting of the Security Council on 7 August 1958,"

Noting the declarations addressed to the President of the General Assembly of 18 August 1958 by the United States regarding United States forces now in Lebanon and their withdrawal and by the United Kingdom regarding British forces now in Jordan and their withdrawal,

Noting the Charter aim that States should practice tolerance and live together in peace with one another as good neighbors,

I

1. *Reaffirms* that all Member States should refrain from any threats or acts, direct or indirect, aimed at impairing the freedom, independence or integrity of any State, or at fomenting civil strife and subverting the will of the people of any State;

2. *Calls upon* all Member States strictly to observe these obligations and to ensure that their conduct, by word and deed, in relation to the general area of the Near East, conforms to the above-mentioned policy;

II

Requests the Secretary-General, in accordance with the Charter, forthwith to make such practical arrangements as he, in consultation with the Governments concerned, may find would adequately serve to help in upholding the purposes and principles of the Charter in relation to Lebanon and Jordan in present circumstances, having in mind section I of the present resolution;

---

* The Swedish Resolution.

† *UN Doc. A/3878,* 18 August 1958.

III

1. *Notes* that the Secretary-General has studies in preparation, for consideration by the General Assembly at its thirteenth session, of the feasibility of establishing a stand-by United Nations peace force;

2. *Invites* the Secretary-General to continue his studies now under way and in this context to consult as appropriate with the Arab countries of the Near East with a view to possible assistance regarding an Arab development institution designed to further economic growth in these countries;

IV

1. *Requests* Member States to co-operate fully in carrying out this resolution;

2. *Invites* the Secretary-General to report hereunder, as appropriate, the first such report to be made not later than 30 September 1958.

(C)

THE ARAB RESOLUTION OF AUGUST 21, 1958‡

The General Assembly,

Having considered the item entitled "Questions concerning the Security Council at its 838th meeting on 7 August 1958,"

Noting the Charter aim that States should practice tolerance and live together in peace with one another as good neighbors,

Noting that the Arab States have agreed, in the Pact of the League of Arab States, to strengthen the close relations and numerous ties which link the Arab States, and to support and stabilize these ties upon a basis of respect for the independence and sovereignty of these States, and to direct their efforts toward the common good of all the Arab countries, the improvement of their status, the security of their future and the realization of their aspirations and hopes,

Desiring to relieve international tension,

I

1. *Welcomes* the renewed assurances given by the Arab States to observe the provision of article 8 of the Pact of the League of Arab States that each member State shall respect the systems of government established in the other member States and regard them as exclusive concerns of these States, and that each shall pledge to abstain from any action calculated to change established systems of government;

2. *Calls upon* all States Members of the United Nations to act strictly in accordance with the principles of mutual respect for each other's territorial integrity and sovereignty, of non-aggression, of strict non-interference in each other's internal affairs, and of equal and mutual benefit, and to ensure that their conduct by word and deed conforms to these principles;

II

Requests the Secretary-General to make forthwith, in consultation with the Governments concerned and in accordance with the Charter, and having in mind section I of this resolution, such practical arrangements as would adequately help in upholding the purposes and principles of the Charter in relation to Lebanon and Jordan in the present circumstances, and thereby facilitate the early withdrawal of the foreign troops from the two countries;

---

‡ *UN Doc. A/3893/Rev. 1,* 21 August 1958.

III

Invites the Secretary-General to continue his studies now under way and in this context to consult as appropriate with the Arab countries of the Near East with a view to possible assistance regarding an Arab development institution designed to further economic growth in these countries;

IV

1. *Requests* Member States to co-operate fully in carrying out this resolution;

2. *Invites* the Secretary-General to report hereunder, as appropriate, the first such report to be made not later than 30 September 1958.

Appendix V

THE HAMMARSKJOLD AND EISENHOWER PROPOSALS

(A)

SPEECH OF MR. HAMMARSKJOLD BEFORE THE GENERAL ASSEMBLY ON AUGUST 8, 1958*

The item on the agenda of this emergency session of the General Asesmbly refers specifically to situations in the Middle East which have arisen only recently. However, seen in their broader context, these situations draw attention to basic problems facing the United Nations in the Middle East. In these circumstances, it may be found useful by the Members of the General Assembly if, at this early stage of the deliberations, I outline some of the basic needs for action in the region, which, in view of the experience of the Secretariat, require urgent attention. It would be premature for me now to indicate along what lines solution might be sought. I hope that in this respect the debate in the General Assembly will prove to be fruitful. An indication of the needs as seen by the Secretariat may serve as a basis on which Members might wish to develop positive and constructive suggestions.

The arrangements by which the United Nations, through the United Nations Emergency Force, assists the Government of the United Arab Republic in Gaza and along the international frontier between Egypt and Israel, and serves to maintain quiet in that area, have worked out in a way which, I believe, may be a source of satisfaction to all Members of the United Nations. Similarly, the United Nations Truce Supervision Organization continues to function, under the terms of reference established by the Armistice Agreements. Although the scope of its activities has been restricted, and in spite of difficulties, this body also represents an essential element in the efforts of the United Nations to stabilize conditions in the area.

On the basis of the resolution of the Security Council of 11 June 1958, the United Nations has organized a third operation in the Middle East, the United Nations Observation Group in Lebanon. It has already rendered very useful service and its further development is, in the light of our experience, fully justified. However, the present operation is related to conditions which may be temporary, and the time may not be distant when a change of those conditions would call for a change of approach. Recent experiences may be taken as indicating that some form of United Nations representation in the country might be a desirable expression of the continued concern of the Organization for the independence and integrity of Lebanon. If that proves to be the case, forms should be sought by which such representation would adequately serve the purposes of the Organization in the region. However, the arrangements that should be made, once the time has come to reconsider the United Nations representation in Lebanon in the light of developments in the country, will depend, ultimately, on the attitude of the Government of Lebanon itself.

Another part of the region which presents specific problems is the Hashemite Kingdom of Jordan, with its central location on the map of the area. In the period through which we are passing, it appears that the United Nations should give special attention to the essential role which this country has to play in the efforts of the Organization to assist in creating conditions for peaceful and constructive development. Under present circumstances, some strengthening of the Truce Supervision

---

* *UN Doc. A/PV. 732,* 8 August 1958, pp. 16-22.

Organization, within the framework of the General Armistice Agreements, may have to be considered. Were it to be felt that special measures would be desirable, in addition to the activities of that Organization, the question would arise how such measures should be developed so that they are adequate in the specific situation prevailing in Jordan. Consideration should also be given to the question how the measures taken might best be co-ordinated with the other United Nations arrangements in the region.

However, activities like those of the United Nations Emergency Force, the Truce Supervision Organization, the Observation Group in Lebanon and such other organs as the General Assembly might wish to consider, are only safeguards created to assist the governments concerned. The developments in which the United Nations and all Member countries within or outside the region are interested can be supported by such measures, but ultimately they must depend on, and will be effectively shaped by, actions of the Member nations in the region.

Arab nations already have co-operated within the Arab League, and they all have subscribed to the principles of mutual respect for each other's territories, integrity and sovereignty; of non-aggression; of non-interference in each other's internal affairs, and of equal and mutual benefit. Were the States concerned in the present troubled situation jointly to reaffirm their adherence to such principles, that step would be of considerable assistance to the general efforts in which the United Nations is engaged. Steps that might be taken in the direction of an agreement or a declaration to that effect, and of accommodations of policies to those principles, should, therefore, have the support of the Organization.

To the extent that the Arab nations would find it possible to translate the principles mentioned into joint practical action, the Organization should be prepared to render assistance of a technical nature and to give the necessary support. This is so especially in the field of economic co-operation, since one of the major aims of the United Nations is to make its contribution to the efforts of the Governments and peoples to improve, in co-operation, their economic and social conditions. By studies made within the Secretariat, and with the assistance of the International Bank, we have, in the Secretariat, tried to prepare ourselves to afford such assistance as the countries concerned may request.

The need for arrangements for economic co-operation within the region has been strongly felt in the work of the United Nations, especially as regards the financial field, where the creation of the proper institutions would considerably facilitate the flow of funds needed in the region. However, arrangements for economic co-operation also in other fields would, in the light of our experience, be helpful. I have in mind especially arrangements giving a proper framework to the co-operation between oil-producing and oil-transiting countries, or made with a view to a joint utilization of water resources.

The need for a closer co-operation in the various fields to which I have just referred could best be met through institutions created by the free initiative of the countries in the region. The Organization could make an essential contribution by extending its encouragement, support and technical assistance to the independent efforts of the nations in the region to fill that need.

Finally, it is clear, in the light of experience, that both the arrangements for direct United Nations representation in various parts of the area to which I have referred, and such arrangements for co-operation as might be made by agreement among the Arab countries, will require the recognition by the world community of the particular problems and possibilities of the region. Most countries in the area have only recently emerged with their present political character of independent sovereign States, with close mutual ties and with a strong sense of the rights and duties which flow from the particular heritage of the Arab peoples. We know that the problems and aspirations of these peoples meet with general respect and understanding. It would be helpful in promoting the purposes of the United Nations in the area if this respect and this understanding were to be given general expression, assuring the peoples there that they may shape their own destinies in the best interest of each nation within the region and of the region as a whole.

It is my belief that, if the General Assembly in its present deliberations could find a way toward furthering developments to meet the needs I have indicated, a basis would be provided on which we could hope to deal with the other serious problems of the area with which the Organization has been engaged for years. First among those problems stands the question of the refugees. It continues to be urgent, but its solution may have to await the creation of the more favourable general conditions which would follow, were the other needs to which I have referred to be successfully met.

(B)

SPEECH OF PRESIDENT EISENHOWER BEFORE THE GENERAL ASSEMBLY ON AUGUST 13, 1958*

Mr. President, Mr. Secretary-General, Members of the General Assembly, and guests: First, may I express my gratitude for the generosity of your welcome.

It has been almost five years since I had the honour of addressing this Assembly. I then spoke of atomic power and urged that we should find the way by which the miraculous inventiveness of man should be not dedicated to his death but consecrated to his life. Since then great strides have been taken in the use of atomic energy for peaceful purposes. Tragically little has been done to eliminate the use of atomic and nuclear power for weapons purposes.

That is a danger.

That danger in turn gives rise to another danger—the danger that nations under aggressive leadership will seek to exploit man's horror of war by confronting the nations, particularly small nations, with an apparent choice between supine surrender, or war.

This tactic reappeared during the recent Near East crisis.

Some might call it "ballistic blackmail."

In most communities it is illegal to cry "fire" in a crowded assembly. Should it not be considered serious international misconduct to manufacture a general war scare in an effort to achieve local political aims?

Pressures such as these will never be successfully practiced against America, but they do create dangers which could affect each and every one of us. That is why I have asked for the privilege of again addressing you.

The immediate reason is two small countries—Lebanon and Jordan.

The cause is one of universal concern.

The lawful and freely elected Government of Lebanon, feeling itself endangered by civil strife fomented from without, sent the United States a desperate call for instant help. We responded to that call.

On the basis of that response an effort has been made to create a war hysteria. The impression is sought to be created that if small nations are assisted in their desire to survive, that endangers the peace.

This is truly an "upside down" portrayal. If it is made an international crime to help a small nation maintain its independence, then indeed the possibilities of conquest are unlimited. We will have nullified the provisions of our Charter which recognizes the inherent right of collective self-defense. We will have let loose forces that could generate great disasters.

The United Nations has, of course, a primary responsibility to maintain not only

* *UN Doc. A/PV. 733,* 13 August 1958, pp. 2-18.

international peace but also "security." But we must not evade a second fact, namely, that in the circumstances of the world since 1945 the United Nations has sometimes been blocked in its attempt to fulfill that function.

Respect for the liberty and freedom of all nations has always been a guiding principle of the United States. This respect has been consistently demonstrated by our unswerving adherence to the principles of the Charter, particularly in its opposition to aggression, direct or indirect. Sometimes we have made that demonstration in terms of collective measures called for by the United Nations. Sometimes we have done so pursuant to what the Charter calls "the inherent right of collective self-defense."

I recall the moments of clear danger we have faced since the end of the Second World War—Iran, Greece and Turkey, the Berlin blockade, Korea, the Straits of Taiwan.

A common principle guided the position of the United States on all of these occasions. That principle was that aggression, direct or indirect, must be checked before it gathered sufficient momentum to destroy us all—aggressor and defender alike.

It is this principle that was applied once again when the urgent appeals of the Governments of Lebanon and Jordan were answered.

I would be less than candid if I did not tell you that the United States reserves, within the spirit of the Charter, the right to answer the legitimate appeal of any nation, particularly small nations.

I doubt that a single free government in all the world would willingly forego the right to ask for help if its sovereignty were imperiled.

But I must again emphasize that the United States seeks always to keep within the spirit of the Charter.

Thus when President Truman responded in 1947 to the urgent plea of Greece, the United States stipulated that our assistance would be withdrawn whenever the United Nations felt that its action could take the place of ours.

Similarly, when the United States responded to the urgent plea of Lebanon, we went at once to the Security Council and sought United Nations assistance for Lebanon so as to permit the withdrawal of United States forces.

United Nations action would have been taken and United States forces already withdrawn, had it not been that two resolutions, one proposed by the United States, the other proposed by the Government of Japan, failed to pass because of one negative vote—a veto.

But nothing that I have said is to be construed as indicating that I regard the status quo as sacrosanct. Change is indeed the law of life and of progress. But when change reflects the will of the people, then change can and should be brought about in peaceful ways.

In this context the United States respects the right of every Arab nation of the Near East to live in freedom without domination from any source, far or near.

In the same context, we believe that the Charter of the United Nations places on all of us certain solemn obligations. Without respect for each other's sovereignty and the exercise of great care in the means by which new patterns of international life are achieved, the projection of the peaceful vision of the Charter would become a mockery.

Let me turn now specifically to the problem of Lebanon.

When the United States military assistance began moving into Lebanon, I reported to the American people that we had immediately reacted to the plea of Lebanon because the situation was such that only prompt action would suffice.

I repeat to you the solemn pledge I then made. Our assistance to Lebanon has but one single purpose—that is the purpose of the Charter and of such historic resolutions of the United Nations as the "Essentials for Peace" Resolution of 1949 and the "Peace through Deeds" Resolution of 1950. These denounce, as a form of aggression and as an international crime, the fomenting of civil strife in the interest of a foreign Power.

We want to prevent that crime—or at least prevent its having fatal consequences. We have no other purpose whatsoever.

The United States troops will be totally withdrawn whenever this is requested by the duly constituted Government of Lebanon or whenever, through action by the United Nations or otherwise, Lebanon is no longer exposed to the original danger.

It is my earnest hope that this Assembly, free of the veto, will consider how it can assure the continued independence and integrity of Lebanon. Thus the political destiny of the Lebanese people will continue to lie in their own hands.

The United States delegation will support measures to this end.

Another urgent problem is Jordan.

If we do not act promptly in Jordan a further dangerous crisis may result, for the method of indirect aggression discernible in Jordan may lead to conflicts endangering the peace.

We must recognize that peace in this area is fragile, and we must also recognize that the end of peace in Jordan could have consequences of a far-reaching nature. The United Nations has a particular responsibility in this matter, since it sponsored the Palestine Armistice Agreements upon which peace in the area rests and since it also sponsors the care of the Palestine refugees.

I hope that this Assembly will be able to give expression to the interest of the United Nations in preserving the peace in Jordan.

There is another matter which this Assembly should face in seeking to promote stability in the Near East. That is the question of inflammatory propaganda. The United Nations Assembly has on three occasions—in 1947, 1949, and 1950—passed resolutions designed to stop the projecting of irresponsible broadcasts from one nation into the homes of citizens of other nations, thereby "fomenting civil strife and subverting the will of the people in any State." That is stated in the language of the resolution. We all know that these resolutions have recently been violated in many directions in the Near East.

If we, the United States, are one of those who have been at fault we stand ready to be corrected.

I believe that this Assembly should reaffirm its enunciated policy and should consider means for monitoring the radio broadcasts directed across national frontiers in the troubled Near East area. It should then examine complaints from these nations which consider their national security jeopardized by external propaganda.

The countries of this area should also be freed from armed pressure and infiltration coming across their borders. When such interference threatens they should be able to get from the United Nations prompt and effective action to help safeguard their independence. This requires that adequate machinery be available to make the United Nations presence manifest in the area of trouble.

Therefore, I believe that this Assembly should take action looking towards the creation of a standby United Nations Peace Force. The need for such a Force in being is clearly demonstrated by recent events involving imminent danger to the integrity of two of our Members.

I understand that this general subject is to be discussed at the thirteenth General Assembly and that our distinguished Secretary-General has taken an initiative in this matter. Recent events clearly demonstrate that this is a matter for urgent and positive action.

I have proposed four areas of action for the consideration of the Assembly—in respect to Lebanon, to Jordan, to subversive propaganda, and to a standby United Nations force. These measures, basically, are designed to do one thing: to preserve the right of a nation and its people to determine their own destiny, consistent with the obligation to respect the rights of others.

This clearly applies to the great surge of Arab nationalism.

Let me state the position of my country unmistakably. The peoples of the Arab nations of the Near East clearly possess the right of determining and expressing their own destiny. Other nations should not interfere so long as this expression is found in ways compatible with international peace and security.

However, here as in other areas we have an opportunity to share in a great international task. That is the task of assisting the peoples of that area, under programmes which they may desire, to make further progress toward the goals of human welfare they have set for themselves. Only on the basis of progressing economies can truly independent Governments sustain themselves.

This is a real challenge to the Arab people and to all of us.

To help the Arab countries fulfill these aspirations, here is what I propose:

First, that consultations be immediately undertaken by the Secretary-General with the Arab nations of the Near East to ascertain whether an agreement can be reached to establish an Arab development institution on a regional basis.

Second, that these consultations consider the composition and the possible functions of a regional Arab development institution, whose task would be to accelerate progress in such fields as industry, agriculture, water supply, health and education, among others.

Third, other nations and private organizations which might be prepared to support this institution should also be consulted at an appropriate time.

Should the Arab States agree on the usefulness of such a soundly organized regional institution, and should they be prepared to support it with their own resources, the United States would also be prepared to support it.

The institution would be set up to provide loans to the Arab States as well as the technical assistance required in the formulation of development projects.

The institution should be governed by the Arab States themselves.

This proposal for a regional Arab development institution can, I believe, be realized on a basis which would attract international capital, both public and private.

I also believe that the best and quickest way to achieve the most desirable result would be for the Secretary-General to make two parallel approaches: first, to consult with the Arab States of the Near East to determine an area of agreement; then to invite the International Bank for Reconstruction and Development, which has vast experience in this field, to make available its facilities for the planning of the organizational and operational techniques needed to establish the institution on its progressive course.

I hope it is clear that I am not suggesting a position of leadership for my own country in the work of creating such an institution. If this institution is to be a success, the function of leadership must belong to the Arab States themselves.

I would hope that high on the agenda of this institution would be an action to meet one of the major challenges of the Near East, the great common shortage—water.

Much scientific and engineering work is already under way in the field of water development. For instance, atomic isotopes now permit us to chart the courses of the great underground rivers. And new horizons are opening in the desalting of water. The ancient problem of water is on the threshold of solution. Energy, determination and science will carry it over that threshold.

Another great challenge that faces the area is disease.

Already there is substantial effort among the peoples and Governments of the Near East to conquer disease and disability. But much more remains to be done.

The United States is prepared to join with other Governments and the World Health Organization in an all-out, joint attack on preventable disease in the Near East.

But to see the desert blossom again and preventable disease conquered is only a first step. As I look into the future I see the emergence of modern Arab States that would bring to this century contributions surpassing those we cannot forget from the past. We remember that Western arithmetic and algebra owe much to Arabic mathematicians and that much of the foundation of the world's medical science and astronomy was laid by Arab scholars. Above all, we remember that three of the world's great religions were born in the Near East.

But a true Arab renaissance can only develop in a healthy human setting. Material progress should not be an overriding objective in itself; it is an important condition for achieving higher human, cultural and spiritual objectives.

But I repeat, if this vision of the modern Arab community is to come to life, the goals must be Arab goals.

With the assistance of the United Nations, the countries of the Near East now have a unique opportunity to advance, in freedom, their security and their political and economic interests. If a plan for peace of the kind I am proposing can be carried forward, in a few short years we may be able to look back on the Lebanon and Jordan crises as the beginning of a great new prosperous era of Arab history.

But there is an important consideration which must remain in mind today and in the future. If there is an end to external interference in the internal affairs of the Arab States of the Near East; if an adequate United Nations Peace Force is in existence; if a regional development institution exists and is at work on the basic projects and programmes designed to lift the living standards of the area; then with this good prospect, and indeed as a necessary condition for its fulfilment, I hope and believe that the nations of the area, intellectually and emotionally, will no longer feel the need to seek national security through spiralling military buildups. These lead not only to economic impotence but to war.

Perhaps the nations involved in the 1948 hostilities may, as a first step, wish to call for a United Nations study of the flow of heavy armaments to those nations. My country would be glad to support the establishment of an appropriate United Nations body to examine this problem. That body would discuss it individually with these countries and see what arms control arrangements could be worked out under which the security of all these nations could be maintained more effectively than under a continued wasteful, dangerous competition in armaments. I recognize that any such arrangements must reflect these countries' own views.

I have tried to present to you the framework of a plan for peace in the Near East which would provide a setting of political order responsive to the rights of the people in each nation; which would avoid the dangers of a regional arms race; which would permit the peoples of the Near East to devote their energies wholeheartedly to the tasks of development and human progress in the widest sense.

It is important that the six elements of this program be viewed as a whole. They are:

(1) United Nations concern for Lebanon.
(2) United Nations measures to preserve peace in Jordan.
(3) An end to the fomenting from without of civil strife.
(4) A United Nations Peace Force.
(5) A regional economic development plan to assist and accelerate improvement in the living standards of the people in these Arab nations.
(6) Steps to avoid a new arms race spiral in the area.

To have solidity, the different elements of this plan for peace and progress should be considered and acted on together, as integral elements of a single concerted effort.

Therefore, I hope that this Assembly will seek simultaneously to set in motion measures that would create a climate of security in the Near East consonant with the principles of the United Nations Charter, and at the same time create the framework for a common effort to raise the standard of living of the Arab peoples.

But the peoples of the Near East are not alone in their ambition for independence and development. We are living in a time when the whole world has become alive to the possibilities for modernizing their societies.

The American Government has been steadily enlarging its allocations to foreign economic development in response to these worldwide hopes. We have joined in partnership with such groupings as the Organization of American States and the Colombo Plan; and we are working on methods to strengthen these regional arrangements. For example, in the case of the Organization of American States, we are consulting with our sister republics of this hemisphere to strengthen its role in economic development. And the Government of the United States has not been alone in supporting development efforts. The British Commonwealth, the countries of Western Europe, and Japan have all made significant contributions.

But in many parts of the world both geography and wise economic planning favor national rather than regional development programmes. The United States will, of course, continue its firm support of such national programmes. Only where the desire for a regional approach is clearly manifested and where the advantage of regional over national is evident will the United States change to regional methods.

The United States is proud of the scope and variety of its development activities throughout the world. Those who know our history will realize that this is no sudden, new policy of our Government. Ever since its birth, the United States has gladly shared its wealth with others. This it has done without thought of conquest or economic domination. After victory in two world wars and the expenditure of vast treasure there is no world map, either geographic or economic, on which anyone can find that the force of American arms or the power of the American Treasury has absorbed any foreign land or political or economic system. As we cherish our freedom, we believe in freedom for others.

The things I have talked about today are real and await our grasp. Within the Near East and within this Assembly are the forces of good sense, of restraint, and of wisdom to make, with time and patience, a framework of political order and of peace in that region.

But we also know that all these possibilities are shadowed, all our hopes are dimmed, by the fact of the arms race in nuclear weapons—a contest which drains off our best talents and vast resources, straining the nerves of all our peoples.

As I look out on this Assembly, with so many of you representing new nations, one thought above all impresses me.

The world that is being remade on our planet is going to be a world of many mature nations. As one after another of these new nations moves through the difficult transition to modernization and learns the methods of growth, from this travail new levels of prosperity and productivity will emerge.

This world of individual nations is not going to be controlled by any one Power or group of Powers. This world is not going to be committed to any one ideology.

Please believe me when I say that the dream of world domination by one Power or of world conformity is an impossible dream.

The nature of today's weapons, the nature of modern communications, and the widening circle of new nations make it plain that we must, in the end, be a world community of open societies.

And the concept of the open society is the ultimate key to a system of arms control we can all trust.

We must, then, seek with new vigour, new initiative, the path to a peace based on the effective control of armaments, on economic advancement and on the freedom of all peoples to be ruled by governments of their choice. Only thus can we exercise the full capacity God has given us to enrich the lives of the individual human beings who are our ultimate concern, our responsibility and our strength.

In this memorable task there lies enough work and enough reward to satisfy the energies and ambitions of all leaders, everywhere.

Index

'Abbūd, Basīl, 162
'Abd al-Naṣīr, Jamal, 27, 29, 39, 40, 41, 42, 43, 44, 46, 51, 52, 60, 62, 63, 66, 91, 172, 178
'Abd al-Nūr, Salīm, 162
'Abdallah, al-Shaykh, 80
Abde, 148
Abū Jawdah, Elie, 155
Abū Shaqrā, Shaykh 'Aql Muḥammad, 135
Aden Protectorate, 128
Afghanistan in the U.N., 100
Afro-Asian bloc in the U.N., 100, 101, 106
al-Aḥdab, 'Azīz, 117, 162
Aiken, Mr., 103
'Aināb, 78
'Akkār, 9, 148, 156
al-'Akkārī, Nāẓim, 159
'Alāyā, Shaykh Muḥammad, 67, 125
Alexandria Protocol, 18
Aley, 3
Algeria, 40
al-'Ali, 165 (Table II)
al-'Amal, 157, 160
Amanus Mountains, 9
American University of Beirut, 8, 111
'Ammān, 108, 154
'Ammūn, Fu'ād, 50, 61, 62, 66, 67, 72
'Ammūns, 83
Anti-Lebanon Mountains, 2, 9, 146
Aqaba, 52
'Aql, George, 60, 66, 67
Arab Gulf, 45, 102, *see also* Persian Gulf
Arab League, 25, 34, 113, 172, 173; Council meeting, 89-91; draft resolution of, 90-1; Pact, 18, 106-7, 172
Arab Liberation Party, 70
Arab nationalism, 40, 44-5, 60, 61, 84, 85, 94, 98, 111; as cause of the crisis, 28-30; recognition by the U.N., 102-3
Arab Nationalists' Movement, 29
Arab News Agency, 139
Arab refugees, 7, 98
Arab Renaissance, 111
Arab states, 37; relations with Lebanon, 18, 26, 34-5, 54; —in the United Nations: attitude towards foreign troops, 99-100; Arab resolution in General Assembly, 106-8
Arabian American Oil Company, 5
Arabian Peninsula, 179
Arabic, 9, 17, 63, 80, 111
Aramaic, 9
al-'Arīḍah, 1, 150
Arislān, Majid, 56, 76
Arislāns, 11
Arman, Mr., 136
Armenian Catholics, 8 (table); 14; 20 (Table I)
Armenian language, 80
Armenian Orthodox, 8 (table); 20 (Table I)
arms supply: government complaint, 138-41; opposition complaint, 136-7
al-'Aryān, 79
al-As'ad, Aḥmad, 49, 62, 79, 160, 165 (Table II), 169
al-As'ad, Kāmil, 49, 60, 62, 64
al-Ashqar, As'ad, 85, 133-4, 159
al-'Aṣī River, *see* Orontes
Atlantic Ocean, 45, 102
al-Aṭrash, Sulṭān Pasha, 142, 143
Australia, 7; in the U.N., 100, 101
Austria, 12, 13
al-'Awar, Bashīr, 64, 91
'Ayn Zaḥaltā, 77
al-Azhar, 29
Aziziye, 150
'Azqūl, 123

Bā'aqlīn, 76
Baghdad, 108, 128, 135, 136
Baghdad Pact, 26, 37, 45, 48, 53, 133, 134, 174
Bahraynis, 78
Bakh'ah, 9
Ba'lbak, 2, 133, 150, 156; balance of forces in, 79-80
Ba'lbak International Festival, 59
Bandung Conference, 105
Banghazi, 89-91 *passim*
Bank of America, 5
al-Barūḥ, 77
al-Basṭa, 41, 49, 73, 80
Ba'th Party, 29, 36, 50, 129, 166
Batlūn, 77
Bayar, Celal, 36, 37, 48
Bayhum, Muḥammad 'Ali, 56, 57
Bayram, 67
Bayt-al-Dīn, 73, 76, 77
al-Bazzī, 'Alī, 22, 49, 161
Beirut, 7, 9, 12, 19, 23, 31, 32, 52, 56-68 *passim,* 71, 76, 78-9, 80, 81, 84, 85, 89, 108, 120, 122, 133, 136, 139, 144, 147, 166-7; balance of forces in, 73-4; climate, 2-3; description, 4-5, 180; US troops in, 115-8; violence in, 72, 156, 158, 161
Beirut al-Masā, 73

Beirut International Airport, 78, 81, 116, 136
Bekaa, *see* al-Biqāʿ
Belgium in the U.N., 100
Bikirki, 10
al-Biqāʿ, 2, 9, 16, 31, 56, 134, 138-9, 146, 159
Bourguiba, 41
Britain, 12, 13, 38, 40, 45, 48, 52, 112, 126, 133, 136; Ambassador of, 65, 115; Fleet, 114; Intelligence Service, 34; in the United Nations, 92, 93, 101, 104, 106; recognition of Iraq régime, 96; troop landings in Jordan, 92, 94, 151; withdrawal, 108-9
Bull, Major General Odd, 144
Būlus, Jawād, 155
Buraimi Oasis, 128
Burma in the U.N., 100
al-Bustānī, Emile, 24
Butrus, Fu'ād, 161
Byzantines, 9

Cairo, 5, 30, 66, 108
Canaanites, 9
Canada in the United Nations, 92, 93, 100, 105
Causes of the crisis, 28-47, 89, 141-3, 169-71
Central Administrative Council, 13
Central Treaty Organization, 174
Chaldeans, 8 (table), 20
Chamoun, Camille, *see* Sham'ūn
Chase Manhattan Bank, 5
China in the United Nations, 91, 93, 100
Christians, 7, 8 (Table), 9, 12; protection mentality as cause of the crisis, 28-30; *see also*: Confessionalism, Maronites
Colombia in the United Nations, 92, 93, 100, 105
"Committee of Union," 159
Communists, 44, 45, 47, 55-6, 59, 64
Compromise solutions, 56, 85-6; causes of failure, 86-7
Concert of Europe, 14
Confessionalism, 16, 21, 32, 130-1, 156, 158-9, 171, 178-9; *see also* Christians, Maronites, Muslims
Congress party, 66
Congress of Parties, Organizations and Personalities in Lebanon, 51
Constantinople, 11
Constitutional Bloc, 50, 69, 167
Constitutional Union Party, 165 (Table II)
Council of Florence, 10
counter-revolution, 156-60
Cyprus, 114, 115
Czechoslovakia, 26

Daily Mail, London, 151
Damascus, 60-3 *passim,* 108, 171
al-Darazī, Muḥammad, 10, 11
Darwīsh, 'Abd al-Raḥmān, 73, 74
Da'ūd Effendi, 14
al-Da'ūq, Aḥmad, 164; Cabinet of, 167-8
Davin, Mr., 103
Dayal, Rajeshwar, 144
Dayr al-Qamar, 12, 25
Denmark in the U.N., 100, 105
dhimmis, 28
Druze, 7, 8 (table), 9, 10-11, 12, 13, 14, 20 (Table I), 42, 49, 50, 57, 67, 73, 76, 77, 135, 142
Dulles, John Foster, 105, 114, 118

East Germany, 26
Eban, Abba, 52, 53
economic development, attitudes towards in UN, 103-4
Economic Research Institute, 8
Ecuador, 144
Eddé, Emile, 17, 22
Eddé, Pierre, 134
Eddé, Raymond, 85, 155, 156, 161, 164, 168, 176
Egan, Mr., 105-6
Egypt, 5, 6, 10, 25, 26, 30, 35, 39-48 *passim,* 52, 55, 56, 57, 59, 61, 84, 85, 128, 134, 170, 179; Constitution of 1956, 40; press campaign against Sham'ūn, 51-3; relations with Lebanon as cause of the crisis, 37-8; *see also* United Arab Republic
Egyptian occupation, 12
Egyptians (Ancient), 9
Eisenhower, 95, 118; address to the United Nations, 97-8, 99, 101, 104
Eisenhower Doctrine, 45, 46, 47, 48-9, 52, 57, 112, 126, 127, 170, 174
Elections of 1957, 56-8; campaign, 53-8; elections of 1960, 163-6
English, 80

Fakhr al-din I, 11
Fakhr al-din II, 11
Far'ūn, Henri, 44, 50, 51, 66, 67, 169
Fārūq, King, 25
Fawzi, Maḥmūd, 100
Fayṣal, King, 26
Fertile Crescent, 17
Fertile Crescent Union, 85

First National City Bank, 5
Fisk, Pliny, 111
France, 10, 38, 45, 48, 52, 80, 126, 133; Ambassador of, 65, 115; in the U.N., 92, 93; Mandate of, 16, 30, 112, 151; occupation of Lebanon by, 12-13
Frangié, *see* Franjiyah
Franjiyah, Ḥamīd, 23, 49, 50, 169
Franjiyahs, 83
Fraydīs, 77
Free Press, 70
French language, 16-17
Fu'ād Pasha, 12, 13

de Gaulle, 95
Germany, 84, 113
Ghālib, 'Abd al-Ḥamīd, 55
al-Ghazālī, Muḥammad, 29
al-Ghusn, Fu'ād, 57
Glubb Pasha, 40
Grand Liban, see Greater Lebanon
Grand Mufti of Lebanon, 70
Greater Lebanon, 16
Greece in the U.N., 100, 103
Greek Catholics, 8 (table), 13, 20 (Table I)
Greek Orthodox 8 (table), 13, 20 (Table I), 21
Greeks, 9
Gregory XIII, Pope, 10
Gromyko, Andrei, 99

Ḥaddād, Fu'ād, 157, 158
al-Ḥājj, 'Abdallah, 23, 24, 49
al-Ḥakīm, 'Adnān, 73
al-Ḥakīm, Caliph of Egypt, 10
Ḥakīm, Yusuf, 73, 74
Halba, 150
Hamādah, Qaḥṭān, 76, 77
Ḥamādah, Ṣabrī, 49, 60, 61, 79, 160, 162, 165 (Table II), 166, 169, 176
Hamawī, Suhayl, 80
Hammarskjöld, Dag, 92, 96, 104, 118, 144, 151, 173; speech before the General Assembly, 97; trip to the Middle East, 108
Ḥamūd, Mu'in, 73
Ḥamzah, 79
al-ḥarakah al-ūla, 12
Harida, 146
al-Ḥaurani, Akram, 60
al-Ḥawādith, 66
Al-Ḥayāt, 163
Ḥaydar, 79
Hermon, 146
Ḥilū, Charles, 50, 155
Hirmil, 150, 156; balance of forces in, 79-80
Ḥitti, Yusuf, 51, 56, 57
Hittites, 9
Holloway, Admiral James L., 116, 117
Hotel Employees and Workers Union, 6
al-Huda, 111
Ḥusayn, King, 26, 41, 92, 99
al-Ḥuṣrī, Sāti', 29

Ibrāhīm Pasha, 12
Iddah, Emile, *see* Eddé
I'īd, Major Jamīl, 117
India, 144; in the U.N., 100, 101-2
International Wheat Agreement, 4
Iran, 127, 177-8; in the U.N., 100, 101
Iraq, 25-26, 35, 37, 38, 41, 45, 51, 78, 84, 90, 127, 133, 136, 170, 177, 178, 179; in the United Nations 92, 93, 94, 106; revolution, 127-8, 135, 151, 173, 174, 175
Iraq Petroleum Company, 5
Ireland in the U.N., 103
Islam, 9
Israel, 1, 5, 52, 107; in the U.N., 100
Italy in the U.N., 100, 104

Jabal Tarbol, 148
Jalbūṭ, Captain Tawfiq, 162
Japan in the United Nations, 92, 93, 100; draft resolution of, 94-5
Jarring, Mr., 92, 93
Jews, 8 (table)
Jizzīn, 64, 162
Jordan, 17, 26, 38, 40, 41, 53, 59, 78, 90, 92, 94, 98, 127, 128, 136, 155, 170, 177, 178, 179; in the U.N., 96, 106
Jubb'adin, 9
Jumayyil, Maurice, 167
Jumayyil, Pierre, 32, 58, 84, 158, 160, 161, 164, 167, 176
Junblāṭ, Kamāl, 22, 25, 34, 42, 48, 49, 50, 57, 62, 63, 66, 67, 72, 73, 75-6, 77, 78, 81, 134, 142, 159, 160, 161, 167, 169, 176
Junblāṭs, 11
Junieh, 166

Kan'ān, Marūn, 162
Karāmī, Nawwaf, 142
Karāmī, Rashīd, 49, 61, 64, 67, 75, 79, 156, 157, 158, 159, 164, 165 (Table II), 166, 169; Cabinet of, 160-1
Karīm, Ṭal'āt, 75
Katā'ib, 50
Khālid, Khālid Muḥammad, 29
Khālid, Muḥammad, 32

al-Khalīl, Kāẓim, 65
khamsīn wind, 2-3
al-Khaṭīb, Anwar, 24, 63
Khāzin, 166
Khrushchev, 95-6
al-Khūrī, Bishārah, 12, 17, 22, 24, 33-34, 50, 65, 66, 70, 81, 83, 155, 167, 169, 176, 177
al-Khūrī, Ilyās, 49, 62, 167
Khūrī, Sāmī, 136
Kisrawān, 166

al-Labābīdī, Ṣalāḥ, 162
Labakī, Kasruwān, 51, 64
Lall, Mr., 101-2
Laḥḥūd, Emile, 26, 62
Laḥḥūd, Salīm, 155
Latakia, 5
Latin American countries in the U.N., 100
Lebanese News Agency, 80
Lebanon: army, role of, 81-3; reaction to U.S. troops, 116-8; Cabinet, institution of, 21; of Karāmī, 160-1; of Da'ūq, 167-8; Chamber of Deputies, 19, 86, 118-9, 121, 122-3, 154, 156, 158, 159, 161; —composition of, 20 (Table I), 165 (Table II); —institution of, 19-20; —President of, 20-1; climate, 2-3; Constitution, 18-9, 65, 66, 121-2; economy, 3-7; electoral laws, 20, 26; geography, 1-2; history, 9-14; in the U.N., 96, 106, *see also* Malik; "list" system, 16; Ministry of Interior, 140; population, 3, 7; President of the Republic, 19, 33, 65, 121-2; *see also* al-Khūrī, Sham'ūn, Shihāb; —succession of, 65-8; Prime Minister, office of, 33; regionalism, 16; religious groups, 7-14, 8 (table)
Liberia in the U.N., 100, 105
Libya, 89, 90; in the U.N., 106
Liṭānī River, 2
Lloyd, Selwyn, 101, 105
Lodge, Henry Cabot, 92-3, 114, 123-4
London, 25
Louis IV, 10
Louis XIV, 10
Luṭfī, 'Umār, 138

Macmillan, 95
al-Madayrij, 77
Maḥjūb, Muḥammad, 90, 91, 106
Majdalānī, Nasīm, 49, 50, 54, 57, 63, 68, 159, 160, 167, 176
Majlis al-Nuwāb, see Lebanon, Chamber of Deputies
Majmū'at, Sulṭān, 142
Mukhaybar, Albert, 134
Malik, Charles, 38, 48, 58-9, 62, 84, 91, 119, 176; accusations against the UAR, 89, 141; in election of 1957, 57; in the U.N., 137, 138-9, 142, 143; UAR press attacks against, 52-3
al-Mālikī, Colonel Adnān, 36, 48
Malta, 114
Ma'lūla, 9
Mamlūks, 11
Ma'n, Aḥmad, 11
Ma'ns, 11
Manṣūrī Mosque, 72, 75
al-Maqāṣid, 61
Mardites, 9, 10
Maronites, 7, 8 (table), 9, 11, 13, 16, 18, 19, 20 (Table I), 21, 32, 36, 42, 46, 50, 61, 63, 68, 75, 83, 84, 86, 111, 130, 133; *see also* Christians, confessionalism
Maronite College, Rome, 10
Maronite Patriarch, 44, 50, 59, 60, 63, 66, 83, 85, 87, 135, 156, 169
Martyrs' Square, Beirut, 74
Marūn, St., 10
Marūn, Yuhanna, 10
al-Mushnūq, 'Abdallah, 62
al-Maṣrī, Nāyif, 166
al-Matnī, Nasīb, murder of, 28, 50, 68-70, 71
al-Ma'ūshī, Badrī, 155
Ma'ūshī, Paul, *see* Maronite Patriarch
McClintock, Robert, 113, 116, 117; *see also* United States Ambassador
Mediterranean Sea, 1, 2, 63, 113, 114, 115, 175
Mediterraneanism, 17
Melkites, *see* Greek Catholics
Middle East Press Review, 111
al-Mīnā, 74
al-Mithāq al-Waṭanī, see National Covenant
Morocco, 40; in the U. N., 106
Mount Hermon, 2, 3, 11
Mount Lebanon, 8, 9-10, 16, 26, 31, 32, 56, 57, 158
Mount Ṣannīn, 1, 3
Mount al-Shaykh, *see* Mount Hermon
Mu'āwiyah, 9
Mu'awwaḍ, René, 50, 159, 160
Mughabghab, Na'īm, 76, 77, 84, 134, 162
al-Mukhtārah, 73, 75, 143
Murphy, Robert, 154-5
al-Murr, Gabriel, 51
Murtada, Shafīq, 62, 63

Muscat, 128
Muslim Lebanon Today, 32
Muslims, 7, 8 (table), 9, 130; attitude towards union with the UAR, 43-4; dissatisfaction as cause of the crisis, 30-3; Shi'a, 11, 13, 16, 18, 20 (Table I), 21, 135, 166; Sunni, 11, 13, 16, 18, 20 (Table I), 21, 30. 49, 86; *see also* confessionalism
Mutaṣarrif, 13
mutaṣarrifah, 13
Mutaṣarrifiyah Period, 12

Nabī 'Uthmān, 79, 80, 134
Najjādah, 50, 69, 73, 80, 81, 165 (Table II)
Najjār, Fu'ād, 161
Nakoura, 146
Naqqāsh, Alfred, 155
Naqqāsh, George, 51
"Nasserism" as a cause of the crisis, 39-44, 44-5
National Bloc, 22, 85, 155, 164, 165 (Table II), 168
National Call Party, 22, 50, 165 (Table II)
National Congress, 23
National Covenant, 17-18, 34, 42, 46, 66, 170, 172, 175, 177, 179
National Liberal Party, 159, 164, 165 (Table II), 168
National Organization, 23, 32, 50, 69, 165 (Table II)
National Socialist Front, 22, 24
Nehru, 95
Nettles, James R., Sgt., U.S.A., 120
Newsweek, 154
The New York Times, 46
New Zealand in the U.N., 100, 103
North Lebanon, 56, 80
Norway, 144; in the U.N., 100, 105-6

Oman, 128
Opposition, view of the crisis, 133-37
L'Orient, 57
Orontes River, 2
Ottoman Turks, 11, 12, 13

Pakistan, 127; in the U.N., 100, 101
Palamas, Mr., 103
Palestine, 9, 17, 112
Palestinians, 64
Panama in the U.N., 92, 93, 100, 105
Paraguay in the U. N., 100, 105
"Patriarch of Antioch and all the East," 10
Persian Gulf, 5, 40, 128; *see also* Arab Gulf
Persians, 9
personal enmities as cause of the crisis, 34
Phalanges, 23, 32, 46, 58, 83, 111, 119, 136, 156, 158-67 *passim;* alliance with the PPS, 85; composition of, 84
"Phoenicianism," 17
Phoenicians, 9
Plaza, Galo, 144
Point Four Program, 112, 163
polarization of Arab politics as cause of the crisis, 38-9
Popular Front, 23, 70
PPS, 36, 46, 48, 64, 72, 76, 77, 78, 79, 80, 81, 83, 159, 161, 162, 164, 176; relations with Sham'ūn, 84-5; role in the crisis, 133-6;
Progressive Socialist Party, 22, 50, 57, 69, 165 (Table II), 166, 167
propaganda war, 80-1; 126-7; 137-8
Protestants, 8, 20 (Table I)
Prussia, 12, 13

Qabr Shmūl, 78
qada, 13
qā'im maqām, 12, 13
qā'im maqāmiyah, 12
Qannūbīn, 10
Qurnat al-Sawda, 1, 3
Qurtbāwī, Father Antoine, 63
Qutub, Sayyid, 29
al-Quwwatlī, 60-61, 62, 171
Quzma, Farīd, 162

Ra'd, In'ām, 162
Radio Beirut, 54, 80, 81
Radio Cairo, 53, 59, 80, 137
Radio Damascus, 59, 80, 137
al-Rāfi'ī, 'Abd al-Majīd, 166
al-Raml Prison, Beirut, 74
Ras al-Nāqūrah, 1
Raslān, Ḥasan, 142
Règlement organique, 13
"The Revolt of the Pashas," 39
Richards Mission, 46
Rizkallah, Nicolas, 136
Rubaiz, Ḥabīb, 51
Russia, 12, 13

Sabara, Muḥammad, 56
Sā'd, Ma'rūf, 62, 64, 67, 75
Sā'd, Ṣalāḥ, 75
al-Sadīq, Shaykh al-Taqī, 135
Sa'īd, Aḥmad, 52
al-Sa'īd, Nūrī, 41, 115
Ṣaida, *see* Sidon

Salām, Miṣbaḥ, 73
Salām, Ṣā'ib, 23, 37, 41, 48, 49, 53, 54, 55, 56, 57, 62, 66, 72, 73, 74, 81, 133, 155, 159, 160, 164, 167, 169
Sālim, Joseph, 51
Sālim, Niqūlā, 64
Sa'ūd, King, 26, 37, 41
Saudi Arabia, 25, 26, 38, 41, 90, 128; in the U.N., 102-3, 106
Sayf, Ghālib, 142
Selim I, 11
al-Sha'b, 53
Shahba, 149
Shahla, Ḥabīb, 21
Shamīṭ, Col. Yusuf, 117
Sham'ūn, Camille, 22-6 *passim,* 30, 32, 34-8 *passim,* 41, 42, 49, 51, 53, 54, 57, 58, 59, 60, 61, 63, 64, 65, 67, 68, 69, 71, 74, 75, 76, 78, 80, 83, 84, 85, 86, 87, 91, 113, 115, 116, 117, 119-23 *passim,* 126, 128, 130, 136, 142, 151, 155, 157, 158, 160, 164, 173, 176; administration of, 30, 31, 32, 48, 50, 53, 55, 66, 134, 164, 169, 172; —characteristics, 25-6; —corruption as cause of the crisis, 33-4; —friendly relations with the United States, 112; —inception, 22-3; international relations of, 26-7; —view of the crisis, 137; question of re-election, 65-6, 154, 169-70; request for troops, 99
Sham'ūn, Fu'ād, 162
Sharī'a Court of Appeals, 53
al-Shihāb, Amīr Bashīr, 11
al-Shīhab, Amīr Bashīr II, 11, 12
al-Shihāb, Bashīr III, 12
Shihāb, Fu'ād, 22, 24, 56, 67, 77, 83, 86, 87, 116, 117, 120, 135, 157, 158, 160, 161, 163, 176; as army commander, 81-2; election to the Presidency, 154-6; threat of resignation, 166-7
Shihāb, House of 11-12
Shihāb al-dīn, Rashīd, 73
Shimlān, 78
Shūf, 11, 73, 134, 142, 162; balance of forces and battles, 75-9; beginning of violence in, 67
Shuqayrī, Aḥmad, 102-3
Shuqayr, Muḥammad, 51
Shuqayr, Shawqat, 142
Sidon, 1, 5, 7, 9, 12, 61, 62, 85, 133; balance of forces in, 75
Sim'ān, Col. Joseph, 162
Sinai campaign, 139
Sinai desert, 52
al-Siyāsah, 60, 73
Skāf, 165 (Table II)
Sobolov, Mr., 94
Le Soir, 51, 58, 64
South Lebanon, 56, 64
Soviet Union, 26, 40, 44, 45, 46, 59, 116, 128-9, 131, 133, 151, 170, 175, 178; in the U.N., 92, 94, 95, 96, 125
Soviet Bloc, 112; in the U.N., 99, 101, 104, 107
Strikes: of May 7, 1957 in Tripoli, 72; of May 30, 1957, 54-5; Phalanges, 158
Sudan, 90, 91, 128; in the U.N., 106
Suez Canal, 40, 52
Suez Canal Company, 40
Suez crisis, 45, 51, 126, 129, 140
al-Ṣulḥ, Riāḍ, 7, 17, 22
al-Ṣulḥ, Sāmī, 23, 32, 37, 38, 48, 52, 54, 56, 59, 60, 67, 68, 74, 84, 86, 91, 134, 141, 154, 176
"Sulṭān Group," 142
Summit meeting proposals, 95-6
Ṣūr, *see* Tyre
Sûreté Générale, 56
Sweden in the U.N., 92, 93, 95; resolution of, 94
Synod of al-Luwzayah, 10
Syria, 1, 4, 5, 6, 9, 10, 11, 12, 14, 16, 17, 18, 24, 25, 26, 32, 38, 40, 41, 42, 43, 45, 46, 47, 48, 51, 55, 56, 57, 61, 75, 77, 79, 80, 84, 85, 114, 126, 128, 134, 135, 139, 141, 149, 151, 170, 171, 173, 179; Decree No. 151 of 1952, 35; Deuxième Bureau, 59, 141, 142: relations with Lebanon as cause of the crisis, 35-7; deterioration of, 59-60
Syriac, 9
Syrian Catholics, 8 (table)
Syrian National Social Party, 17
Syrian Orthodox, 8 (table)
"Syrianism," 17

Tannūkhs, 11
Tapline, 5
Taqī al-dīn, Bahīj, 51
Taqlā, Philippe, 44, 49, 50, 161, 167
Taurus Mountains, 9
The Telegraph, 68, 69
Third Force, 65-6, 69, 86, 158; composition of, 50-1
The Torch, 80
Tripoli, 1, 5, 7, 9, 61, 62, 63, 64, 72, 79, 85, 133, 134, 146, 156, 158, 166; balance of forces in, 74-5
Tripoli, Libya, 89
The True Nature of the Lebanese Revolt, 34

Tunisia, 40, 41, 128; in the U.N., 106
Turkey, 36-37, 46, 48, 59, 80, 113, 127, 133, 136, 170, 177-8; in the U.N., 100, 101
al-Tuwaynī, Ghassān, 23, 24, 51
Twining, General Nathan, 114
Tyān, Emile, 155
Tyre, 7, 61, 62, 63-4, 133

United Arab Republic, 44, 66, 68, 113, 116, 127, 133, 135, 145, 167, 170, 177; attitude towards union with Lebanon, 42-3; denial of Lebanese allegations in U.N., 93-4, 106; effect of formation in Lebanon 60-5; intervention in crisis, 171-2; Lebanese accusation of intervention, 89; participation of government authorities in crisis, 143; participation of nationals in crisis, 141-3; *see also* arms supply, Egypt, propaganda war, Syria
United National Front, 51, 53, 54, 56, 58, 60, 61, 62, 64, 68, 69, 71, 72; formation and objectives, 48-50
United Nations, 7, 25, 46, 113, 130, 140, 172, 173, 175, 180; Charter, 97, 98, 105, 106, 121, 126; —Article 51, 93, 94, 99, 123, 124-5, 174; "Essentials for Peace" Resolution, 97, 98, 125; General Assembly meeting, 96-108; —attitude on foreign troops, 98-101; —attitude on U.N. Police Force, 101-2; —differences between the Seven State and Arab draft resolutions, 106-7; Japanese draft resolution, 94-5, 125; "Peace through Deeds" Resolution, 97, 98, 125; Police Force, 98, 107; Secretary General, 95, 98, 105-6, 107, *see also* Hammarskjöld; Security Council meeting, 89, 90, 91-5, 118, 123, 124, 137, 142, 143, 144, 150, 172, 174; Seven State draft resolution, 105-6; Soviet draft resolution, 94, 104-5; Swedish resolutions, 92, 93, 114, 124, 143; United States draft resolution, 92-3, 94
United Nations Observation Group in Lebanon (UNOGIL), 92, 93, 96, 105, 108, 109, 114, 125, 127, 135, 174; description of, 143-4; evaluation of, 150-2, 172-3; reports of, 143-50
United Parliamentary Bloc, 157
United Press, 154
United States, 6, 7, 26, 52, 107, 133, 163, 170, 178; Ambassador of, 65, 115, 133, *see also* McClintock; Congress, 118; Information Library, Tripoli, 72; intervention, 115; —justification, 121-6, 173-4; —motives, 173-4; ——as regards Lebanon, 126-7; ——as regards the Middle East, 127-8; ——as regards the Soviet Union, 128; —objectives, 129-30; ——achievement of, 174-5; in the U.N., 92-3, 96, 104, 105, 106; *see also,* Eisenhower, Lodge; Navy Department, 113; Pentagon, 129; recognition of Iraq, 96; relations with the Arab states as cause of the crisis, 45-7; relations with Lebanon: —attitude in the U.N., 114-5; —history of, 111-3; —post-crisis, 178; —prior to intervention, 113-5; Sixth Fleet, 113, 115, 175; State Department, 113, 129; troops in Lebanon 93, 94, 113, 151; —behavior of, 119-21, 174; —civilian reaction to, 119; —landings, 92, 115-6; —occupation of Beirut International Airport, 116; —political negotiations with, 117; —political reaction to, 118-9; —relation with Lebanese army, 116-8; —withdrawal of, 108-9
'Usayrān, 'Ādil, 23, 66, 86, 155, 159, 162, 165 (Table II); telegrams concerning U.S. troops, 118-9, 123
USS Boston, 115
USS Des Moines, 115
USS Essex, 115
USS Saratoga, 115
al-'Uwaynī, Ḥusayn, 49, 51, 67, 72, 73, 159, 160, 161

Voice of Arabism, 80
Voice of the Arabs, 40, 52, 80, 137
Voice of Free Lebanon, 80
Voice of Lebanon, 80, 158
The Voice of Reform, 79, 80, 134
Voice of Revolution, 81

Wade, Brigadier General Sidney, 117
West Africa, 7
Western Powers in UN, attitude toward foreign troops, 98-99
al-Yāfī, 'Abdallah, 23, 37-8, 41, 48, 49, 53, 57, 60, 61, 66, 72, 159, 160, 164, 167, 169

Yamūt, Shaykh Shafīq, 53
Yemen, 39, 90; in the U.N., 106

Zaḥlah, 7, 57, 85, 133, 158
al-Zayn, 'Abd al-Karīm, 73, 135
al-Zayyāt, Aḥmad, 29
Zurich, 136
Zuwayn, Maurice, 161, 166
Zuwayn, Simon, 162